SOCIAL
INEQUALITIES

NEW APPROACHES TO SOCIOLOGY

The **New Approaches to Sociology** series actively responds to the call to decolonise the curriculum by developing progressive and critical textbook titles that seek a plurality of perspectives and worldviews, take a global outlook and embed a strong historical awareness of the context within which scholarly knowledge has been produced. The Series Editor is Nasar Meer, Personal Chair of Race, Identity and Citizenship at the University of Edinburgh.

Recent titles in the series

Social Inequalities
Anya Ahmed, Lorna Chesterton, Deirdre Duffy

Race, Ethnicity, & Society
Tina Patel

Consultative Board Members

Professor Anya Ahmed, University of Salford

Dr June Bam-Hutchison, University of Cape Town

Professor Anna Elia, Calabria, Italy

Professor Daniel Faas, Trinity, Dublin

Professor Pauline Leonard, University of Southampton

Professor Per Mouritsen, Aarhus University

Professor Karim Murji, University of West London

Professor Lene Myong, University of Stavanger, Norway

Professor Dr. Parvati Nair, United Nations University Institute on Globalization, Culture and Mobility

Professor Erica Righard, Malmö University

Professor John Solomos, University of Warwick

Professor Meenakshi Thapan, University of Dehli

NEW
APPROACHES TO
SOCIOLOGY

SOCIAL
INEQUALITIES

Anya Ahmed,
Lorna Chesterton
& Deirdre Duffy

Los Angeles | London | New Delhi
Singapore | Washington DC | Melbourne

Los Angeles | London | New Delhi
Singapore | Washington DC | Melbourne

SAGE Publications Ltd
1 Oliver's Yard
55 City Road
London EC1Y 1SP

SAGE Publications Inc.
2455 Teller Road
Thousand Oaks, California 91320

SAGE Publications India Pvt Ltd
B 1/I 1 Mohan Cooperative Industrial Area
Mathura Road
New Delhi 110 044

SAGE Publications Asia-Pacific Pte Ltd
3 Church Street
#10-04 Samsung Hub
Singapore 049483

Editor: Natalie Aguilera
Editorial assistant: Rhoda Ola-Said
Production editor: Ian Antcliff
Marketing manager: Ruslana Khatagova
Cover design: Francis Kenney
Typeset by: TNQ Technologies
Printed in the UK

**Library of Congress Control Number:
2022942561**

British Library Cataloguing in Publication data

A catalogue record for this book is available from
the British Library

ISBN 978-1-5297-7215-9
ISBN 978-1-5297-7216-6 (pbk)

At SAGE we take sustainability seriously. Most of our products are printed in the UK using responsibly sourced
papers and boards. When we print overseas we ensure sustainable papers are used as measured by the PREPS
grading system. We undertake an annual audit to monitor our sustainability.

This book is dedicated to Alison Ahmed Barrett who has spent her life working to make the world a fairer place for young people in Manchester.

Brief Contents

Author Biographies   XV

**Introduction: Understanding Social Inequalities in the Context of
Decolonisation**   1
Anya Ahmed and Lorna Chesterton

1   **Theories and Concepts**   9
    Anya Ahmed, Lorna Chesterton and Deirdre Duffy

2   **Social Class**   26
    Nicola Ingram

3   **Race, Racism and Decolonising Knowledge**   39
    Dyuti Chakravarty

4   **Gender**   56
    Peace Kiguwa

5   **Sexuality**   72
    Lee Gregory

6   **Ageing**   88
    Anya Ahmed, Lorna Chesterton and Sarah Campbell

7   **Decolonising Disability Research and Disabling War**   102
    Susie Balderston

8   **Health**   117
    Deirdre Duffy

9   **Unequal Mobilities and Global Social Inequalities**   131
    Anya Ahmed, Lorna Chesterton and Nafhesa Ali

10 Neoliberalism, Hegemony and Government Responses to Social Inequality in the UK   **147**

Steve Iafrati

11 Researching Inequalities   **163**

Ruby C. M. Chau

12 Conclusion   **179**

Anya Ahmed and Lorna Chesterton

Glossary   183
Index   187

Detailed Contents

Author Biographies   xv

**Introduction: Understanding Social Inequalities in the Context of
Decolonisation**   1
Anya Ahmed and Lorna Chesterton

1   Theories and Concepts   9
      Anya Ahmed, Lorna Chesterton and Deirdre Duffy
      Learning Objectives   9
      Framing Questions   9
      Introduction   9
      Gender and Economic Inequality   13
      Post-colonial Critiques of Modernity   18
      Critical Race Theory   20
      Intersectionality   21
      Chapter Summary   22
      Conclusion   22
      Questions to Reflect Upon   23
      Further Reading   23
      References   23

2   Social Class   26
      Nicola Ingram
      Learning Objectives   26
      Framing Questions   26
      Introduction   26
      What Is Social Class and How Has It Been Historically Understood?   27
      Intersectionality   31
      Thinking About the Case Study Through an Intersectional Lens   34
      Chapter Summary   36
      Conclusion   36
      Questions to Reflect Upon   37
      Further Reading   37
      References   38

3 Race, Racism and Decolonising Knowledge   39
Dyuti Chakravarty
Learning Objectives   39
Framing Questions   39
Introduction   40
A Starting Point   40
Mapping the Terrain of Theories of Race and Racial Inequality   41
Colonial Difference and Biological/Construction of Race   43
Colonial Matrix of Power, Disciplinary Knowledge and Epistemic Racism   46
'Decolonise not Diversify'   50
Chapter Summary   51
Conclusion   51
Questions to Reflect Upon   52
Further Reading   52
References   52

4 Gender   56
Peace Kiguwa
Learning Objectives   56
Framing Questions   56
Introduction   56
Social Inequality: How Does Gender Matter?   57
Feminist Re(imaginations): Looking Back and Looking Forward   58
Decolonial and Afro-Feminisms: What Relevance for Engaging
Gender Inequalities?   64
Chapter Summary   68
Conclusion   68
Questions to Reflect Upon   68
Further Reading   69
References   69

5 Sexuality   72
Lee Gregory
Learning Objectives   72
Framing Questions   72
Introduction   72
The Social Construction of 'Homosexuality'   73
Heteronormative Assumptions and Welfare Provision   76
Homophobia, Transphobia and the 21st Century   79
Assimilation through Equality?   80
Intersectionality With Class and Race   82
Chapter Summary   84
Conclusion   84

Questions to Reflect Upon   85
Further Reading   85
References   86

6   Ageing   **88**
Anya Ahmed, Lorna Chesterton and Sarah Campbell
Learning Objectives   88
Framing Questions   88
Introduction   88
Constructions of Ageing   89
Ageing Well   90
Transnational Experiences of Ageing   91
An Intersectional Perspective on Ageing   94
Raising Awareness of Inequalities and Their Impacts Upon Ageing   95
Ageing in a Migration Context   95
Chapter Summary   96
Conclusion   97
Questions to Reflect Upon   97
Further Reading   97
References   98

7   Decolonising Disability Research and Disabling War   **102**
Susie Balderston
Learning Objectives   102
Framing Questions   102
Introduction   103
Background   105
Disability Legislative and Policy Responses in Relation to War   106
Colonial Models of Disability   107
Social and Collective Models of Disability   110
An Intersectional Perspective: Gender, Ethnicity and Disability in War 112
Disability, Colonialism and Peace-Building   113
Chapter Summary   114
Conclusion   114
Questions to Reflect Upon   114
Further Reading   114
References   115

8   Health   **117**
Deirdre Duffy
Learning Objectives   117
Framing Questions   117
Introduction   117

Health and Social Inequalities   118

Understanding the 'Language' of Health and Inequality   118

Challenging Traditional Health(y) Policy   123

Challenging Medical Hegemony   125

Decolonialist Criticisms of Global Health Policy   127

Chapter Summary   128

Conclusion   129

A Question to Reflect Upon   129

Further Reading   129

References   130

9   Unequal Mobilities and Global Social Inequalities   131
Anya Ahmed, Lorna Chesterton and Nafhesa Ali

Learning Objectives   131

Framing Questions   131

Introduction   132

Mobilities and Migration   132

Forced Migration   133

Forced Migration in Response to Climate Change (Climate Migration)   134

Economic Migration   136

Retirement (Lifestyle) Migration   138

The UK Immigration Context   139

Chapter Summary   140

Conclusion   140

Questions to Reflect Upon   141

Further Reading   142

References   142

**10 Neoliberalism, Hegemony and Government Responses to Social
     Inequality in the UK   147**
Steve Iafrati

Learning Objectives   147

Framing Questions   148

Introduction   148

Social Policy, Ideology and Social Inequality   149

Inequality in UK Society   152

Neoliberal Responses to Inequality   154

Discussion   155

Chapter Summary   157

Conclusion   157

Questions to Reflect Upon   158

Further Reading   158

References   158

11 Researching Inequalities   **163**

Ruby C. M. Chau

Learning Objectives   163

Framing Questions   163

Introduction   163

Ethnocentric Interpretations of Confucian Ideas and Counterarguments   166

Ethnocentric Views and Social Inequalities   171

Cross-cultural Research Approaches   172

Chapter Summary   175

Conclusion   176

Questions to Reflect Upon   176

Further Reading   176

References   177

12 Conclusion   **179**

Anya Ahmed and Lorna Chesterton

References   180

Glossary   183

Index   187

Author Biographies

Professor Anya Ahmed

Anya Ahmed is Professor of Wellbeing and Communities in the Department of Social Care and Social Work at Manchester Metropolitan University. A social scientist with over 25 years of academic experience, she previously worked as a housing practitioner, trainer and consultant. Her research focuses on the experiences of marginalised communities (with a specific focus on minoritised ethnic populations) and she has led a range of funded projects on housing and homelessness, migration, ageing and health and social care. Much of her work involves interrogation of the theoretical, conceptual and applied nature of 'community' in national and international contexts. Anya is also a Non-Executive Director at Merseycare NHS FT, Chair of the Somali Adult Social Care Agency (SASCA) in Manchester; a member of the Customers and Communities Committee at Mosscare St Vincent's Housing Association; and a Trustee for Knowledge for Change (K4C) a charity which organises ethical international student placements.

Dr Nafhesa Ali

Dr Nafhesa Ali is a Sociologist and Research Associate at the University of Manchester. She is currently leading research for the 'Towards Inclusive Environmental Sustainability (TIES)' Leverhulme-funded project at the Sustainable Consumption Institute (SCI). Nafhesa has expertise in gender, migration, creative methods and drawing attention to how minoritised communities are positioned in their everyday lives in relation to their varying and diverse intersections. Nafhesa previously worked in the NHS as a Mental Health Practitioner with a particular focus on inclusive practices for carers. Nafhesa continues to work on increasing engagement between academia, voluntary and community organisations, and policy makers. Nafhesa's recent publications include two books, *Storying Relationships* (2021) and *A Match Made in Heaven: British Muslim Women write about Love and Desire* (2020) and journal publications in Sexualities, Ethnic and Racial Studies, Ethnicities and Cultural Geographies. Past publications include *Asian Voices: First Generation Migrants* (2010).

Dr Susie Balderston

Dr Susie Balderston is a disabled scholar, activist and Research Fellow in the School of Law University of Strathclyde. She was formerly a Research Associate and Research Fellow at the UNESCO Centre for Violence and Society at Lancaster University. There she evaluated third sector services to prevent and tackle violence, including for the European Commission, a sex worker outreach project and a Routine Enquiry for domestic violence with National Citizens Advice.

Before joining academia, Susie mentored commissioning and service improvements in policing, social care and health across England and was Policy & Training Director for a user-led, not-for-profit organisation of disabled people. Susie authored a Shadow Report about disabled women and criminal justice for the UN Inquiry into Systematic Human Rights Violations in the UK. She has served as an advisor to EHRC, NIHR and an EU DAPHNE project about disabled women after violence. She has been part of Care and Treatment Review Teams for high and medium secure offenders and out of area social care assessments.

Dr Sarah Campbell

Dr Sarah Campbell is a Senior Lecturer in Integrated Health and Social Care within the Department of Social Work and Social Care at Manchester Metropolitan University. She is also a social scientist and researcher, working for 14 years in academic research in the field of social and cultural ageing and lived experiences of dementia on several UKRI-funded studies. Sarah received her PhD from the University of Manchester in 2019, titled: Atmospheres of Dementia Care: Stories told through the bodies of men, an ethnographic study using sensory and embodied narrative analysis. Her current research is a participatory arts-led research study titled Uncertain Futures exploring the inequalities faced by women over 50 in relation to work. This project has been funded through Manchester Art Gallery and MICRA (Manchester Interdisciplinary Collaboration on Ageing) and in collaboration with the University of Manchester, Manchester Art Gallery, Artist – Suzanne Lacy, and a group of 15 women who form an advisory group and who support the work as co-researchers. Prior to working within academic research, Sarah has worked as a researcher and research trainer at the Mental Health Foundation and also within the voluntary sector as a group facilitator and trainer, and as a freelance researcher. Her research background spans 20 years in the Health and Social Care sector. Her work is underpinned by participatory methodologies and using creative methods to support the inclusion of marginalised voices within research. She is the book reviews editor for *Dementia: The International Journal of Social Research and Practice*.

Dyuti Chakravarty

Dyuti Chakravarty is a final year PhD candidate at the School of Sociology in University College Dublin. She specialises in postcolonial and decolonial feminist theories. She is completing her dissertation titled 'Break the Cage: the body politics of respectability and autonomy in contemporary women's movements in India and Ireland' through a comparative analysis of two movements – Pinjra Tod (right to mobility in India) and Repeal the Eighth (reproductive rights in Ireland). Dyuti has collaborated with artist Eimear Walshe on an *Arts Council of Ireland*, funded project to commemorate the legacies of Irish–Indian suffragette Margaret Cousins. She has also worked on a recent World Health Organization abortion policy implementation study in Ireland and is part of a new Irish Research Council New Foundations project titled *Negotiating difference on a shared island: agonism, commonality or critical constitutionalism*. Dyuti was also a co-organiser of Ireland's first Working-Class Studies Conference in November 2021.

Dr Ruby C M Chau

Dr Ruby Chau is an Associate Professor in Public and Social Policy in the School of Sociology and Social Policy at the University of Nottingham. She is an international scholar with experience in conducting 18 funded research studies in various East Asian and European countries and territories. Her main research interests are Chinese communities in the UK, cultural sensitivity in health and social care, comparative social welfare, de/familisation policies, and women and welfare. She has published more than 40 articles in international refereed journals and seven monographs including a joint-authored book on 'Women, Welfare and Productivism in East Asia and Europe' due to be published in 2022. Dr Chau is active in the social policy community by serving on the Executive Committee of the Social Policy Association, co-editor of *Social Policy and Society* (2021–2025) and member of the Editorial Board of *International Social Work*, *Journal of Women and Aging* and *Sociology*. Her community involvement includes supporting various community organisations by serving as their trustee and honorary adviser. She was a consultant (2019–2021) of a community project in Sheffield which contributed to the city's success in becoming a member of the WHO Global Network of Age-Friendly Cities and Communities. With a professional background in social work and a career in social policy research, she is passionate about promoting social inclusion, social equality and wellbeing for socially disadvantaged groups, including ethnic minority communities, homeless people, people with disabilities, older people and women.

Dr Lorna Chesterton

Dr Lorna Chesterton is a Social Scientist and Researcher in the Department of Social Care and Social Work at Manchester Metropolitan University. Lorna's work centres on social aspects of ageing and dementia with marginalised groups, exploring how people's culture, ethnicity, beliefs and socio-economic situations impact upon their health and access to services. Her work has been grounded in a person-centred approach to research and care, valuing the contribution which individuals' personal experience can make to research and future service provision. As an academic, she has been involved in research involving interprofessional learning, communities of practice and several research studies in care home initiatives. Lorna's background is in nursing, having worked for many years as a specialist practitioner in primary care and was honoured to receive the title of Queen's Nurse in 2012. Her community involvement includes work with voluntary groups and serves as a Trustee for the Somali Adult Social Care Agency, based in Manchester.

Dr Deirdre Duffy

Dr Deirdre Duffy (she/her) is a Reader in Critical Social Policy, Manchester Metropolitan University. She is an international expert on reproductive justice and reproductive governance, with a special interest in barriers and facilitators to abortion care. Her work has been used as an evidence-base to support expanding access to abortion in Colombia, the Republic of Ireland and Northern Ireland. In 2022, Deirdre was appointed as lead researcher on the Irish government's review of healthcare providers' perspectives and experiences of the recently-transformed abortion care system. Prior to this Deirdre was Co-Investigator and stream lead on the World Health Organization Human Reproduction Programme's ground-breaking implementation study of abortion care in the Republic of Ireland following the removal of the constitutional recognition of the 'right to life of the unborn'. Deirdre has collaborated with non-governmental organisations, activists and researchers globally and is passionate about feminist research practice.

Dr Lee Gregory

Dr Lee Gregory (he/him) is an Associate Professor at the School of Sociology and Social Policy, University of Nottingham. Lee is a co-investigator of the Nuffield funded project exploring LGBTQ+ experiences of access to welfare support, assets and debts in Britain and has also co-authored the forthcoming paper in the *Journal of Social Policy*, Social Policy and queer lives: coming out of the closet? He has previously published *Exploring Welfare Debates: key concepts and questions* (Policy Press) as well as, with Pete Alcock, the upcoming fifth edition of *Social Policy in Britain* (Bloomsbury Academic). His primary research areas are within the topics of poverty, inequality, LGBTQ+ experiences of welfare, welfare theory, social mobility and asset-based welfare (in particular youth savings initiatives). Lee has previously been a member of the Social Policy Association Executive Committee (as ECR lead and later Membership Secretary) and previously sat on the editorial board for the *Social Policy and Society* and currently sits on the editorial board for the *Journal of Social Policy*. He is also a Trustee of Academics Stand Against Poverty (UK chapter).

Dr Steve Iafrati

Dr Steve Iafrati is an Assistant Professor at the University of Nottingham. Following completion of his PhD studies, Steve worked within the voluntary sector and then as a Neighbourhood Manager within local government, affording him valuable insights into the ways in which people's lives were frequently shaped by factors external to their control. Returning to academia Steve worked as a senior lecturer in Social Policy where he continued to focus on issues related to poverty and social exclusion. In doing so, he sought to combine the lived experiences of people experiencing vulnerability with academic debate and the context of policymaking. Steve has published research in areas covering hate crime, food poverty and housing, as well as experiences of diversity within welfare. In 2016, Steve joined the executive of the Social Policy Association (SPA) and, as vice-chair, oversaw commissioning of research to examine the position of race and ethnicity within Social Policy research and teaching. Subsequently, Steve wrote the SPA action plan that has guided the SPA to improve diversity at conferences, increase awareness of race and ethnicity in the SPA's journals, and use SPA opportunity grants to support relevant projects. Steve continues to research housing and is currently involved in working with local government to examine hidden homelessness within Black and minoritised communities.

Professor Nicola Ingram

Nicola Ingram is Professor of Sociology of Education at Manchester Metropolitan University and Director of the Education and Social Research Institute. Her research is focused on young people and social inequalities in education and work. She has published widely on these issues and her recent books include: *Working-Class Boys and Educational Success: Teenage Identities, Masculinities and Urban Schooling* (Palgrave MacMillan 2018); *Educational Choices, Aspirations and Transitions in Europe* (Routledge 2018); and *Higher Education, Social Class and Social Mobility: the Degree Generation* (Palgrave MacMillan 2016). Nicola is on the board of Trustees of the British Sociological Association (BSA) and is co-founder and co-convenor of the BSA's Bourdieu Study Group. She is on the editorial board of the *Sociological Review*, *Sociology* and the *British Journal of Sociology of Education*.

Dr Peace Kiguwa

Peace Kiguwa (PhD) is Associate Professor in Psychology at the University of the Witwatersrand, South Africa. Her research interests include critical social psychology, affective politics of gender and sexuality, racism and racialisation and the nuances of teaching and learning. Her collaborative research projects have included focus on young women's leadership in Higher Education and the Destabilising Heteronormativity project. She is currently Editorial Board member on three accredited journals publications and has served as Chair of the Sexuality and Gender Division of the Psychology Society of South Africa (PSYSSA) and is current Executive Member of the Society. She is recent recipient of the Oppenheimer Memorial Trust Rising Star Fellowship at Wits University and is current lead researcher on the African Futures project as part of the Fellowship.

INTRODUCTION

Understanding Social Inequalities in the Context of Decolonisation

Anya Ahmed and Lorna Chesterton

Defining and Problematising Social Inequality

Social inequality is a complex concept, referring to the multidimensional inequality created by uneven distribution and access to resources and opportunities (Elenbaas, Rizzo, & Killen, 2020). It is shaped by structural factors, for example being excluded from opportunities in education or occupation and through bodily inscribed identities such as race and gender which impact on social and economic disparity (Bullock, 2019). Consequentially, certain individuals, communities and populations have access to fewer opportunities for social mobility and experience a lack of equality of outcome (Wilkinson & Pickett, 2017). Social inequality operates on several spatial levels, within and between regions and nations and globally. There is increasing disparity between the most and least socially advantaged, a situation which is continually perpetuated and underpinned by social divisions (Warwick-Booth, 2018).

Measuring social inequality is recognised as being problematic, and there is little consensus on what is the most effective way to do this (Warwick-Booth, 2018). Social inequality is complex and includes multiple structural dimensions, such as income, occupation, social capital, health and education, to name but a few. Measuring these separate dimensions of inequality then allows policymakers and society more broadly to understand the influences on individuals and population groups, and how different dimensions reinforce and compound one another (Binelli, Loveless, & Whitefield, 2012). However, measuring the separate dimensions of inequality such as poverty, whilst undoubtedly important, does not capture its complexity and the systems and structures which shape it. There is often a cultural and power imbalance in debates of social inequality, as those with power, class and status define and explain the phenomenon from a privileged vantage point, without acknowledging that such a vantage point exists (Berreman, 2015; Walker, 2009).

Recognising that power is fundamentally linked to social inequality brings us to critically examine how it has been portrayed historically in Sociology and the social sciences. Auguste Comte is generally credited as being the creator of Sociology, developing a discipline which would study 'the social realm'. Whilst Comte theorised about social order, social dynamics and social progress, his overarching mission was to assemble a group of experts, which could help manage and control society (Go, 2017). The study of social order, then, was a very helpful tool when managing threats from lower classes which threatened the privileged (Hund, 2014). Throughout the 19th century, European male elites used such sociological theories to understand and manage resistance from those with less power, for example the working classes and women (Owens, 2015). These theoretical positions were also used to explain the situation facing 'natives', or non-Europeans and provided intellectual reasons to justify colonial actions which oppressed and dispossessed colonised people (Bhambra et al. 2018). Similarly in the United States, sociological theory was used to justify and vindicate slavery (see Fitzhugh, 1854) and the poor treatment and oppression of immigrant workers (Hughes, 1854), essentially protecting the interests of the white male elite (Go, 2013).

Decolonising Social Inequality

This book offers a critical re-reading of canonical approaches to understanding social inequalities and responds to the call from university administrations, academics and students to decolonise the curriculum and challenge its lack of diversity and 'Eurocentric domination' (Hussain, 2015). Situating social inequalities within a global and historical context, each chapter will embed an epistemological critique of knowledge, its origins, contexts and influential shifts (Saini & Begum, 2020). Importantly, the book presents an intersectional approach to understanding diversity and social inequalities and in so doing, allows for alternative knowledge sources and voices to be heard.

Historically, Western accounts of imperialism, colonialism and slavery enabled Europe and Western thought to dominate (Bhambra, 2007), and this obscures the fact that knowledge is socially constructed, and metanarratives/social theory are embedded in power relations and structures. In this way, new historical understandings of social inequalities cannot be added to pre-existing ones without in some way calling into question the validity and legitimacy of previous paradigms (Bhambra, 2007). We also address the erroneous and entrenched paradigmatic assumption that there are differences between the Western world and the rest of the world and how this has framed theory about the social world for generations. Of course, these assumptions are often underpinned by the narrative that Western structures were or would become universal (Bhambra, 2007), allowing the West to develop a Eurocentric and privileged position.

This departure from more traditional ways of observing social inequalities will allow us to critique the perspectives and contexts of central sociological theories such as Marxism, functionalism and feminism etc., before examining different sociological frameworks, from Black feminist scholars, critical race scholars and intersectional theorists. This will furnish the reader with different perceptions and viewpoints, which embrace the diversity of today's modern society. In exploring alternative knowledge sources, we will increase intellectual rigour and facilitate greater understanding of social inequality and the histories of Black and indigenous populations across the world. Importantly, this book will help to challenge sociological knowledge sources and see how the colonial legacy has influenced Western political thought, policymaking and subsequent impacts on society as a whole and on marginalised groups.

Recognising that Sociology has strong Eurocentric roots, with sociological epistemes which have been intrinsically situated in Western ideas and hierarchies, demonstrates how it has been able to marginalise, omit or repress other worldviews, and sources of knowledge. Therefore, in bringing about an epistemic shift in sociology, teaching should cultivate critical thinking, which is open to multiple and different perspectives, and become able to question established hegemonic standpoints. We would contend that Sociology should be viewed as part of the global economy of knowledge, and as such should be reflective of global inequality and marginalisation. By critiquing traditional explanations of social inequalities which position Western thought and thinking as universal and objectively 'true', we will instead focus on how different realities, experiences and histories shape knowledge and its production. Throughout the book we will argue that social inequalities will be perpetuated if we do not account for this.

In the context of decolonising Western institutions and the curriculum, an intersectional perspective offers a different and important approach to understanding diversity, whilst observing the impact of social and political policy and the subsequent social inequality. Utilising an intersectional framework will demonstrate how social categorisations such as race, class, sexuality and gender overlap and combine to produce different forms of discrimination and oppression. An example of this would be that a white woman and a Black woman whilst being the same gender do not experience the same prejudices and discrimination within their daily lives, since being a 'woman' and being 'Black' are identities which do not exist independently of each other. Adopting this framework allows for a better understanding of how oppression works and therefore can be instrumental in eliminating these issues.

From a broader perspective, understanding how historical colonial knowledge sources and political drivers have influenced theory and practice will offer useful insights into how discrimination and oppression have developed in societal thinking and behaviour and why it continues to pose a threat to reducing disparity. We will show how a Eurocentric approach, from a predominately elite white male standpoint has often excluded and compounded inequality and disadvantage for individuals and groups. Using case studies, we will give students a real-world view of how individuals have encountered discrimination and disadvantage and bring in evidence from often unheard sources in

Western contexts, which accurately capture historical events and the impacts on individuals and communities.

By focusing on colonialism and the politics of knowledge production and drawing on Subaltern studies we aim to present a deeper understanding of the subjectivities of those who have been historically marginalised in Western debates. In this way we challenge the dominant narratives of the causes of social inequalities, drawing from historical colonial relations as a framework to explain and understand the present. It is important to fully contextualise social inequalities in the present in colonial histories of the past (Bhabba, 1992). We will critique and situate colonialism as not just the conquest and domination of nations but also in terms of its epistemological impacts and bias of thought and categorisation of social inequalities (Bhambra, 2007). We address this issue of epistemological hubris and explore how structural inequalities intersect with social locations or positionalities to create multiple jeopardies.

Throughout the book, we take critical view of neoliberal economic policy and highlight that globalisation has disproportionately affected the most vulnerable in society and across the world. We explore how social policy is intrinsically linked to the process of globalisation and how this has contributed to social inequalities. An examination of the interplay between these processes, the political forces which underpin them, and globalised capitalism will illuminate some of the often-silenced disparities in income which affect the poorest population groups in the UK and across the world. By looking at the links between globalisation and inequality, we discuss the consequences and how these relate to the Global North–South divide.

Chapter by Chapter Summary

Chapter 1 Theories and Concepts

In this chapter, Anya Ahmed, Lorna Chesterton and Deirdre Duffy provide an overview of the dominant social theorists, such as Durkheim, Comte and Weber, who presented their work within the context of global colonialism. They explain how the dawn of postcolonialism posed threats to these established sociological canons, and address these challenges by focusing on lesser known, previously ignored scholars, in particular subaltern studies whose work bring new insights and important knowledge to sociological debate. This chapter examines several influential theories, such as Marxism, feminism and conflict theories which have all observed societal divisions derived from identity, class and positionality and how these impact upon inequality, disadvantage and marginalisation. The chapter highlights the need to understand these theoretical concepts, within the temporal and spatial contexts of their production.

Chapter 2 Social Class

Nicola Ingram explores the multiple dimensions of class and how the interplay of power and economic factors culminates in social inequalities. She also explores the social and psychological impacts of the class system on behaviours, attitudes and outcomes. This chapter problematises the concept of class and examines how social locations and social processes shape and perpetuate resulting negative outcomes. The chapter also considers how constructions and imaginings of class identities and experiences have informed and are shaped by social policy. The chapter provokes students to consider how social policy sustains classed relations and both produces and reinforces classed narratives and divisions. The chapter also considers issues of intersectionality and how class-oriented analysis of social relations – particularly the work of Marx and Weber – obscure raced and gendered inequalities.

Chapter 3 Race, Racism, and Decolonising Knowledge

Dyuti Chakravarty examines the distinct concepts of race and ethnicity, and how they intersect with individual identity, collective identity and power. With a focus on the importance of decolonising institutions and curriculums she examines the path towards reconceptualising the institutional and collegial dialogue on research and education to be inclusive of cultures, ethnicity, race and knowledge systems. In appraising the narratives and knowledge used within institutions and curriculums she discusses the need for alternative knowledge sources and diverse voices to be heard, to allow students the opportunity to develop new understandings. To that end, this chapter discusses Critical Race Theory and how it relates to society and culture and the interplay between race, law and power.

Chapter 4 Gender

In this chapter, Peace Kiguwa explores the different factors which contribute towards gender inequality and the impacts of culture, ethnicity, economic structure and social organisation. In discussing gender inequality, she explores issues of sexual exploitation, violence and ritualistic practice. Using Black feminist theory to critique other, more traditional theories, she looks at concepts of patriarchy, oppression and the exploitation of women. Drawing on Afro feminisms and Latin American Feminisms which emphasise the invisibility of women in social economic and political spheres because of colonialism, imperial and dominant Western frameworks, she frames feminism as an intersectional struggle/endeavour which is more than addressing patriarchy: it is concerned with social class, gender, race, religion and white privilege. Kiguwa argues that traditional feminism does not address the reality of other cultures, classes and religions, nor does it take account of slavery and the colonial past and the role these play in shaping experiences.

Chapter 5 Sexuality

Lee Gregory discusses the dominant cultural narrative affecting the lesbian, gay, bisexual and transgender (LGBTQ+) community. He examines the homophobia and heterosex-ism, which make this heterogeneous group susceptible to abuse and violence and has prevented access to social and legal structures. He also looks at how the factors of class, race and ethnicity intersect and lead to inequality. The chapter seeks to deepen our understanding of LGBTQ+ poverty and LGBTQ+ discrimination as broader social issues. Gregory draws on 'queer theory' as a means to undo the presumptions that empower the heteropatriarchal conditions that shape the social, economic and political conditions in which LGBTQ+ people, particularly those of colour, suffer from unequal opportunity and representation. The chapter also considers the co-option and deradicalisation of LGBTQ+ identities by social narratives of equality. For example, it considers how equality initiatives such as equal marriage represent an extension of heteronormative frames rather than recognition of LGBTQ+ intimacies.

Chapter 6 Ageing

In this chapter, Anya Ahmed, Lorna Chesterton and Sarah Campbell present a critical discussion of ageing and migration and the impacts of post-colonialism on social inequalities experienced across the life course. They focus on age as a heterogeneous category and experience; the intersections of migration regimes with welfare regimes; and on how other social locations intersect with age. The chapter considers cross-cultural conceptions of ageing, how positive and successful ageing approaches privilege certain types of embodied experience and highlights how the materiality of older age is different according to bodily inscription. This chapter also examines how socioeconomic and political factors intersect with ethnicity, gender, sexuality and social class to result in poor health and social outcomes in the UK. They look at the narrative around ageing and explore why this has taken a predominantly white affluent focus, which neglects marginalised groups, and invariably the oldest old (fourth age) in our society.

Chapter 7 Decolonising Disability Research and Disabling War

Susie Balderston presents a critical appraisal of social perspectives of and policy for people with disabilities. Drawing on critical disability studies as well as activist contestations, the chapter aims to provoke students to reflect on their own perceptions of disability as well as expand their awareness of the unequal realities of disabled people's lives and the position of disability in policy debates. The chapter takes a broad lens. In addition to offering an introduction to divergent models of disability – the medical and social – it explores the complexity of disability as a social policy issue. Through the chapter, students will encounter significant debates and contested territories within disability studies including discrimination against people with learning difficulties, the intersecting inequalities of gender and disability, the systemic exclusion of disabled voices from service design, and the ideological demonisation of people with disabilities within political debates. The chapter will also introduce students to resistance and political interventions led by people with disabilities, encouraging them to challenge their own beliefs regarding the position of disabled voices in social policy debates.

Chapter 8 Health

In this chapter, Deirdre Duffy introduces and disrupts dominant narratives of health policy and inequality. The chapter's objective is to push students to think beyond assumed health policy 'truths'. Taking public and population health as its departure point, the chapter interrogates the historic inequalities embedded in global and national health policy. The chapter encourages students to think critically about the logics underpinning campaigns for improved population health and the linkages between narratives of 'healthy societies' and the policing of particular communities. The chapter underlines how contemporary global health initiatives and discourses of population health target populations outside of the Global North and the linkages of this focus and philosophies of eugenics and social Darwinism. It also introduces students to global debates in health policy such as vaccine hesitancy, health governance and the global pharmaceutical inequalities.

Chapter 9 Unequal Mobilities and Global Social Inequalities

Anya Ahmed, Lorna Chesterton and Nafhesa Ali explore how macro structures enable and constrain mobilities, and how geographical and social location shape migration experiences. They discuss the relationship between global social inequality and mobilities and how forced, economic and lifestyle migration, although premised on a desire to improve one's life are differently shaped by macro structures. This chapter also looks at the global rise of right-wing groups, which publicise and practice an opposition to immigration, xenophobia and nationalistic policy.

Chapter 10 Neoliberalism, Hegemony and Government Responses to Social Inequality in the UK

In this chapter, Steve Iafrati focuses on political ideology and how this shapes social policy responses both in the UK, and globally and the consequential health and social outcomes. He looks at how a top-down approach impacts on marginalised communities, arguing that this often fails to recognise the needs of the most vulnerable, and therefore fails to deliver services, resulting in an increase in social inequalities. He examines how social policy and social theory has predominantly underpinned beliefs about culture based on a Western viewpoint and consequently created policies to address a homogenous society, where cultural beliefs are often seen as barriers to progress.

Chapter 11 Researching Inequalities

Ruby Chau begins this chapter by exploring the role of culture and the part it plays in societal organisation. She premises that culture can be seen to influence beliefs, behaviours, access to services and as a form of capital in relation to class structure and status. Within the context of decolonising the curriculum, this chapter will challenge students to understand culture, as a product of the histories that have shaped it and see positionality as a critical issue. Through a Confucian lens, she examines how cross-cultural research approaches can be used to develop understanding of specific areas of social inequality across different cultures.

Chapter 12 Conclusion

In this final chapter, Anya Ahmed and Lorna Chesterton reflect upon the common threads highlighted by the contributors to the book. They acknowledge the lasting legacy and impact of colonialism and the need to interrogate social inequalities through a different lens.

References

Berreman, G. D. (2015). *Inequality: Comparative aspects: International Encyclopaedia of the social & behavioural sciences* (2nd ed., *Vol. 11*, 894–898). doi:10.1016/B978-0-08-097086-8.12093-8

Bhambra, G. (2007). *Rethinking modernity: Postcolonialism and the sociological imagination*. Berlin: Springer.

Bhambra, G. K., Gebrial, D., & Nişancıoğlu, K. (2018). *Decolonising the university*. Pluto Press: London.

Binelli, C., Loveless, M., & Whitefield, S. (August 2012). What is social inequality and why does it matter? In APSA 2012 annual meeting paper.

Bullock, H. E. (2019). Psychology's contributions to understanding and alleviating poverty and economic inequality: Introduction to the special section. *American Psychologist, 74*(6), 635.

Elenbaas, L., Rizzo, M. T., & Killen, M. (2020). A developmental-science perspective on social inequality. *Current Directions in Psychological Science, 29*(6), 610–616.

Fitzhugh, G. (1854). *Sociology for the south, or the failure of free society*. Richmond, VA: A. Morris.

Go, J. (2013). Sociology's imperial unconscious: The emergence of American sociology in the context of empire. *Sociology and Empire*, 83–105.

Go, J. (2017). Decolonizing sociology: Epistemic inequality and sociological thought. *Social Problems, 64*(2), 194–199.

Hughes, H. (1854). *Treatise on sociology*. Philadelphia, PA: Lippincott, Grambo and Co.

Hund, W. D. (2014). Racism in white sociology. *Racism and Sociology, 5*, 23.

Hussain, M. (2015). *Why is my curriculum white?* National Union of Students. Retrieved from https://www.nus.org.uk/en/news/why-is-my-curriculum-white/

Owens, P. (2015). *Economy of force: Counterinsurgency and the historical rise of the social*. Cambridge: Cambridge University Press.

Saini, R., & Begum, N. (2020). Demarcation and definition: Explicating the meaning and scope of 'decolonisation' in the social and political sciences. *The Political Quarterly, 91*(1), 217–221.

Walker, C. (2009). New dimensions of social inequality. Postdoctoral Research Project. Retrieved from http://www.ceelbas.ac.uk/research/socialinequality

Warwick-Booth, L. (2018). *Social inequality*. SAGE. London.

Wilkinson, R. G., & Pickett, K. E. (2017). The enemy between us: The psychological and social costs of inequality. *European Journal of Social Psychology, 47*(1), 11–24.

1

THEORIES AND CONCEPTS

Anya Ahmed, Lorna Chesterton
and Deirdre Duffy

Learning objectives

- To recognise the origins of sociological thinking and how different sociological theories have influenced our understanding of society
- To identify perspectives which have been absent from debate
- To understand how colonialism has shaped sociological thought

Framing questions

- What are the roots of social inequality?
- How have different social thinkers explained inequality and its impact on individuals and communities?
- If we know society is unequal, what stops us from addressing inequality?

Introduction

This chapter will provide an overview of the theories and concepts which have shaped sociological thinking over its history. In acknowledging that sociological theory is constantly evolving, we will consider how theories are often built upon predecessors' work and then act as a catalyst for new thought. The chapter commences with an introduction to Comte and Durkheim, who theorise on how society is ordered and its social evolution, before discussing Max Weber, and Karl Marx, whose work would go onto influence many world leaders and societies into the present day. In providing such commentary the chapter considers where and from whom these theories derive, and question if sociology has omitted to draw on the perspectives of those who were not in privileged societal positions, due to their ethnicity and gender. It is therefore essential that theory should be included from feminist perspectives which are often absent from sociological debate. However, as feminism gained popularity and traction within society, there remained a Western centric approach, omitting the voices of other women who differed through race, class or other diversity. Subaltern studies, then, bring a wealth of new perspectives to the chapter, with links to colonialism and the harm and legacy it created in its wake. This then leads us to consider post-colonial thinking and challenges us to consider concepts of modernity and inequality. In decolonising sociological theory, it would be remiss not to bring in the work of Crenshaw and intersectionality to better understand the fundamental concerns of difference and diversity which again have been absent both from theoretical feminist scholarship and sociological thought more broadly. In taking such a broad epistemological perspective of sociological concepts, it is hoped that students will be prompted to interrogate the theories and context of the sociological canons and read then differently.

Auguste Comte (1798–1857) and Emile Durkheim (1958–1917): The Ordering of Society

The two key concerns of Comte and Durkheim, who are generally regarded as the 'founding fathers' of sociology, were how society was ordered and social order. The first question looked at the organisation of society and the position of individuals and communities relative to each other. Why are kings and governments 'higher up' in the social pecking order than farm labourers? If anything, the people who produce our food are more important to our survival than monarchs and politicians. According to Comte and Durkheim, the order of society was influenced by a combination of factors, some of which were related to society's needs, some to nature and some to belief.

Comte described this in what we now call his theory of social evolution. It is worth noting that Comte was not necessarily interested in explaining society but in establishing what he called a 'science of society' or sociology (Table 1.1). Like other sciences – for example physics, biology, chemistry, mathematics – sociology's objective was to identify the underpinning laws of social organisation (social physics). In his 1822 essay 'Plan of the Scientific Operations Necessary for Reorganizing Society', Comte argued that there were three basic laws of social organisation. Importantly for Comte, these laws did not operate in all societies at the one time. Instead, society evolved through them (social evolution) as we became more rational and scientific. Table 1.1 gives you a brief outline of Comte's three stages (theological-military, metaphysical-judicial and scientific-industrial).

According to Comte's 'law of three stages', society had developed into its 'modern' form – which Comte saw as dominated by industry, urban living and scientific thinking – once it moved beyond explaining social order according to God's will (theological) or natural laws (metaphysical). As we became more industrial and scientific, those who were able to drive forward industry and science rose to the top of the social pecking order. The emergence of a scientific-industrial society resulted in a new organisation of society with what we might now call 'professionals' (think doctors, business owners, scientists) at the top and everyone else below them.

Table 1.1 Presents Comte's Three Laws of Social Organisation

Phase	Time Period	Ordering	Social Unit	Material Phase
Theological phase	Before 1300	Domestic order	Family	Military • Social organisation is mainly of a military nature • Social stability is maintained by military
Meta-physical phase	1300 A.D. Till 1800 (Middle Ages – Renaissance)	Collective order	State	Legalistic • Influenced by churchmen and lawyers
Positive phase	From 1800	Universal order	Race-humanity	Industrial • Represents the scientific way of thinking • Influenced by industry and science

Durkheim built on this perspective. In his 1893 thesis, *The Division of Labour*, Durkheim argued that there were two forms of social organisation – mechanical solidarity and organic solidarity. In mechanical societies, society was organised by underlying cultural mechanisms (social facts). These facts included belief systems (God's will) and ideals, which were considered fixed or irrefutable (natural laws). In contrast, organic societies were organised according to what society needed in order to function (Table 1.2) and meet shared needs. Returning to the king/farm labourer question, kings had no role in either Comte or Durkheim's societies!

Karl Marx (1818–1883): Industrialisation, Capitalism and Class

Perhaps one of the most famous social theorists, Karl Marx was a German philosopher and staunch critic of the political and cultural establishments of the day. His most famous and influential work, *The Communist Manifesto* was published in 1848 and introduced the concept of socialism, which Marx saw as a result of the struggles which were inherent in a capitalist system. In his later work, *Das Kapital* he provides a critique of capitalism, laying down theories on commodities, labour markets, and the division of labour.

Marx's writing explored the differences between groups in society, class systems and hierarchies which all reflected inequality. For Marx, it was not just that people had different roles, it was that a hierarchy existed. Unlike Durkheim the division of labour, according to Marx, was not the outcome of a society trying to function effectively but the outcome of a factory-owning class (the bourgeoisie) attempting to gain the upper hand socially, politically and economically. Marx also saw a new 'rationality' or 'logic of

Table 1.2   Presents Durkheim's 'Division of Labour'

Society	Type	Description	Function	Ethos
Traditional society	Mechanical solidarity	• Based on **simple** division of labour • Social independence based on shared values • Strong group identity	Simple organism or machine, People are functionally equivalent or substitutable	Society is in the individual
Modern society	Organic solidarity	• Based on **specialised** division of labour • Social interdependence	Complex organisms People are not interchangeable	The individual is in society

society' developing with industrialisation; however, he argued that this rationality was built by elites to legitimise their position. It was not that they were more intelligent or more productive or more valuable than people who worked in their factories which meant they were wealthier; it was that their wealth and position allowed them to define what made a person valuable. Essentially, for Marx, the reason a CEO earns more than someone who works in a factory is because in the logical landscape which industrialisation created – capitalism – being a CEO is seen as more important.

Max Weber (1864–1920)

Max Weber was an influential sociologist, whose work was set against the backdrop of industrialisation. Weber's focus lay on the structure of society, and the determinants of class, status and power. Like Marx Weber (1958) saw that class was based on economic factors, with society being divided between owners and workers, while status was determined by non-economic factors such as family, education and religion. Power then was determined by both class and status, and that this underpinned society. Weber (1958) theorised that both structural and action approaches were necessary to gain a full understanding of society and social change. Using three pivotal arguments, he posited that there first needed to be an empathetic understanding concerning human action; that human action was governed by four basic types of motivation and that structure shaped human action since every society encourages certain types of motivation (Table 1.3).

Weber believed that societal thinking was dominated by efficiency and in doing so, it had started to ignore the issues of ethics, affection and tradition, which created social problems. Weber's (1958) work *Protestant ethic and spirit of capitalism* showed how religion could promote social change, using the example of Calvinism, a strict protestant religion, which taught followers that extolled the virtue of working hard, saving money and entrepreneurialism, while frivolous spending was sinful. Weber compared these cultural values as creating the environment in which capitalism could thrive.

Table 1.3 Presents Max Webber's Four Ideal Types of Social Actions

Action	Motivation
Traditional Social Action	Actions which are controlled by tradition, 'the way it has always been done'
Affective Social Action	Actions which have been determined by an individual's emotional state, with no thought to the consequences of the action.
Value Rational Social Action	Actions which have been determined by a conscious belief in the value of action (e.g. religious motivation).
Instrumental-Rational Social Action	Actions designed to achieve a certain result.

Gender and Economic Inequality

Much of the 'introductory' material for students of Sociology and social inequalities frame the discipline canonically. By this we mean that it presents Sociology as being established by a set of key thinkers. People like Comte, Durkheim, Weber and Marx are put forward as laying the foundations for how we analyse and understand why, how and in what ways society is unequal. The brief reviews above will give you an indication of these foundations and the main differences between them. Like Comte and Durkheim, Marx saw society as separated into hierarchies with business owners and industrialists as a new 'elite'. Where Marx disagreed with Comte and Durkheim was in how he viewed these hierarchies. Whereas Comte argued the hierarchies were a sign of a more 'rational' society and Durkheim positioned them as ordered; Marx contended that these hierarchies were another form of exploitation. We were not becoming more 'enlightened', we were changing the rules of the social game. Society was still unequal; the only difference between a peasant farmer and a factory worker was the place they worked.

But there were gaps in this literature. The most obvious gaps were inequalities relating to gender and inequalities relating to race. In fact, one of the biggest problems with Comte's later work in particular is that while he acknowledges that men and women[1] are different, he argues that this difference is natural and positive. Comte believed that women were emotional, not rational and by allowing them to stay in the home and not participate fully in social decision-making reflected how much they were respected! Pederson (2001) summarises:

> Whether Comte was praising reason or emotion, however he consistently linked men with thought and women with feeling. [...] He consistently linked his assessments of women's emotional nature to explanations of why women were unfit to participate in public life. Even in the religion of humanity, which revered women for their spiritual insight, women might achieve their greatest honour only if they remained, in Comte's contradictory phrase 'free in the sacred retirement of their homes'. [...] Which is to say, not entirely free at all. (Pederson, 2001, p. 235)

---

[1] We use cis terminology here reflecting Comte's representation of gender.

Similarly, while Marx recognised that the experience of class-based social inequality was different for men than for women, he did not discuss these differences in depth. Nor did Marx look at the impact of industrialisation and the emergence of capitalist economies on women. Feminist activists and theorists have been very critical of Marx's work for precisely this reason. How social inequalities 'appear' in the context of gender, sexuality and race will be discussed in more depth in later chapters. Yet it is important to give some theoretical background.

Charlotte Gilman Perkins (1860–1935): Gender, Economics and Social Order

An important, and in some ways under referenced, early feminist intervention to the debate around the impact of industrialisation on social order came from the American commentator Charlotte Gilman Perkins. Like Comte and Durkheim, Gilman Perkins was very interested in how society was organised and how this effected individuals and communities. What made Gilman Perkins different from Comte and Durkheim was that she not only positioned the different contributions made by men and women as unnatural, she also saw it as undesirable. In the introduction to her seminal text 'Women and Economics' published in 1898 Gilman Perkins pointed out that humans were the only species where contributions were not linked to ability but to gender. For Gilman Perkins (1898/1972), the gendered division of labour – where women did more 'caring' work and men more 'industrial' work – was not, as Comte had suggested, because of women were just more caring. It was because the cultural norms (i.e. the social facts) of the human race had evolved to a point where caring work could not be seen as anything other than 'women's work'.

More than that, Gilman Perkins (1898) argued that this 'naturalisation' had become so entrenched in social relations that it could not be addressed without substantial economic disruption. According to Gilman Perkins (1898), the emergence of sexual difference as a social fact had limited women's accumulation of knowledge needed to engage fully with industrialised society. Women were not just dependent on men; society was dependent on men. As Gilman Perkins explained in Women and Economics:

> To take from any community its male workers would paralyze it economically to a far greater degree than to remove its female workers. The labour now performed by the women could be performed by the men [. . .] but the labour now performed by the men could not be performed by the women without generations of effort and adaptation [. . .] This is not owing to lack of the essential human faculties necessary to such achievements, nor to any inherent disability of sex, but to the present condition of woman, forbidding the development of this degree of economic ability. (Gilman Perkins, 1898, pp. 4–5)

That said, like Marx, Gilman Perkins presented this form of social organisations as fundamentally damaging and prohibiting substantive societal progress. By denying women, as a class, the necessary social support to engage fully in industrialised society and, indeed, forcing women out of the workplace when they married or had children, indicated that society was preventing itself from benefitting from 'collective industry' and 'a union between man and woman such as the world has long dreamed of in vain' (Gilman Perkins, 1898, p. 145).

What is useful about Gilman Perkins' writing in terms of decolonisation is that it deals explicitly not just with inequality and industrialisation but with dependency. Applying Gilman Perkins analysis to the history of stolen independence reveals how dependency is reinforced by industrialisation and the expansion of capitalist economies. A key argument proposed in Women and Economics is that the more society 'naturalises' a division of labour where women stay at home and men make money, the harder it is for women to gain independence.

Indeed, Gilman Perkins observes that the more a 'less free' position is projected as being a desirable social state for a particular social group, the more acceptable it becomes to take whatever freedoms that they may have away from them. As Gilman Perkins outlined in literary works such as *The Yellow Wallpaper* as well as more 'academic' analyses like *Home*, the projection of dependence on men as women's ultimate destination meant that it seemed normal for financially independent women to have this independence removed.

Another element of Gilman Perkins' work which is useful for understanding how capitalism restricts particular groups into a state of subjugation is her analysis of the devaluing of the kinds of work women do. Echoing Marx, Gilman Perkins highlighted how social evolution – specifically the industrialisation and the growth of capitalism in the 19th century – disconnected the economic value of work from its difficulty or social value. Whereas Durkheim had described the value of labour as based around social need, Marx and Gilman Perkins argued that labour value was dictated by the accumulation of wealth. Essentially, work that generated more money was paid better.

While Marx demonstrated this argument through looking at wages in industrial workplaces, Gilman Perkins used the example of 'women's work' such as cleaning, cooking and dressmaking. She argued that even though these forms of labour were incredibly hard physically, were socially important and required skill, they were not well paid. The ultimate proof of the disconnect between social value (which Marx labelled use value) and economic value (which Marx labelled surplus value), for Gilman Perkins, was the fact that 'the women who do the most [domestic] work get the least money, and the women who have the most money do the least [domestic] work' (Gilman Perkins, 1898, p. 8).

Silvia Federici: The Position of Women in Capitalist Society
Silvia Federici (1974) adds to the understanding of gender and class and the connection between feminism and Marxism in her work, *Wages Against Housework*.

They say it is love. We say it is unwaged work.

They call it frigidity. We say it is absenteeism.

Every miscarriage is a work accident

Homosexuality and heterosexuality are both working conditions [...]

Neuroses, suicides, desexualisation: occupational diseases of the housewife
(Federici, 1974, p. 74)

Federici (1974) framed her ideas within the context of the 1970s and the second wave
feminism which was taking place, leading her to question and reconstruct Marxist theories, situating housework and reproduction as being essential sources of capital accumulation. Adopting this standpoint meant that women were re-positioned as
revolutionary subjects in the economic and political system. The idea then, of wages for
housework, was to force a restructure of social relations, which would end the biological
determinism which seemed to underpin these activities, and potentially destabilise
capitalism.

Gilman Perkins' and Federici's engagement with the position of women in capitalist
society brought them both to two equally important and equally uncomfortable critiques
of dominant projects of 'equalising society'. The first was the scale of changes that needed
to happen for the project of addressing inequalities to become meaningful.

The second issue was how much our understanding of 'progress' prevented meaningful
engagement with social inequality. Importantly Gilman Perkins and Federici levelled this
critique as much at those supposedly fighting against gendered oppression as anyone else.
As Federici made explicit in *Wages Against Housework*, one of the greatest challenges
facing 1960s and 1970s feminist politics was how to stop interpreting housewives as
uneducated or unfree. The problem for Federici was not that women who stayed at home
needed to be freed but that their work needed to be recognised as valuable. By prioritising
a political project of 'getting women out of the kitchen', the feminist movement was
reinforcing the ideologies and systems that reinforced women's position at the bottom of
the social hierarchy.

Gilman Perkins' work in Women and Economics also challenged standard themes in
feminist politics. A key focus of her writing was unpacking the 'unity' of women as a
social group. According to Gilman Perkins, the idea that all women were disadvantaged in
the same way was not an accurate depiction of reality. Some women were privileged and
benefited from capitalist inequality; some women depended on the (limited) wages they
received through engaging in 'women's work' to survive. If progress meant either more
capitalism or removing women's work, then at least one 'group' of women would end up
in a worse position than before!

Angela Y. Davis: Women, Race and Class

The 'unity' of women was further critiqued by the Black feminist theorist Angela Y. Davis
in her seminal work, *Women, Race and Class* (2011). Like Gilman Perkins, Davis focused
her analysis on the US experience. In *Women, Race and Class*, Davis outlined how the
history of womanhood and gender relations was different for Black women, particularly

those who had been enslaved and exploited in the Southern United States, than white women. Reviewing personalised accounts of former enslaved women and historical legal texts, Davis noted how enslaved people were often treated as 'genderless'. The system of colonialist capitalism that facilitated the slave trade and enslavement was more likely to deny feminine characteristics and maternal roles than impose them. Where these women were assigned caring roles or positioned as womanly, it was usually part of gendered violence (i.e. rape as punishment) or exploitation by white slave-owners. After the transatlantic slave trade became illegal, female slaves were valued as mothers only insofar as they could produce more slaves. US legal precedent established that, even when fathered by white slave-owners, the children of enslaved women were classed as slaves. Enslaved women did not have parental rights; when they were involved in childcare it was most likely for children who were not their own.

By tracing the history of enslaved Black communities, Davis raises a critical point to remember when analysing social inequalities – marginalisation and social disadvantage is closely tied to the legacies of colonialism and capitalism. The profitability of female slaves and their children altered the experience of gendered inequality for these groups. The feminine qualities and oppressions discussed by white women, Davis argues, are equally rooted in industrialisation, capitalism, and colonialism but in a very different way. Whereas enslaved females were expected to perform the same tasks as males; white female slave-owners, and later bourgeois and working-class women, were assigned very different roles to white men. High birth rates among enslaved women, following the end of the slave trade, was desired as a means of capitalist, commodifiable reproduction (of more slave workers). By comparison, high birth rates among white working class were seen as problematic and connected with the problem of the urban poor such as overpopulation.

Gurminder Bhambra: Modernity and Post-colonialism

Structuring her ideas around connected histories, Gurminder Bhambra rejected Western constructions of universality and truth and instead presented a fundamental recon-struction of the idea of modernity in contemporary sociology. She criticises the abstrac-tion of European modernity from its colonial context and the way that non-Western 'others' have been disregarded, and so aimed to establish a dialogue in which 'others' could speak and be heard.

Bhambra (2007) argues that the western framing of modernity relies on two basic assumptions, that of 'rupture' and 'difference', where 'rupture' represents the shift from agrarian past to industrial present, and that this is combined with the belief that Europe is different from the rest of the world. Qualifying this she contends that the dominant sociological theorists, such as Marx, Durkheim and Weber, had become preoccupied with explaining the challenges and issues of European society, as it was seen to be different from earlier agrarian societies (rupture) and unique within the world (difference).

Wallerstein (1997) contends that the social sciences have always exhibited 'Eurocen-trism' and communicated this through their histography, parochial universalism, assumptions about Western civilisation, orientalism and in attempts to impose a theory of progress. Bhambra (2007) adds to this criticism and argues not for a reorientation in interpretation of rupture/difference, but the need to challenge further the idea of Europe and what it was assumed to have done:

> Eurocentrism is the belief, implicit or otherwise, in the world historical significance of events believed to have developed endogenously within the cultural-geographical sphere of Europe. (Bhambra, 2007, p. 5)

A challenge therefore presents itself to sociologists to consider the specialness of Europe, its modernity, history and knowledge production. Indeed, classic theories of modernity are Eurocentric, and modernity is often conflated with Europe which has been shaped and framed by 'the politics of knowledge production' (Bhambra, 2007, p. 9). Delanty (2004) adds to this by asserting that modernity emerged from Europe and has become a global phenomenon, which can be modified by local tradition, but which is generally understood to be the expression of the European experience.

Modernity then remains a problematic concept, which according to Geonkar (2002) encompasses different and often conflicting theories, experiences, norms and beliefs. Trouillot (1991) turns our attention to importance of knowledge production, and the politics which underpin it, which can shape, interpret and construct representations of the past, and how the past relates to the future, which in effect can silence colonial encounters. Anthropologist, Trouillot (1991) contended that unequal power structures can construct historical narratives which shape how societies remember the past. Indeed, the development of social theories today is impacted by our understanding of the past. It is therefore critical that there is a recognition of 'others' alongside an acknowledgement that they were previously written out and their voices silenced.

Post-colonial Critiques of Modernity

Post-colonialism is often used as an umbrella term to encapsulate the political, economic, social and historical impact of European colonial rule. Post-colonial theory often utilises critical reflection to uncover the damage done by the creation of a colony. Common to all post-colonial theory is the belief that in order to understand the world we must acknowledge the impact of imperialism and colonial rule. The important word here is 'Post' as it must be understood, not just in terms of temporality but as a marker to show the change in conceptual thinking and understanding about the world. However, Quijano's (2000) work on 'coloniality of power' perspective observes that we remain in a colonial world which requires a break in narrow-minded thinking if decolonisation is to be achieved. With Appiah (1991, p. 348) conceiving the 'post' in post-colonial as a 'space-clearing gesture'.

Post-colonial theory, then, should, according to Bhambra (2007), be used to challenge dominant narratives, and foster inclusivity by analysing the links between knowledge, politics and power. Jardine (2000) furthers this by observing the importance of the context in which social sciences operate and derive meanings. Nandy (1983) asserts the importance of viewing epistemological issues, where cultures are taken over, and subjugation of minds as well as bodies occur, which has been observed, for example, in Africa with the actions of religious missionaries.

The colonial relationship fundamental to Europe and 'others' is based on the assumptions of cultural superiority of the colonisers, and it has been through the empire that European ideas were perpetuated throughout the world. Asher (2017) observes that colonial discourse has represented the world in simple binaries such as modernity/tradition, civilized/barbaric and the west/the rest. By using such representations colonial interventions are erased (Asher, 2017). Vázquez (2009) and Mignolo (2011) also outline and interrogate how the process of colonisation involved and was reinforced by the formation of a matrix of power which positioned European, colonising histories, knowledges and practices as superior to those of colonised peoples and nations. Vázquez argues that the absorption of modernity as neutral and rational ignores the violence of the colonial 'modernising' project which involved, among other things, the theft of land, the denial of indigenous languages and the destruction of historical texts.

To counter this, Vázquez argues that we need to pursue decoloniality and openly resist the binaries of modernity/tradition and so on. De-colonialist and post-colonialist theorists such as Vázquez and Quijano propose that this can be partially – but not wholly – achieved through memorialising and remembering the violence of modernity. It is also important, these theorists argue, to disrupt Western chronologies of social development, which position the Enlightenment and Industrial Revolution as the starting point of social and sociological analysis. Instead, they propose the first land-grabs of the Americas and Africa, by European imperialist nations, initially Spain and Portugal but later Britain and France, as the 'beginning' point for discussions of the origins of social inequalities and relationships. The reason for doing so is to foreground the role of colonialism and the transatlantic slave trade in the formation of many of the social inequalities sociological theory considers (including the inequalities covered in this book).

Spivak and Mohanty: What Stops Us From Addressing Social Inequality?

The ways in which marginalised or subaltern subjects have been represented is a central tenet in Gayatri Spivak's work and linked to issues in relationships between the West and the rest of the world. Spivak's (1988) work eloquently argues that colonial discourse stops the subaltern from having a voice. She also criticises the way that imperialism is depicted as the establisher of a good society, using the example of the codification of Hindu law concerning widows by the British in colonial India. Spivak (1988, p. 297) describes this as espousing woman as 'an object of protection from her own kind' or as an act of 'white men saving brown women from brown men'.

Chandra Mohanty, a post-colonial and feminist theorist, has been critical of Western feminism for its representation of women in the third world. She claims that there has been a propensity to categorise all 'Third World Woman' as one, coherent group which in effect ignores their historical and geographical differences, thus robbing them of their identity. Mohanty (1988) asserts that by creating these categories of 'Western Woman and Third World Woman', the Western Woman is depicted as strong, liberated, educated and superior whereas the Third World Woman is viewed as weak, oppressed, lacking in education, and inferior. Such representation, Mohanty explains, damages the solidarity of women as a whole. Mohanty's (2003) work asserts the need to convert relations of difference into relationships of solidarity.

In bridging these divides in relations, representations and communication, Spivak (1988) and Mohanty (2003) have much to offer in respect of transcending boundaries of difference. Spivak (1988, p. 295) suggests that those with privilege need 'to learn to speak to (rather than listen to or speak for) the historically muted subject of the subaltern woman' on an equal level, in effect, unlearning privilege and experiencing loss. For Mohanty (2003) it is about building coalitions and solidarity through a discourse which is caring and ethical. Moreover, van Dijk affirms that inequality can be created and maintained by discourse, where access to communication sources such as the media can be used to control and manipulate the minds of the lower classes.

Critical Race Theory

Critical Race Theory (CRT) originated in America in the mid-1970s and provides an analytical framework grounded in critical theory, by cross-disciplinary intellectuals, activists and civil rights scholars (Rollock & Gillborn, 2011). Originally stemming from the Critical Legal Studies (CLS) movement, which argued that the law was not objective or apolitical, CLS explored how the law served the wealthy at the expense of the poor, an idea which resonated with Marxist theory. The CRT theorists however did not want to abolish laws, instead they wanted to critique the law, society and race, and ground its conceptual framework in the lived experiences of people of colour. By exploring experiences of racial oppression, CRT posits we can better understand racial dynamics, and see how past issues/policies which were overtly racist continue to negatively impact on people's lives through inequalities.

Critical Race Theory is underpinned by Five key tenets, which are: (1) that racism is ordinary and not aberrational and has become deeply entrenched in the social order, public policy and organisational structures as well as being codified in law (Delgado & Stefancic, 2001); (2) interest convergence, whereby racism advances White Supremacy, allowing them to retain positions of power (Bell, 1980); (3) Race is socially constructed, which has been used to oppress and exploit people of colour; (4) The voices of people of colour – recognising the value of insights and experiences of racism and what it means to be racially minoritised (Delgado, 1989); (5) Intersectionality: which we will explore in more detail in the next section.

Over several decades, Critical Race Theorists have fought to challenge the racial disparities, inequalities and discrimination which exist and are reinforced by legal systems and public policies (Sawchuck, 2021). However, despite CRT taking a moral and ethical stance to improve equality, it has become embroiled in controversy in recent years, with efforts by right wing politicians to have it banned in schools. In September 2020, Donald

Trump, then American president, issued an executive order which prohibited diversity and inclusion training which was deemed to be divisive, which included CRT. In defiance, around 100 civil rights groups signed a petition opposing the order (George, 2021). President Biden rescinded Trump's order on taking office, but similar attempts to ban CRT continue to be attempted by Republican-controlled state legislatures (Fortin, 2021). The debate around CRT was also echoed in British politics, as 'equalities minister' Kemi Badenoch declared that the Conservative party 'stands unequivocally against Critical Race Theory', and that any teacher promoting elements of CRT such as 'white privilege' and 'inherited white guilt' without offering counter arguments are breaking the law (Meghji, 2021). Although, Meghji and Niang (2022) note that UK policymakers could use CRT's structural understanding of racism to tackle the socioeconomic disparity and inequalities evident in the United Kingdom, highlighted by the disproportionate mortality rates from people from Black and minoritised groups during the COVID-19 pandemic. The next section describes Intersectionality, a concept which underpins CRT and seen as a way of identifying and addressing inequality and discrimination.

Intersectionality

Intersectionality describes the analytical framework developed by Kimberle Crenshawe in 1989, which demonstrates how aspects of a person's identity overlap and combine to create different forms of discrimination or privilege (Crenshawe, 1989). Conceptualised as an analytical tool, intersectionality has its roots in Black feminism and CRT and aimed to address the marginalisation of Black women (Carbado et al., 2013). Crenshawe developed the framework to highlight ways in which antidiscrimination law, feminist theory and politics ignored the vulnerabilities of women of colour, especially those from deprived communities and in relation to violence against women (Crenshaw, 1991). Observing the multiple oppressions which intersect, the approach allows insight into to how these inequalities overlap and compound one another, while being affected contextually by historical, social and political factors. Indeed, intersectionality underlines the need to understand systems of inequality and discrimination as cumulative experiences, which impact people across their life-course (Collins, 2009) and how systems of power exert the greatest impact on the most marginalised and vulnerable in society. Cooper (2016) notes that intersectionality provides an analytical tool to study the dynamics of power to 'illuminate the diverse ways in which relations of domination and subordination are produced'.

Intersectionality is increasingly being considered as a policy framework to explore and highlight inequalities, and power structures in policymaking, practice and process (Hankivsky et al., 2014; Kapilashrami & Hankivsky, 2018). Indeed, intersectionality would allow policymakers to expose and work towards eliminating deep-rooted structures of discrimination, which compound disadvantage (Hankivsky et al., 2014). Moreover, this approach would facilitate identification of multiple dimensions of identity and disadvantage, in order to uncover any interconnected systems of oppression that are impacting upon people's agency and opportunities (Holman et al., 2021).

Collins (2009) considers intersecting systems of power and the hierarchical power relations as being the two main factors of what she calls 'the matrix of domination'. The intersecting systems of oppression include: race and structural racism; gender and patriarchy, age and ageism, class, sexual orientation; and other systemic oppressions. Hierarchical power relations include macro-, meso- and micro-level domains of power which are all strengthened and perpetuated by the hegemonic (ideological) domain of power (Collins, 2009).

■■■■■■■■■■■ **Chapter summary** ■■■■■■■■■■■

The chapter has taken an overarching perspective of key sociological theorists:

- August Comte: The three laws of social organisation
- Emile Durkheim: The division of labour
- Karl Marx: Industrialisation, capitalism and class
- Max Weber: Four ideal types of social action
- Charlotte Gilman Perkins: Gender, economics and social order
- Silvia Federici: The position of women in Capitalist societies
- Angela Y Davis: Women race and class
- Gurminder Bhambra: Modernity and post-colonialism
- Post-colonial critiques of modernity
- Spivak and Moharty: What stops us from addressing social inequality
- Critical Race Theory

Conclusion

This chapter has first looked at the early theorists which have shaped sociological thinking and discourse. Until recently, theories and concepts have very much been based on Western perspectives, and experiences, often at the expense of the rest of the world, who have not been given the opportunity of an audible voice. The chapter has shown how discourse can create a powerful asymmetry in representing and building relations in a post-colonial society. Western discourses have been seen to reinforce false stereotypes and infer cultural superiority often as a way of legitimising development programmes by the developed world.

The chapter has also presented a feminist perspective to draw attention to important female sociological theorists who offer a very different viewpoint from the long annotated 'old guard' of sociology. However, early feminist scholars failed to give attention to the role of racism and its role in oppressing women of colour (Ruparelia, 2016). Therefore, it was important that this chapter encompassed subaltern studies and pioneers in critical race feminism who in recent decades have challenged why white women's experiences have been universalised and allowed them a privileged position in society. The chapter has importantly contextualised these theories, which has inevitably drawn on the political influences which were apparent, up to modern day.

Questions to Reflect Upon

- We have seen how the key sociologists have examined the relationship between individuals and society, and how they have reached different or sometimes converging understandings for the causes of societal problems. While we must recognise the context of these theories from their own vantage points in history, they are nonetheless speaking from a position of privilege, as a white man. How might this have skewed our knowledge and understanding?
- The chapter has presented a diverse discourse from thinkers across the world in order for readers to contrast lesser-known theories against established Western perspectives. To decolonise completely, sociology needs to globalise. Consider how discourses of contemporary social problems from non-Western societies can be re-situated alongside Western perspectives.

Further Reading

Bhambra, G. (2007). *Rethinking modernity: Post-colonialism and the sociological imagination*. Springer (This book reconstructs the idea of modernity and its portrayal in Sociology and through a critique of post-colonial theorists demonstrates the importance understanding social theory.)

Collins, P. H. (2021). *Black feminist thought: Knowledge, consciousness, and the politics of empowerment*. Routledge (Patricia Hill Collins explores the work and theories of Black feminist intellectuals and writers).

Delgado, R., & Stefancic, J. (2001). *Critical race theory: An introduction*. New York, NY: University Press (Richard Delgado and Jean Stefancic explain in accessible terms what Critical race theory is all about and explore its origins.)

Federici, S. (1975). *Wages against housework*. Bristol: Falling Wall Press (Silvia Federici explores the nature of women's domestic labour and the social consequences which are attached to it.)

Spivak, G. C. (1988). Can the subaltern speak? In C. Nelson & L. Grossberg (Eds.), *Marxism and the interpretation of culture* (pp. 21–78). University of Illinois Press (Gayatri Spivak explores the ethical problems of how western cultures investigate other cultures and the prejudice and privilege underpinning this.)

References

Appiah, K. A. (1991). Is the post-in postmodernism the post-in postcolonial? *Critical Inquiry*, *17*(2), 336–357.

Asher, K. (2017). Spivak and Rivera Cusicanqui on the dilemmas of representation in postcolonial and decolonial feminisms. *Feminist Studies*, *43*(3), 512–524.

Bell, D. A. Jr. (1980). Brown v. Board of education and the interest-convergence dilemma. *Harvard Law Review*, *93*(3), 518–533. doi:10.2307/1340546.

Bhambra, G. (2007). *Rethinking modernity: Postcolonialism and the sociological imagination*. New York, NY: Springer.

Carbado, D. W., Crenshaw, K. W., Mays, V. M., & Tomlinson, B. (2013). Intersectionality. *Du Bois Review, 10*, 303–312. doi:10.1017/S1742058X13000349

Collins, P. H. (2009). Emerging intersections: Building knowledge and transforming institutions. *Emerging intersections: Race, class, and gender in theory, policy, and practice*, pp. vii–xiv.

Collins, P. H. (2021). *Black feminist thought: Knowledge, consciousness, and the politics of empowerment*. New York, NY: Routledge.

Cooper, B. (2016). Intersectionality. In L. Disch & M. Hawkesworth (Eds.), *The Oxford handbook of feminist theory* (pp. 385–406). Oxford, UK: Oxford University Press.

Crenshaw, K. (1989). *Demarginalizing the intersection of race and sex: A black feminist critique of antidiscrimination doctrine, feminist theory, and antiracist politics* (Vol. *1989*, p. 139). University of Chicago Legal Forum.

Crenshaw, K. (1991). *Race, gender, and sexual harassment*. s. Cal. l. Rev., 65, 1467.

Davis, A. Y. (2011). *Women, race, & class*. Vintage. New York.

Delanty, G. (2004). Is there a European identity? *Global Dialogue, 5*(3/4), 76–86.

Delgado, R. (1989). Storytelling for oppositionists and others: A plea for narrative. *Michigan Law Review, 87*, 2411–2441.

Delgado, R., & Stefancic, J. (2001). *Critical race theory: An introduction*. New York, NY: University Press.

Fortin, J. (27 July 2021). Critical race theory: A brief history. *The New York Times*. Retrieved 10 March 2022, from https://www.nytimes.com/article/what-is-critical-race-theory.html

Gaonkar, D. P. (2002). Toward new imaginaries: An introduction. *Public Culture, 14*(1), 1–19.

George, J. (11 January 2021). A lesson on critical race theory. *Human Rights Magazine*. Retrieved 10 March 2022, from https://www.americanbar.org/groups/crsj/publications/human_rights_magazine_home/civil-rights-reimagining-policing/a-lesson-on-critical-race-theory/

Gilman, C. P. (1898). *Women and economics: The economic factor between men and women as a factor in social evolution*. Boston, MA: Maynard and Company.

Hankivsky, O., Grace, D., Hunting, G., Giesbrecht, M., Fridkin, A., Rudrum, S., & Clark, N. (2014). An intersectionality-based policy analysis framework: Critical reflections on a methodology for advancing equity. *International Journal for Equity in Health, 13*(1), 1–16.

Holman, D., Salway, S., Bell, A., Beach, B., Adebajo, A., Ali, N., & Butt, J. (2021). Can intersectionality help with understanding and tackling health inequalities? Perspectives of professional stakeholders. *Health Research Policy and Systems, 19*(1), 1–15.

Jardine, N. (2000). *The scenes of inquiry: On the reality of questions in the sciences*. Oxford, UK: Oxford University Press.

Kapilashrami, A., & Hankivsky, O. (2018). Intersectionality and why it matters to global health. *The Lancet, 391*(10140), 2589–2591.

Meghji, A. (2021). *Decolonizing sociology: An introduction*. Cambridge: Polity Press.

Meghji, A., & Niang, S. M. (2022). Between post-racial ideology and provincial universalisms: Critical race theory, decolonial thought and COVID-19 in Britain. *Sociology, 56*(1), 131–147.

Mignolo, W. D. (2011). *The darker side of western modernity: Global futures, decolonial options*, New York, NY: Duke University Press.

Mohanty, C. (1988). Under western eyes: Feminist scholarship and colonial discourses. *Feminist Review, 30*(1), 61–88.

Mohanty, C. T. (2003). *Feminism without borders: Decolonizing theory, practicing solidarity.* Durham, NC: Duke University Press.

Nandy, A. (1983). *The intimate enemy: Loss and recovery of self under colonialism.* Delhi; Oxford, UK: Oxford University Press.

Pedersen, J. E. (2001). Sexual politics in Comte and Durkheim: Feminism, history, and the French sociological tradition. *Signs: Journal of Women in Culture and Society, 27*(1), 229–263.

Quijano, A. (2000). Coloniality of power and eurocentrism in Latin America. *International Sociology, 15*(2), 215–232.

Rollock, N., & Gillborn, D. (2011). *Critical race theory (CRT), British Educational Research Association online resource.* Retrieved 9 March 2022, from https://www.bera.ac.uk/publication/critical-race-theory-crt

Ruparelia, R. (2016). The invisibility of whiteness in the white feminist imagination. In *Shades of whiteness* (pp. 77–89). Brill. New York.

Sawchuck, S. (18 May 2021). What is critical race theory, and why is it under attack? *Education Week.* Retrieved 10 March 2022, from https://www.edweek.org/leadership/what-is-critical-race-theory-and-why-is-it-under-attack/2021/05

Spivak, G. C. (1988). Can the subaltern speak? In C. Nelson & L. Grossberg (Eds.), *Marxism and the interpretation of culture* (pp. 21–78). Illinois, IL: University of Illinois Press.

Trouillot, M. R. (1991). Anthropology and the Savage slot: The politics and poetics of otherness. *Recapturing anthropology: Working in the present.* Santa Fe, NM: School of American Research Press.

Vázquez, R. (2009). Modernity coloniality and visibility: The politics of time. *Sociological Research Online, 14*(4), 109–115.

Wallerstein, I. (1997). Eurocentrism and its avatars: The dilemmas of social science. *Sociological Bulletin, 46*(1), 21–39.

Weber, M. (1958). The protestant ethic and spirit of capitalism (T. Parson, Trans.), Scribner's, New York in B. Dyck and D. Schroeder: 2005,Management, theology and moral point of view: Towards an alternative to the conventional materialist-individualist ideal-type of management. *Journal of Management Studies, 42*(4), 70.

2

SOCIAL CLASS

Nicola Ingram

━━━━━━━━━━ Learning objectives ━━━━━━━━━━

- To consider the different ways in which class has been historically understood
- To understand the differences between material, social and cultural framings of social class
- To critically evaluate conceptualisations of social class through the lens of intersectionality
- To consider ways of understanding class-based inequalities together with race, ethnicity and gender

━━━━━━━━━━ Framing questions ━━━━━━━━━━

- What is social class and how has it been historically understood?
- Is social class an economic, cultural or social categorisation?
- How can conceptualisations of social class take account of race, ethnicity, gender and other axis of inequality?
- What theoretical approaches can we take to thinking complexly and intersectionally about class?

Introduction

This chapter explores the multiple dimensions of class and how the interplay of economic and cultural factors culminates in social inequalities. It will problematise uni-dimensional conceptualisations of class and examine social positions as well as social processes, highlighting how they may shape and perpetuate negative outcomes. The chapter will also consider issues of intersectionality and how class-oriented analyses of social relations – particularly the work of Marx and Weber through to Bourdieu – obscure racialised and gendered inequalities. It introduces students to thinking about class complexly, using Bourdieu's forms of capital, but to understand capitals as not only classed, but as gendered and racialised. The aim of this chapter is to provide a grounding in thinking intersectionally about class.

What Is Social Class and How Has It Been Historically Understood?

There are different perspectives on social class on how it is defined and how it is measured. These are often in contestation with one another. What underpins each of these, however, is the idea that society is organised within a social structure of different class fractions and that these are hierarchically arranged. The dynamics of this structure and how it is formed is what is up for debate. This chapter provides a basic overview of some of the key theorists of class as well as contemporary perspectives. It will briefly discuss Marx, Weber and Bourdieu before outlining more recent perspectives which take account of gender and race as key dimensions of inequality that cannot be neatly separated from class. Early social theorists such as Marx and Weber remain important to understanding the development of thinking about class inequalities. Their perspectives, however, as privileged white men, tended to neglect the significance of gender and race inequalities, which has more recently been remedied through feminist, decolonial and anti-racist scholarship.

Karl Marx (1818–1883) was a German economic and political theorist whose work championed the significance of social class conflict and the alienation of workers. Marx is famous for his critical writings on capitalism, and his work has had a lasting influence on thinking about the connection between work and society. Marxist perspectives on social class underscore the importance of the relationship between the owners (the Bourgeoisie) of the means of production (all the things that are needed in order to produce – e.g. land, premises, equipment, technology) and those who need to sell their labour (the Proletariat). From a Marxist perspective the Bourgeoisie are the owners of the means of production, who then rely on the paid labour of the proletariat in order to enhance their own material capital. The proletariat are not owners of the means of production and therefore need to sell their labour for material gain (i.e. wages). Their labour power is the only commodity that they possess and so they must enter into an employment arrangement, which is deemed to be an arrangement of exploitation. Using this key division to understand the class structure brings material circumstances to the fore as a defining principle of class division. In a capitalist mode of production those who need to sell their labour in order to generate a means to exist are regarded as working-class. The neat dualistic classification is obviously based on the structures of early capitalist social formation where the division between owners and non-owners of the means of production was clearly defined and less complexly differentiated. In contemporary societies, still governed by the capitalist mode of production, stratification between workers has become more complex, so much so that we would not regard all those who sell their labour as working-class. Marxism, however, has made a fundamental contribution to our understanding of how class works, in particular, it necessitates an important focus on the material circumstances of workers, the value of their labour, and the relationship between work and exploitation. In class terms Marxism highlights social division and inequality through material economic power relations.

Max Weber (1864–1920) was a German historian and political economist whose work was influential in the development of the discipline of sociology. Weber was interested in social status as a way of thinking about social stratification within society. As we have noted throughout this book, society is organised hierarchically into unequal social strata. Weber recognised that economic resources were a key means through which society was divided. From a Weberian perspective, social status and political power were, however, also fundamental in considering how society was stratified. Weber identified four different social classes. These were the working-class (who were wage labourers); the petite-bourgeoisie (those who were self-employed); the propertyless intelligentsia (e.g. writers, artists, teachers who do not own the means of production); and entrepreneurial property owners. These different classes cannot be reduced to their economic positions alone as status and political affiliation/position are fundamental in determining status and power. This approach allows for an understanding of how cultural resources, such as education, are crucial in thinking about the class structure. For example, while writers and artists may not have historically earned a significant amount of money through their work, their position in the class hierarchy would have been greater than factory or farm workers as they gained status through their role in directing cultural knowledge production. Like Marx, Weber was interested in power relations and its role in determining social structure. Unlike Marx, he highlighted, however, the significance of status and political power – i.e. cultural resources (through education, religious standing, political influence, knowledge production), not just economic power, in thinking about how we might consider the class structure to be organised. Both Marx and Weber were influential on the thinking of a more recent theorist of class, Pierre Bourdieu, whose legacy has had a lasting impact on how scholars conceptualise social class.

Pierre Bourdieu (1930–2002) was a French sociologist and anthropologist whose work is fundamental to approaches to class analysis in the 20th and 21st centuries. Bourdieu continues to have a strong influence in the development of thinking about social class and social stratification, particularly within European and American sociology. Bourdieu's writing has been adopted widely because of its focus on how class divisions are produced by, woven through, and visible in socio-cultural arenas outside of what we see as formal 'workplaces'. Bourdieu takes the foundational precepts of thinkers like Marx and Weber and extends the arguments around stratification and hierarchies to explain why situations where status markers are not stated explicitly can still be riven with uneven power relations. As we will discuss below, Bourdieu is important as it forces us to reflect on what we, individually and collectively, see as hallmarks of status. More pointedly, by applying Bourdieu to our own conduct, we can become aware that, even when we claim to resist class-based hierarchies, our attitudes towards each other and how we interact with the world are clearly marked by classed thinking.

A Bourdieusian approach to social class brings together both economic and cultural resources (similar to Weberian approaches) as important factors in determining social stratification. It also includes *social* resources as a third factor. Bourdieu refers to these as three forms of capital which are lynchpin concepts in his conceptualisation of the class structure. For Bourdieu, a person's position in social space is the outcome of their unique combination and volume of economic, cultural and social capital. Economic capital refers to material resources such as property, income and inheritance, and is the most straightforward form to measure. Bourdieu (1986, p. 242) defines economic capital as material possessions that are 'immediately and directly convertible into money and may be institutionalized in the form of property rights'. They include property, income and inheritance and are important for the acquisition of other forms of capital (i.e. cultural and social).

The other forms of capital are more complex. Cultural capital has three forms, what Bourdieu (1986) calls 'the embodied state', 'the objectified state' and 'the institutionalised state'. The embodied state refers to dispositions 'of body and mind' and may be regarded as ways of speaking, posture and projections of confidence. These forms of bodily expression can be seen as a resource as people are valued according to their presentations of self – their posture, their body language, manner, accent and expression. The objectified state refers to cultural goods such as books, paintings, clothing, cars and shoes. These objects signify a person's taste and have value (and values) attributed to them. For example, the way a person dresses is often used as a shorthand means of assuming their social class status, and can lead to snobbery and discrimination against the working-classes. The institutionalised state refers to titles conferred through valued institutions e.g. the status of Bachelor of the Arts conferred through the acquisition of a degree certificate. The final form, social capital, refers to valuable social connections, such as gatekeepers to job opportunities, or people with valuable knowledge of a desirable employment field that a school leaver/graduate would like to enter. Bourdieu defines social capital as 'the aggregate of the actual or potential resources which are linked to possession of a durable network of more or less institutionalized relationships of mutual acquaintance or recognition' (Bourdieu, 1986, p. 248). They are essentially valuable social connections, valuable in the sense that they can be utilised/exchanged for other forms of capital, and ultimately enhance the accumulation of economic capital.

For all three forms of capital their value is only realised in the process of exchange. For example, having a high volume of economic capital may enable someone to purchase an elite education at a private school (and thus economic capital can be exchanged for both cultural and social capital); or a degree certificate can be used to access graduate employment (thus cultural capital can be exchanged for economic capital); or knowing the right people may help when applying for a job as they may be able to provide advice and guidance in relation to navigating within a chosen field or profession (thus social capital can be exchanged for economic capital). Bourdieu's mapping of the social space is not as linear as his predecessors' conceptualisations of class, as his model positions people by *forms* as well as *volume* of capitals. In other words, it is not just about how much capital a person has, but what forms of capital they have, and crucially, how they can exchange it. He conceptualised social space as a quadrant with two axes, the X axis for forms of capital and the Y axis for volume of capital (see Figure 2.1 for a Bourdieu inspired example of a map of social space). If we look at Figure 2.1, we can see that different professions can

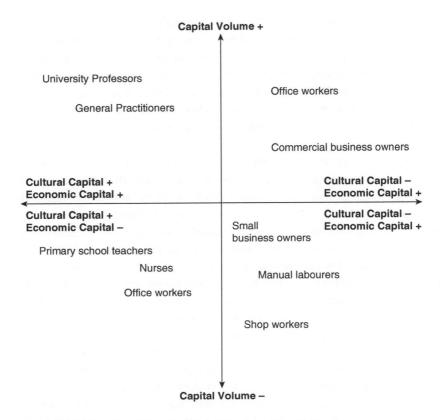

Figure 2.1   Presents a Bourdieusian Mapping of Social Space

be positioned according to volumes of both economic and cultural capital. For example, primary school teachers can be regarded as having reasonably high volumes of cultural capital (institutionalised in a university degree) while scoring lower in terms of economic capital. Conversely, shop owners may have high volumes of economic capital but without high volumes of cultural capital. Bourdieu's way of conceptualising social class draws on Weber's thinking about status, and moves the debate on from thinking about class in purely economic terms. In this way, employment status, which is often the measurement used in defining social class can be seen as encompassing different forms of capital, and class can therefore be thought of as both an economic and cultural phenomenon. A critique of this approach to mapping cultural capital is that it takes a deficit approach to thinking about the working-class as lacking, or having lower levels of cultural capital. Bourdieu's work is actually more subtle than this, in that he uses the term symbolically recognised cultural capital, and conceptualises capital as a relational good within a socially constructed value system. Therefore, while the working-classes possess forms of cultural capital, it is not necessarily valued highly in the social spaces of the dominant classes (Ingram, 2009). When we think about high and low volumes of cultural capital we need to remember that the symbolic recognition of the capital is important for determining its value.

Intersectionality

Intersectionality is a way of thinking about multiple dimensions of disadvantage together rather than as separate components. The term, coined by Kimberlé Crenshaw in 1989, has become a key framework for considerations of interlocking forms of oppression. It facilitates thinking about inequalities as having multiple dimensions that cannot be reduced to a single axis or considered in isolation. From a social class perspective, an intersectional approach would recognise the interaction between social class and other dimensions of identity and inequality (e.g. gender, race, ethnicity, disability). While the contributions of Marx, Weber and Bourdieu have been fundamental to conceptualisations of class they, each in different ways, neglect to fully account for other axes of disadvantage that interact with that of social class. In other words, thinking about class-based disadvantage as a single axis issue leads to the side-lining of race, ethnicity, gender and disability, even though each of these aspects of experience are integral to how class works (Bohrer, 2019, pp. 159–82). Of the three theorists outlined above, Bourdieu provides the theoretical tools most adaptable to a consideration of multiple dimensions of disadvantage (e.g. embodied cultural capital as a concept arguably necessitates thinking about class, race, gender and disability), but his work has been critiqued for neglecting gender (Adkins & Skeggs, 2004) and for not fully accounting for race and ethnicity (Wallace, 2017). Each of these axes of disadvantage are complex in their own ways, and there is a tendency for research to highlight the significance of one over the other. Crenshaw (1989, p. 140), however, makes a strong case against focusing on a single dimension of disadvantage, arguing that to do so entails an assumption that a person is privileged in other dimensions. That is, if we only see one dimension of disadvantage then we are not recognising, and de facto denying, the significance of other dimensions. Crenshaw is a law professor in the United States of America and is best known for her concept of intersectionality, which essentially means thinking about multiple forms of disadvantage together, rather than as single issues. In particular, when coining the term, she was interested in the intersection of race and gender. She writes:

> Because the intersectional experience is greater than the sum of racism and sexism, any analysis that does not take intersectionality into account cannot sufficiently address the particular manner in which Black women are subordinated. (Crenshaw, 1989, p. 140)

Her work is very influential within the social sciences, and is the basis of critique for studies of social class that fail to account for other forms of disadvantage. For example, popular discourses present social class as an identity position that belongs to white citizens. Class is discussed as if it applies to the white working-class only and racialised minorities are therefore presented without a class attribution. This way of thinking contributes to the discourse about white working-class failure that has seeped into political agendas in the global north, where right-wing nationalist populism has constructed whiteness as form of contemporary disadvantage (Mondon & Winter, 2020).

Instead of recognising disadvantage as located in class, whiteness is (mis)presented as an identity position that leads to poor outcomes such as educational failure. This discourse seeks to disrupt anti-racist developments in society by racialising class in a way that denies its structural disadvantages. Whites are constructed as 'race victims' (Gillborn, 2008, p. 229) rather than victims of an oppressive class system. Intersectionality is a useful concept for countering these problematic discourses. From an intersectional perspective we can consider how class and race interact for the white working-classes to generate disadvantage in terms of social class without generating disadvantage in terms of race. In other words, whiteness does not reinforce class-based inequalities and in fact may help mitigate them in some cases. Class and race are interactive in generating advantage and disadvantage rather than interchangeable.

Intersectionality is also key for pushing against analyses of gender that privilege the perspectives of white middle class women. Nash (2008, p. 2) claims that 'Intersectionality, the notion that subjectivity is constituted by mutually reinforcing vectors of race, gender, class, and sexuality, has emerged as the primary theoretical tool designed to combat feminist hierarchy, hegemony, and exclusivity'. While challenges to the feminist tradition of foregrounding gender as a discrete site of inequality have existed for decades through for example the work of Black feminists (Collins, 2000; Davis, 1981; Spelman, 1988), the term intersectionality has become popularised as a theoretical tool for engaging with issues of gender, class and race simultaneously and in a way that recognises their co-constitution. This has had a significant influence on thinking about social class in recent decades, and many studies attend to class in a way that doesn't isolate it from other aspects of identity and axis of disadvantage.

In her seminal text, *Formations of Class and Gender*, Bev Skeggs (1997) takes an intersectional approach and provides a robust analysis of working-class women's life experiences and perspectives. Using a Bourdieusian lens, Skeggs highlights the way that gender and class are enmeshed. Her work provides a good example of the use of Bourdieu's concept of capitals to analytically bring together gender, class and race. She writes:

> Gender, race and class are not capitals as such, rather they provide the relations in which capitals come to be organized and valued. (Skeggs, 1997, p. 9)

For Skeggs, forms of capital are given value in a relational way. For example, gender itself is not a form of capital but different ways of doing or presenting gender carry different values. We can think about the way that different classed and racialised presentations of femininity (clothing, style, manner of speaking) carry different levels of capital in society and are accorded more or less value. In this way we can see that while gender is not a form of cultural capital, cultural capital is gendered and classed and racialised. The difference is important.

Intersectional approaches to disadvantage can work with conceptualisations of class that focus on both material circumstances (economic capital) and cultural factors.

The following story is one of class, race and gender inequality. It draws on data from the Paired Peers project (Bathmaker et al., 2016), which is a major study of social class and higher education inequalities in the UK. Read through Adele's story and consider how you might use an intersectional class lens to think about issues of disadvantage and the graduate labour market.

━━━━━━━━ **Case study** ━━━━━━━━━━━━━━━━━━━━━

The story of Adele

Adele studied history and international relations at the University of the West of England, a Post 92 university in Bristol, in the United Kingdom. Post 92 universities are newer universities within the UK higher education system and are so-called because they were granted university status after 1992. Many were formerly polytechnic colleges and generally they are associated with widening university participation to under-represented populations, such as the working-class and some ethnic minority groups.

Before moving to Bristol to study, Adele lived with her mother in Wales. Her mother worked in retail and raised her and her sister on her own. Her father left when she was nine months old. Adele describes her ethnicity as mixed race white and Afro-Caribbean, her mother is white Welsh and her father is Jamaican. She completed her studies with a 2.1 and upon leaving university Adele continued with a job she had secured during the course of her degree, after completing a paid internship. She was working as a fundraising officer for a small charity in Bristol and upon graduation they offered her a full-time position with an £18,000 salary. It was not necessarily the job she aspired to do, but earning money was important to her as her family did not have the economic capital to support her while she waited for the right opportunity to present itself, or for her to explore and consider her options. It was taken-for-granted that she would support herself, and she didn't entertain the possibility of not working.

While she felt 'lucky' that she had a job that she liked, she also recognised that in not taking time to pause she was closing herself off to other possibilities such as travel.

> . . . I was just here continuing on with my job, which I really enjoyed and I really liked and I was quite lucky in the fact that I. . .unlucky and lucky. Lucky that I had a job that I could go into which I liked and that paid, unlucky in the fact that maybe I didn't really kind of have time to have a break, go travelling, really kind of discover what I wanted to do. . .So it's kind of weird, I don't know how I ended up in the charity sector, I was just kind of like. . .I don't understand how it happened, I just kind of like. . .I obviously just got lucky. I didn't get lucky because I did work my arse off in that internship and then they offered me a full time job.

After a year or so of working in the job, Adele began to wish for more challenging employment:

> Although it's not challenging me I am happy, I'm not going to work, like 'oh God I hate it' and I've been lucky enough to not being stuck for work since I left university, I've gone straight into work and haven't left. I'm just at that stage where I kind of want to develop

(Continued)

a bit more and possibly go on to do something else in the charitable sector. But I do think I'm on the right track, I just don't know how long that track is and where the end point is and I kind of think, you know it's not a race and I'm just kind of grappling with that and trying to not beat myself up for, you know perhaps not earning more or not being in a higher position.

After three years of working in the charity sector in Bristol with aspirations for something more challenging Adele is offered a job as a corporate account manager for a charity based in London. She lands the job after numerous applications and after 'about 10' interviews in London, a lot of disappointment, and a battle with the 'disheartening' nature of the struggle. She recalled some of her negative experiences of interviews:

As soon as I walked in I just felt like they had disengaged immediately. I don't know if it's because they looked at me and thought 'well no we don't like the look'.

As soon as I walked in I think I was like 'no, it's not for me' perhaps I think sometimes that affects your performance in an interview as well.

It took Adele 'a long time and a lot of interviews to kind of understand what would suit' her, which entailed weathering 'a lot of "nos"' and left her thinking 'is this for me?' Despite her experience, her tenacity and a clear plan of direction that emerged over three years, Adele's experiences of rejection in her employment area of choice leave her questioning herself. She wonders if it is for her because she is made to feel that she does not belong.

Adele's efforts finally pay off and she has a positive interview experience where before the interview she met her prospective colleagues and felt a connection:

I had to do a presentation, it was one of the best presentations I've done, I was cracking jokes and I had a ... you know we were talking beforehand, like personally, just about different things, and that kind of set the scene and it made me a lot more relaxed when I was doing my presentation. But other presentations, like my leg's been going and I've been really ... and I was just like 'oh', it just made so much more of a difference.

Thinking About the Case Study Through an Intersectional Lens
Class Position

Adele's mother works in retail, which from a Marxist perspective makes her working-class, as she has to sell her labour. From a Weberian perspective the job has low social and economic status. If we look again at Figure 2.1, from a Bourdieusian perspective, Adele's family are in the lower right-hand quadrant, denoting low economic and low symbolically recognised cultural capital. Adele, however, gained a degree and had an administrative job in the charity sector. This puts her in the lower left quadrant of Figure 2.1 as her degree carries symbolic value, her job has status, but it is not highly paid. This puts her in a similar position in social space to primary school teachers, with higher levels of cultural capital and lower economic capital. However, positioning Adele according to her economic and social position does not allow us to fully engage with the complexity of the inequalities that she experiences as a mixed race woman from a working-class background.

Intersectionality and Different Forms of Capital

Adele has a good degree from a UK university, which is a form of institutionalised cultural capital. However, her story shows how institutionalised cultural capital does not work on its own in the graduate labour market. Both economic capital and embodied cultural capital can be seen to be at play in the way that Adele's graduate labour market journey unfolds. Adele does not have the economic capital to afford the luxury of time to be strategic about launching her graduate career (see Ingram, Abrahams, & Bathmaker, 2018 for a further discussion of time and stop gaps), and is not presented with a range of pathways and choices on graduation. Her parameters are therefore delineated by her class position. This shows the importance of the various forms of capital and how they work together to create opportunities and outcomes.

Confidence and Competence: Issues of Race, Class and Gender

Adele, as a mixed race, white, working-class woman, does not get to believe in her own capabilities in a way that is free from doubt. As evident above, she constructed her immediate graduate labour market success as luck while at the same time recognising that she had worked hard for her achievements. In response to her success three years later she pits the notion of fate against hard work. She says: 'is it meant to be or was it my hard work?' which is very different to thinking that she is entitled to her success because of her competence and developed skills, knowledge and experience. As shown by Ingram et al. (forthcoming) white middle-class male graduates are happy to claim their skills and competencies while also recognising their privilege, but they don't use their privilege to undermine their own success. Adele, on the other hand, partially explains her success through fate, undermining her own role in making it happen. In considering the possibility of her outcome being as a result of fate, Adele misrecognises the inequalities that she has experienced on the graduate labour market through her embodied racialised, classed and gendered markers of cultural capital.

Intersectionality and Embodied Cultural Capital

Shilling (1992) stresses the relative values of different forms of physical capital and argues that the dominant class defines what is a worthy orientation towards bodily presentation. Concomitantly they define corporeal unworthiness and so 'other' bodies can be easily devalued. Adele's negative interview experiences have transmitted messages of her embodied unworthiness – her ethnicity, class and gender are worn on her body and have not fitted with that of the employing institution (and by default those that comprise the organisation). Her repeated experiences of walking into the interview room and immediately feeling like she did not fit ('they had disengaged immediately', 'no, it is not for me') suggest that her embodied cultural capital did not align with the employers. Nirmal Puwar, in her book, *Space Invaders*, writes about the ways in which certain bodies that present racialised, gendered and classed cultural capital are read as trespassers and not belonging.

> Social spaces are not blank and open for anybody to occupy. ... Some bodies have
> the right to belong in certain locations while others are marked out as trespassers
> who are, in accordance with how both spaces and bodies are imagined,
> circumscribed as being "out of place". (Puwar, 2004, p. 8)

In Adele's case, the argument can be made that her cultural capital as a mixed race, working-class women was not being recognised as valuable in the space of her interviews. This is how unconscious bias works, it is intersectional, and it is easy for those with privilege to deny its existence. It allows bodies that are white to be invisible and to pass without notice or recognition of being out of place (Ahmed, 2007).

Chapter summary

This chapter outlines key social theories of class, drawing on the work of sociological theorists, and includes the following:

- Explores the work of Marx, Weber and Bourdieu
- Explains how class is woven through and reproduced by everyday interactions
- Using a case study, the chapter shows how we need to understand class-based inequalities as connected with race and gender
- Intersectionality and different forms of capital
- Confidence and competence: issues of race, class and gender
- Intersectionality and embodied cultural capital

Conclusion

This chapter has provided an introduction to theoretical perspectives on social class, with an overview of the key thinkers Marx, Weber and Bourdieu. It has drawn out their different conceptualisations of the class structure, highlighting similarities and differences in their thinking. Crucially, the chapter has outlined the complexities of Bourdieusian framings of social class, with a focus on Bourdieu's three forms of capital, which build upon and expand Marxist and Weberian approaches to social class by considering the importance of economic/material factors, status/cultural factors and social connections. The chapter has subsequently provided an overview of the concept of intersectionality as a key intervention in the theoretical space of narrowly focused class analysis that is neglectful of, for example, issues of race, ethnicity and gender. The work of both Crenshaw and Skeggs has been presented as critical to advancing scholarship and thinking on intersectionality, with particular reference to both race and gender. The chapter has then provided a case study, using data from the Paired Peers project, which highlights issues of intersectionality through the story of a mixed-race working-class woman attempting to make it on the graduate labour market in the UK in the mid-late 2000s. Different ways of analysing the case study have been presented, using an intersectional approach and considering the framings of social class presented earlier in the chapter. Overall, the chapter shows the complexity of social class and the different and contested ways in which it might be conceptualised. Moreover, the importance of not considering social class in isolation from race, ethnicity and gender has been demonstrated.

Questions to Reflect Upon

- How important are material circumstances or economic capital in defining class position, opportunities and outcomes?
- How important are cultural resources or forms of cultural capital in defining class position, opportunities and outcomes?
- How important are race and gender in considerations of social class position, opportunities and outcomes?

Further Reading

Ingram, N (2009). Working-class boys, educational success and the misrecognition of working-class culture. *British Journal of Sociology of Education*, *30*(4), 431–434 (This paper explores how individual working-class identities, selfhoods and dispositions [Bourdieu's 'habitus'] are troubled by institutional educational habitus. It is based on a study of white working-class boys in Belfast, Northern Ireland, in two separate schools: a high-achieving grammar school and secondary school. The boys come from the same community and have been separated by an exam taken at aged 11. The paper is useful as it shows how working-class cultural capital is undervalued and/or misrecognised within middle-class institutional habitus [the grammar school]).

Nash, J. C. (2008). Re-thinking intersectionality. *Feminist Review*, *89*(1), 1–15 (This paper revisits intersectionality. It discusses the limitations of Crenshaw's original concept and considers how it can be strengthened. This paper is important as intersectionality can be approached uncritically. As you progress through your studies it is important to consider the gaps within theories as well as the contribution they make.)

Skeggs, B. (1997a). *Formations of class and gender: Becoming respectable*. London: SAGE (This work is based on research with working-class women in the North of England and contends that feminism needs to centre class more in discussions of how identity, gender and inequalities are formed. Using ethnographic research Skeggs outlines how women negotiate classed and gendered inequalities. This work is important as it bridges a gap between feminism and working-class cultural studies.)

References

Adkins, L., & Skeggs, B. (2004). *Feminism after Bourdieu*. Oxford: Blackwell.

Ahmed, S. (2007). A phenomenology of whiteness. *Feminist Theory, 8*(2), 149–168.

Bathmaker, A. M., Ingram, N., Abrahams, J., Hoare, A.,Waller, R., & Bradley, H. (2016). *Higher education, social class and social mobility: The degree generation*. London: Palgrave Macmillan.

Bohrer, A. J. (2019). *Chapter four: Intersectional critiques of Marxism. Marxism and intersectionality: Race, gender, class and sexuality under contemporary capitalism* (pp. 159–182). Bielefeld: Transcript Verlag.

Bourdieu, P. (1986). The forms of capital. In J. Richardson (Ed.), *Handbook of theory and research for the sociology of education* (pp. 241–258). Westport, CT: Greenwood.

Collins, P. H. (2000). *Black feminist thought* (2nd ed.), New York, NY: Routledge.

Crenshaw, K. W. (1989). Demarginalizing the intersection of race and sex: A Black feminist critique of antidiscrimination doctrine. *University of Chicago Legal Forum, 1989*, 139–168.

Davis, A. (1981). *Women race and class*. New York, NY: Random House.

Gillborn, D. (2008). Coincidence or conspiracy? Whiteness, policy and the persistence of the black/white achievement gap. *Educational Review, 60*(3), 229–248.

Ingram, N. (2009). Working-class boys, educational success and the misrecognition of working-class culture. *British Journal of Sociology of Education, 30*(4), 431–434.

Ingram, N., Abrahams, J., & Bathmaker, A. M. (2018). When class trumps university status: Narratives of Zoe and Francesca from the paired peers project. In P. J. Burke, A. Hayton, & J. Stevenson (Eds.), *Widening participation in higher education: Towards a reflexive approach to research and evaluation*. London: Trentham.

Mondon, A., & Winter, A. (2020). *Reactionary democracy: How racism and the populist far right became mainstream*. London: Verso.

Nash, J. C. (2008). Re-thinking intersectionality. *Feminist Review, 89*(1), 1–15.

Puwar, N. (2004). *Space invaders: Race, gender and bodies out of place*. Oxford: Berg.

Shilling, C. (1992). Schooling and the production of physical capital. *Discourse: Studies in the Cultural Politics of Education, 13*(1), 1–19.

Skeggs, B. (1997). *Formations of class and gender: Becoming respectable*. London: SAGE.

Spelman, E. (1988). *Inessential woman: Problems of exclusion in feminist thought*. Boston: Beacon Press.

Wallace, D. (2017). Reading 'race' in Bourdieu? Examining Black cultural capital among Black Caribbean youth in South London. *Sociology, 51*(5), 907–923.

3

RACE, RACISM AND DECOLONISING KNOWLEDGE

Dyuti Chakravarty

━━━━━━━━ Learning objectives ━━━━━━━━

- To consider racism beyond individual acts of prejudice and bigotry.
- To understand the persistence of colonial matrix of power (CMP) in our curriculums that shape our understanding of the 'developing' world and of minoritised communities in the 'developed' world. This will help us understand the concept of epistemic racism.
- To envision ways of prioritising racial justice within the university and beyond.

━━━━━━━━ Framing questions ━━━━━━━━

- How can we question the nature of 'objectivity' in academic disciplinary knowledge and expose the intricate links between colonialism and academic knowledge production?
- What does it mean to raise questions around 'whiteness' in existing academic curriculum and to demand for 'decolonising the curriculum'?
- How is the call for 'decolonising the university' essentially a call for racial justice in universities?

Introduction

This chapter will examine the intersections of race and ethnicity and their interplay with institutional disciplinary knowledge received in the Western academy. Central to this chapter is a key issue in current social (in)equalities theory and research, the call to 'decolonise the curriculum'. Drawing on decolonial theory and literature on race, the chapter outlines how these calls are essentially about 'de-centring Europe' (Ngugi, 1989) from our disciplinary/academic knowledge production, to create a space that allows us to co-design knowledges with the communities that we inhabit. It will conclude with a discussion on how endeavours to decolonise the university would require a 'fundamental overhaul of the whole epistemological model underlying the current educational system' (Cotton, 2018, p. 6).

The debate around decolonising the curriculum may appear to be of minor academic concern. However, the chapter uses different case studies that allow us to disentangle the relationship between colonialism and our established belief systems. To this extent, the chapter unpacks the role that the discourse around 'colonial difference' and knowledge or epistemic superiority played in justifying colonialism's supposed 'civilisational' benefits at the cost of underplaying the reality of conquest, slaughter and plunder of resources. Through decolonising the curriculum we will look at the lasting effects of the discourse around colonial difference implicit in disciplinary knowledge production in perpetuating 'epistemic racism' that devalues experiences, cultural practices and forms of expressions of non-white/people of colour.

These issues are complex and challenging. Even so, through engaging with them we can expand our understanding of racism that goes beyond the popular conception of individual prejudice, bias and bigotry. By working through the case studies in this chapter, you will be able to talk about and identify a critical argument within decolonial theories of race and racism – that racism is systemic and that the 'world is built in the image of White supremacy' (Andrews, 2021, p. 11) and that academic knowledge production has played a pivotal role in rationalising this world-order marked by a 'colonial matrix of power' (Mignolo, 2018).

A Starting Point

In 2015, a young student activist at the University of Cape Town (UCT) in South Africa threw faeces at a bronze statue of British imperialist, Cecil Rhodes. This act of disruption sparked the formation of #RhodesMustFall (#RMF) student movement the same year. The movement primarily led by Black students at UCT sought to decolonise the university by confronting its inherent structures of racism and patriarchy (Ahmed, 2019). Soon, calls for #RMF reverberated across the University of Oxford centred mainly around the statue of Cecil Rhodes at Oriel College. Questions around the 'whiteness' of the existing curriculums and further calls to decolonise the curriculum gripped universities across the United Kingdom and the rest of Europe. At the heart of these calls were questions around epistemologies – 'whose knowledge counts as legitimate?' and thus, a desire for knowledge justice (Feldman, 2020).

Calls for decolonisation of the Western academy are often met with half-hearted and incomplete initiatives around diversity and inclusion. To be clear, I use the term 'Western academy' as a short-hand to refer to the tradition of university education across Euro-America and much of the Global South that has retained colonial systems of education and knowledge production. The epistemic injustice perpetuated through disciplinary university curriculums has material consequences for students from essentially minoritised, racialised backgrounds. However, these questions remain inadequately addressed. In fact, the deficits in disciplinary knowledge received in the Western academy, continues to perpetuate 'white ignorance' (Mills, 2007, p. 26) and 'epistemic violence' (Heleta, 2016, p. 2). It also contributes to racialised people's experiences of 'bodies out of place' (Puwar, 2004). To paraphrase Alana Lentin's (2018) words, it is thus important to understand the 'historical conjunctures' at which conceptions of race as biology gave rise to racism (p. 862). In other words, it is imperative for us to understand how certain groups of people were racialised and how this process of racialisation gave rise to racism. It is also important to remember that paradigms of race, perfected at the height of European colonialism, were fundamental to different disciplinary traditions of knowledge production. Feldman (2020), among other scholars, argues that the current architecture of disciplinary knowledges received in universities are dominated by the legacies of Anglo-European colonialism and Eurocentrism. It would also be remiss of me to ignore Eurocentrism's stranglehold over universities in the Global South. Even in countries that have a long tradition of putting up strong anti-colonial resistance and earning a hard-fought independence from European colonialism, universities and disciplinary curriculums continue to remain Eurocentric (Feldman, 2020, p. 142).

Mapping the Terrain of Theories of Race and Racial Inequality

The killing of a 46-year-old Black man in Minneapolis, Minnesota, in the hands of a white police officer, Derek Chauvin, in the summer of 2020, sparked widespread protests across different parts of the world. People took to the streets chanting 'Black Lives Matter' to expose the systemic nature of racial injustices against Black and other racial and ethnic minorities in Global North countries. The United Kingdom also witnessed people pulling down statues of slaveowners. The protests generated a fresh demand for studies in Critical Race Theory (CRT) as a way to understand and cultivate a struggle against racism beyond the framework of individual acts of prejudice and bigotry. CRT involves 'studying and transforming the relationship among race, racism and power' (Delgado & Stefancic, 2017, n.p.). However, such demands for studies in CRT received backlash from the conservative establishments in countries like the United States of America and the United Kingdom. Commentators and politicians accused those introducing elements of CRT in the classroom of 'promoting partisan political views' (Kemi Badenoch, at the British House of Commons, October 2020). However, in the midst of this cacophonous scepticism around CRT, it is important to remember the longer trajectory of a critical mass of scholarship on race and racism. Such race critical scholarship goes back to the beginning of the 20th century with the works of scholars like W.E.B. Du Bois, a Harvard University-trained sociologist, credited for popularising the concept of 'double-consciousness' in his 1903 publication, *Souls of Black Folk*. He also predicted that 'problem of the Twentieth Century is the problem of the colour-line' (1903 [1994], p. 1).

The mid-20th century witnessed critical theoretical works of non-white intellectuals like Aime Cesaire, Frantz Fanon, Albert Memmi and Oliver Cromwell Cox to name a few. While the Martinican intellectual, Aime Cesaire is associated with the Negritude movement, the writings of Frantz Fanon alongside those of Albert Memmi would come to influence the field of postcolonial theory. Oliver Cromwell Cox is associated with the tradition of Black Marxism. However, what links the writings of all these intellectuals is their analysis of the 'racial conception and racist expression' which constituted the 'colonial condition' (Goldberg, 2009, p. 1273). The period from mid-1970s onwards witnessed a proliferation of scholarship on race and racism, from different corners of the world. With post-structuralism gaining ground from the 1970s onwards, race came to be generally accepted as a social construct. However, the lived realities of race and racism, despite liberal efforts at diversification for the purposes of 'social upliftment', tell a different story. Scholars like Stuart Hall (1980) in the United Kingdom have been instrumental in theorising the complex structures and linkages between different phenomena that contribute to the varying degrees of oppression that constitute the lived experiences of race. Hall, in his article, 'Race, Articulation, and Societies Structured in Dominance' (1980) argues that the lived experiences of race are not 'simply "coloured" by race; they work through race' (Hall, 1980 [2019], p. 214; also cited in Lentin, 2018, pp. 862–3).

In the United States, the 1980s witnessed the flourishing of CRT. Critical legal scholars like Derrek Bell, Richard Delgado, Charles Lawrence, Mari Mastuda and Patricia Williams were central to its foundation. CRT, as Bell (1995) points out, emerged as 'a body of legal scholarship' by a majority of scholars of colour, 'ideologically committed to the struggle against racism, particularly institutionalised in and by law' (p. 898). Using tools of 'storytelling, narrative, allegory, interdisciplinary treatment of law, and the unapologetic use of creativity', critical race writers and lecturers are committed to a redemptive vision of 'liberation from racism through right reason' (Harris, 1994 cited in Bell, 1995, p. 899). Richard Delgado (1990) argues that critical race scholars ought to:

(1) insist on 'naming our own reality'; (2) believe that 'knowledge and ideas are powerful'; (3) be ready to 'question the basic premises of moderate/incremental civil rights law'; (4) borrow from the 'insights from social science on race and racism'; (5) critically examine 'the myths and stories powerful groups use to justify racial subordination'; (6) contextualise treatment of doctrine; (7) criticise legal legalisms; and (8) have an interest in 'structural determinism – the ways in which legal tools and thought-structures impede law reform' (cited in Bell, 1995, p. 899).

CRT, however, has been charged for its 'American parochialism', and its concerns with 'more or less restricted considerations of legal structures, conditions, and rationalities in the US context' (Essed & Goldberg, 2002, p. 4). Essed and Goldberg (2002) contend that CRT has been short of ensuring 'its applicability and implications of its key concepts outside of that context, or perhaps more importantly (because more constitutively) to thinking its central concepts through their globalizing significance and circulation' (pp. 4–5). Most recently, Ali Meghji in his book, *Decolonizing Sociology* (2021) argues that current CRT scholarship fails to acknowledge the legacies and histories of colonialism in their understanding of contemporary racism. He argues, another popular rival theory – Michael Omi and Howard Winant's (1994) racial formation theory – also holds that in societies such as the US, colonialism and imperialism are no longer pertinent in their racial projects. Both of these key 'race studies' paradigms, therefore, go against the concept of coloniality – that the world is still shaped by the colonial matrix of power (2021, p. 23). Drawing on Anibal Quijano's concept of the 'coloniality of power' which articulated the 'global hegemonic model of power', Mignolo argues that the colonial matrix of power (of which modernity/coloniality is a shorter expression) 'was constituted, managed, and transformed from its historical foundation in the sixteenth century' with the colonisation of the Americas to the present (in Mignolo & Walsh, 2018, p. 3). Goldberg (2015) offers an 'interactive' methodology to study race and racism. Such a methodology recognises that 'the racial ideas and arrangements circulate, cross borders, shore up existing or prompt new ones as they move between established political institutions' (p. 254, cited in Lentin, 2018, p. 862). Thus, there is a need to place local racism in the transnational historical conjunctures of race and racism.

When thinking about race, it is easy for us to fall prey to a universalising mode of 'racial naturalisation' that is 'bound to finding colour prejudice recurrent from Latin America to East Asia' (Goldberg, 2009, p. 1274). Goldberg (2009) instead argues that we should think about racial arrangements in a relational manner, thereby complexifying the white/black binary that we have in our minds when we think of the race. He argues, '[w]ho counts as "black" and who "white" differs from one place to another, as too do specific meanings attached to the designations and their placements' (2009, p. 1275). In order to understand the construction of race – i.e., the meaning inscribed to racial categories – and resultant racism experienced by people denied entry into the 'privilege of Whiteness' (Bhopal, 2018), Lentin (2018) advocates for the use of 'flexible, multi-tentacled and historically grounded' definitions of race (p. 862). Such an understanding would move beyond popular perceptions of racism as individual acts of prejudice and bigotry to a more systemic analysis of the same. As she further argues, such definitions would also be fool proof against charges of 'anti-white racism' or 'reverse racism' (Lentin, 2018, p. 862).

Colonial Difference and Biological/Construction of Race

Yes, European civilization and its agents of the highest caliber are responsible for colonial racism. (Frantz Fanon, 2008 [1952], p. 70)

The previous section of this chapter discussed some of the most prominent debates and theories around race and racism. However, to appreciate these debates and theories, one must understand that constructions of race and racialised identities, based on certain observable or phenotypical characteristics of different ethnic groups, were systematically deployed to justify the construction of a 'global racial hierarchy'. This will help us further understand how the construction of such a hierarchy deployed not just biology, but also geography or even concepts such as time and progress to rationalise prejudicial treatment of those placed at the bottom of this hierarchy. These different aspects of racial construction will be discussed in this section.

It is important to remember that race was deployed as 'a technology for the management of human difference', to produce, reproduce and maintain white supremacy on both local and planetary scales (Lentin, 2020, p. 5). The role of colonialism cannot thus be underplayed in the perpetuation of race aimed to construct and maintain political structures that justified the subjugation of 'non-white'/'non-European' subjects. Ali Meghji (2021) draws on the work of decolonial theorists such as Maria Lugones amongst others, to point out how the 'coloniser invented the colonised' by focusing on the complex interplay between 'power, knowledge (epistemology) and being (ontology)'. Such machinations had both epistemological and ontological consequences that have far outlived the formal end of colonisation by the second half of the 20th century.

Mignolo (2012) among others have argued that colonial empires were actively invested in the endeavour of knowledge production that deemed colonised people as inherently different from, or rather inferior to the colonisers (also cited in Meghji, 2021, p. 3). Such constructions of *colonial difference* were contingent upon the creation of a master category of race and an agreement of a 'racial contract' among 'people who count' for the perpetuation of a 'political system, a particular power structure of formal or informal rule, socioeconomic privilege, and norms for the differential distribution of material wealth and opportunities, benefits and burdens, rights and duties' (Mills, 1997, p. 3). In the 16th century, Spanish colonisers used blood as marker of biological race to draw links between indigenous blood and lack of reason among indigenous peoples to rationalise and justify the colonisation and dispossession of the latter from their lands (Lewis, 2012 cited in Meghji, 2021, p. 3). The 18th century witnessed the proliferation of race science, which paved the way for a more rigid conceptualisation of racial categories. The meticulous documentation of different ethnicities codified into racial categories by colonial administrations, show how keen they were to use racial categories as tools of governance to create and maintain a hierarchy with the power of white superiority remaining intact (for further reference see Stoler, 1995; Young, 1995). As Meghji (2021) points out, this conceptualisation of race and the increasingly common-sense knowledge around a 'global racial hierarchy' allowed for the perpetuation of a colonial world order. W.E.B. Du Bois (1967 [1899], pp. 386–7) described this global hierarchy at the helm of the colonial world order accordingly:

We grant full citizenship in the World Commonwealth to the 'Anglo-Saxon' (whatever that may mean), the Teuton and the Latin; then with just a shade of reluctance we extend it to the Celt and Slav. We half deny it to the yellow races of Asia, admit the brown Indians to an ante-room only on the strength of an undeniable past; but with the Negros of Africa we come to a full stop, and in its heart the civilized world with one accord denies that these come within the pale of nineteenth-century Humanity.' (cited in Meghji, 2021, pp. 3–4)

As mentioned at the beginning of this section, apart from blood and blood quantum, geography, and teleology – or as the *Oxford Dictionary of Sociology* defines it as 'process by the end-state towards which it is directed' – were as central to racial categorisations that were used to create, maintain, and perpetuate white superiority. The colonial world order was maintained around the idea that people in different regions of the world are at different temporal stages of human development. Defined as *coloniality of time* (Mignolo, 2012), the idea of teleological progression in human development, was the rationale behind the 'White Man's Burden' (Kipling, 1899) used to justify Euro-America's colonial domination of the rest of the world. Sylvia Wynter (2003) argues that such an endeavour was sustained through a reliance on European knowledge systems and origin stories which conjured a singular image of the 'rational' Man (cited in McKittrick, 2015). Understood as *coloniality of being* (Wynter, 2003), McKittrick (2015, p. 10) reflects how:

> such systems and stories produce the lived and racialised categories of the rational and irrational, the selected and the dysselected, the haves and the have-nots as asymmetrical naturalized racial-sexual human groupings that are specific to time, place, and personhood yet signal the processes through which the empirical and experiential lives of all humans are increasingly subordinated to a figure that thrives on accumulation.

The principle of *coloniality of being*, thus, allowed imperial powers to espouse and support liberal legislation 'at home' in Europe, such as the 1789 French Declaration of the Rights of Man and of the Citizen, while denying the same to others in the colonies (Meghji, 2021). Thus, the concepts of *colonial difference* along with *coloniality of time* and *being*, serve as a set of 'racialising assemblages' (Weheliye, 2014, p. 3 cited in Lentin, 2020, p. 6) that, work in tandem to ensure the maintenance of political structures and institutions which exclude 'non-white subjects' from being considered fully human (Lentin, 2020, p. 6). However, it is worth mentioning how other structures of power – namely gender, sexuality, class and ability – are deployed in the perpetuation of colonial difference that guide racial logics of oppression, ranking and exclusion. As Lentin (2020, p. 6) points out, 'the categorisation and ranking of humans into putatively natural groupings along racial, gendered, and classed lines grew in necessity at the start of the modern era, in Europe'. In fact, it would be remiss of one to not mention how race and capitalism not just developed together, but rather inextricably from each other, as they matured within the context of European colonial domination over the rest of the world (Lentin, 2020, p. 6).

It is also important to remember that, in the late 18th century, with the birth of modern nation-states in Euro-America, racism and nationalism entered into a reciprocal relationship (Lentin, 2020, p. 6). Sivamohan Valluvan (2019, p. 23) argues that the nation, in its bid to 'offer modernity a fundamental lens' that renders *community*, with a sense of 'shared entity of belonging beyond those whom we know and congregate with at any given moment' visible, does so at the cost of excluding some people. He draws on the scholarships of Yuval-Davis and Floya Anthias, and Homi Bhabha to argue that 'nation-states do not simply reflect pre-existing framings' of a particular ethnic group as a nation (Valluvan, 2019, p. 24). In fact, he argues that 'states that actively produce and entrench ideas of nation, conceptions of the national subject ... are in turn, necessarily exclusionary' (2019, p. 24). Thus, it is not uncommon to witness western nationalism's articulation of communal aspirations and problems by scapegoating various 'alien' ethno-racial communities (p. 13). As an oppressive and discriminatory project, race unfurls within a nation-state, by also producing eugenicist hierarchies of the 'deserving' and 'undeserving' poor (Shilliam, 2018, cited in Lentin, 2020, p. 6).

Colonial Matrix of Power, Disciplinary Knowledge and Epistemic Racism

Academic disciplines are not impervious to the outside world and hence to the colonial matrix of power which continues to constitute the world we inhabit (Meghji, 2021). In order to understand the persistence of *colonial matrix of power*, one needs to be cognisant of the epistemic and ontological hierarchical organisation of the world that continues into the present, much after the formal end of colonialism. In fact, the western academy has played an undeniably major role in laying the epistemic foundation of hegemonic knowledge production that has had knock on effects on establishing 'common sense' ideas and stereotypical societal representations of much of the 'Third World'. In order to consider the role of coloniality (used as a shorthand for *colonial matrix of power*) in disciplinary knowledge production and the persistence of *epistemic racism*, one requires shifting their understanding of the historiography of modernity itself (Bhambra & Holmwood, 2021).

The historiography of modernity typically looks at the emergence of the modern world through the 'processes associated one the one hand with the eighteenth-century American Revolution and French Revolution and, on the other, with industrialisation, in Britain and elsewhere, in the subsequent century' (Bhambra & Holmwood, 2021, p. 4). As Bhambra (2007) argues, such historiography is seen as 'underpinned by earlier cultural changes across Europe brought about by the Renaissance, the Reformation and the scientific revolution' (cited in Bhambra & Holmwood, 2021, p. 4). Such narratives conflate Europe with modernity while denying the role of rest of the world in these world-historical processes. This denial of the place of the rest of the world is often done by underplaying the role of colonialism and colonial extractivism in its development.

For many theorists, the period of the 18th-century Enlightenment is associated with the 'emergence of a distinctive European voice' (Bhambra & Holmwood, 2021, p. 4). This is in fact at the heart of the assumptions around *rupture and difference* (Bhambra, 2007) that separated 'the West from the rest' (Hall, 1992 cited in Bhambra & Holmwood, 2021, p. 4). However, it is important to historicise the Enlightenment itself, which is often celebrated as a key period in Euro-American history for perpetuating the theories of individual rights and freedom. Documents like the US Bill of Rights and the French Revolution's Declaration of the Rights of Man are celebrated as examples of Western intellectual framework's contribution to the arena of human rights. However, Kehinde Andrews (2021) argues that these theories cannot be separated from the context in which these were produced. With Columbus's voyage in 1492, which arguably marked the beginning of the West as we understand, Europeans managed to carry a monolithic idea of 'civilisation' with them. Kehinde Andrews (2021) reminds us that the period of Columbian exchange coincided with the fall of the Moorish Empire in Spain and with that the erasure of the influence of non-European knowledge production on Europe itself. While the influence of the Muslim world with Arabic as the language of knowledge until the 15th century is undeniable (Moller, 2019, cited in Andrews, 2021), Andrews (2021, pp. 13–14) argues that:

> Once Europe asserted its domination, this was no longer allowed to be the case. Erasure of non-Europeans was at the core of the Western project in terms of both actual slaughter and symbolic destruction [...] By burning books and libraries and Whitewashing history, Western intellectual thought was able to start from a clean slate of White supremacy. It is likely that the Enlightenment scholars genuinely believed they had inherited their knowledge solely from Europe, given the source of material they were working from.

In fact, following the decline of the Moorish Empire in Spain coupled with the periods of Renaissance and colonial expansion, Europeans were able to cast themselves as the 'embodiment of human perfection, perfectly proportioned and rendered through mathematics, science, aesthetics at the centre of the universe' (Feldman, 2020, p. 145). Through the violent conquest of both the physical and metaphysical, white European civilisation was able to claim and maintain itself as the centre of all worldviews, while freely appropriating those who were colonised (Feldman, 2020). At the height of the colonial enterprise, Western social sciences and humanities 'factualised' Eurocentric mythologies (Mudimbe, 1989) through the genesis of the 'canons' of Western knowledge (cited in Feldman, 2020, p. 146). These in turn can be traced to the 'tales of Anglo-European explorers and travellers, artists and writers, philosophers and idealists, eventually to anthropologists and social scientists' (Feldman, 2020, pp. 146–7).

Mudimbe (1989) in his work on *Inventing Africa*, demonstrates how the interconnected and mutually reinforced relationship between the disciplines of Art and (white) African Studies, formed the basis for social scientific cartography of heirarchisation (cited in

Feldman, 2020, p. 147). In fact, anthropological research at the time of colonisation involved the simple transcription and codification of difference 'in and through the lexicon of Social Darwinism' (Mudimbe, 1989, p. 30; also cited in Feldman, 2020, p. 148). The theological, biological and anthropological destinies of Africa, were mapped onto theories of evolution, thus contributing to the reification of the category of 'primitive' (Mudimbe, 1989, p. 30). Commenting on the epistemological racism inherent to anthropological research, he further points out:

> The novelty resides in the fact that the discourse on 'savages' is, for the first time, a discourse in which an explicit political power presumes the authority of a scientific knowledge and vice-versa. Colonialism becomes its project and can be thought of as a duplication and a fulfilment of the power of Western discourses on human varieties. (Mudimbe, 1989, p. 29)

Commenting on the beginnings of the academic discipline of sociology, Ali Meghji (2021) draws on the works of revisionist historians of sociology to demonstrate how deeply interested sociologists were in issues pertaining to colonialism. They were also committed to reinforce the myth of colonial difference used to justify the colonial enterprise's 'civilising mission'. As Meghji (2021) argues, introductory sociological teaching of Emile Durkheim – hailed as one of the members of 'holy trinity' of canonical sociology alongside Karl Marx and Max Weber – usually revolves around his thesis on 'social evolution from mechanical into organic solidarity, as primitive societies become "advanced"'. However, as scholars like Fuyuki Kurasawa (2013, p. 194) point out, Durkheim's thesis on 'primitive life-worlds' was based on the explorations and ethnographies of aboriginal peoples in the North America and Australia. The colonised were treated as 'the past in the present' who provided the frame for 'sociological models around the idea of colonial difference.

Drawing on Julian Go's (2009) work on American sociology's interest in colonialism, Meghji (2021, p. 8) points out that,

> British sociologists were [also] interested in issues including marriage patters across Africa (Leach, 1953), colonial resistance in South Africa (Kuper, 1953), how to strengthen British colonial administration (Freidman, 1951), the value of 'colour' in Jamaica (Henriques, 1951) and the ethnic demography of East Africa (Sofer & Ross, 1951).

Through its engagement with these topics, sociology was a key discipline in 'producing and reproducing colonial difference' (Meghji, 2021, p. 8). Commenting on colonial education in South Africa, scholars like Heleta (2016) and Feldman (2020) point out that its purpose and objective was to maintain colonial order through the education of White elites to rule and Black people to be ruled. In fact, Lord Thomas Babington Macaulay's

Minutes on Education in India (1835) reflects the purpose of colonial education even further:

> I feel with them that it is impossible for us, with our limited means, to attempt to educate the body of the people. We must at present do our best to form a class who may be interpreters between us and the millions whom we govern, – a class of persons Indian in blood and colour, but English in tastes, in opinions, in morals and in intellect.

The genealogy of colonial education for the purpose of maintaining colonial order illuminates the ways in which *epistemic racism* or the racist disregard of otherised peoples' 'epistemic capacity (Maldonado-Torres, 2004, p. 34, cited in Feldman, 2020, p. 149) was institutionalised into university curriculums. The role of the western academy in 'establishing epistemic foundation and political legitimacy for racial hierarchy circulated within the academy for years' (Crenshaw, 2011, p. 1258) is thus undeniable. Such academic training devalues and supplants other forms of knowledges, including indigenous knowledges and cultural practices, forms of creativity and so on, thereby undermining the 'subjectivities, experiences and bodies' of students of colour (Nyamnjoh, 2012, cited in Feldman, 2020, p. 149). Race awareness and race critical pedagogical approaches in classrooms are the only way to deal with epistemic racism inherent in Eurocentric curriculums and universities modelled around the European framework. Without centring race in pedagogical approaches, global justice educators will fail to acknowledge the persistence of coloniality in curriculums and not further the cause of transformative learning.

■ Case study ■

On 13 March 2021, University College Dublin's (UCD) student newspaper, *College Tribune*, ran a report on the African Scholars Association of Ireland's (AfSAI) open letter to its management team lodging a complaint against the organisation of a module on African American literature module offered by the UCD School of English (Eiland, 2021). The module in question: 'Writing Black: African American Literature and Racial Consciousness', was being offered by a White tenured male member of faculty with little demonstrable scholarship on the Black literature. AfSAI registered its complaint against the organisation of this particular module which they argue 'effectively reproduces the structural racism that disadvantages Black scholars within the academy'. They raise the issue of lack of racial diversity across academic departments in UCD, with no tenured Black academics in the School of English which made the module on 'Writing Black' available to students.

Despite UCD's focus on social justice and public support of the #BlackLivesMatter movement, AfSAI notes that the university has failed in its commitment to upholding anti-racism in its academic practice. They point to UCD's public anti-racist posturing through such modules, and thus indulging in an 'unacknowledged appropriation of Black scholarship'. As it further points out, out of the two modules in UCD that centre Black experience, it

(Continued)

is the module taught by a white scholar that receives institutional support in the form of employment security. The other module, which is arguably the first Black Studies course to be ever taught in Ireland, is taught by a Black scholar employed on a precarious hourly-paid contract.

The letter calls for accountability on UCD's part by calling for the School of English to 'rescind its decision to offer modules on Blackness that are taught by white staff' who have not conducted any 'substantive scholarship on Black race consciousness or Blackness'. They demand accountability on UCD's recruitment practicing and their lack of commitment to making sustainable opportunities for Black scholars with expertise in race critical scholarship to teach in UCD. The letter thus, calls for a complete redevelopment of UCD's Equality, Diversity, and Inclusion (EDI) structure, with a focus on race, racial discrimination racism and anti-racism, and calls for greater expertise in issues of racial equity within management structures.

'Decolonise not Diversify'

Discussions around 'decolonising the curriculum' as a way to initiate the process of 'decolonising the university' must first begin by acknowledging the role that colonial intellectuals in the Western/European University played in developing theories of racism, that 'bolstered support for colonial endeavours and provided ethical and intellectual grounds for dispossession, oppression and domination of colonised subjects' (Bhambra, Gebrial, & Nisancıoğlu, 2018, p. 5). In fact, European universities and institutions higher education served the purpose of training colonial administrators to rule over colonised populations across the world. Thus, the Western/European University has not always been the paragon of progressive ideas as we might think. Works to decolonise must thus begin with historical contexualisation of the University and the *epistemic racism* inherent in many academic disciplines including the social sciences and humanities which became one of the mediums through which Europe articulated its singular vision of 'rights of Man' that excluded the rights of colonised populations.

In fact, universities as educational institutions that inculcate skills that enable people to compete for specialised occupations, being exclusive elite spaces that contribute to the feelings of isolation and alienation for students from racialised backgrounds. Despite its pretence of offering an equalising opportunity to students from all backgrounds, many research studies have found that universities reproduce racial inequalities. Universalising arguments around 'meritocracy' often ignore the interactions between networks of social relations 'at social, political, economic and ideological levels that shape life chances of various races' (Bonilla-Silva, 2015, p. 1360). In fact, in many cases universities deploy mechanisms of racial exclusion to 'enhance their own position of elitism to maintain their power' (Bhopal, 2018). These mechanisms can take the form of 'unconscious bias' betrayed by admissions officers dealing with non-anonymised university applications (Bhopal, 2018). Despite policies around affirmative action or positive discrimination in the United States for example, aimed at countering racial and gender discriminations, universities continue to remain a 'White middle-class' space, where students are required to adopt a particular way of writing, speaking and use of academic language (Bhopal, 2018). As Bhopal (2018) further argues, 'Universities measure a particular type of success that is possessed by those from white middle-class backgrounds.' Such conditions often make it incumbent on the smaller number of racialised students who enter these spaces to leave their diverse credentials at the revolving door of the university (Ahmed, 2021). In fact, such an environment contributes to feelings of isolation, unworthiness and shame, often associated with misrecognition (Burke, 2015, cited in Bhopal, 2018). As Burke argues, '[i]nclusion tends to be more about fitting into the dominant culture than about interrogating that culture for the ways that it is complicit in the social and cultural reproduction of exclusion, misrecognition and inequality' (cited in Bhopal, 2018, n.p.).

The universities responsible for ensuring wider participation among its student body require adopting an ethical framework that allowed the space for a true interrogation into the dominant culture and styles of writing and speaking that are permitted in an academic environment. However, the equality, diversity and inclusion frameworks adopted by universities have fallen short in addressing these issues. In fact, the Black Lives Matter protests from the summer of 2020 along with fresh demands to 'decolonise the academy/curriculum' were only met with more inadequate and half-hearted diversity initiatives without a proper interrogation into the structures of racial inequality embedded in the academic environment itself. The boxed case-study referred to in this chapter, is a classic example to demonstrate this point. The university in this case failed to grapple with issues around structural racism and a demand for racial justice at the heart of such demands.

■■■■■■■ **Chapter summary** ■■■■■■■

This chapter provides an overview of contemporary decolonialist perspectives of racism and racial inequalities and includes the following:

* Illustrates how academic knowledge and the 'academy' reinforces racialised, colonialist inequalities
* Case study examples of efforts to 'de-centre' Western ways of knowing, particularly the 'decolonising the university' movement
* Discussion of how calls to 'decolonialise the university' are connected with projects to address racial injustices

Conclusion

It is important to remember that movements like #RhodesMustFall in South Africa and the various #DecolonisetheCurriculum campaigns across Europe, led primarily by students of colour, laid an epistemic charge against the content of university knowledge, which 'remains principally governed by the West for the West' (Bhambra et al., 2018, p. 5). By allowing for a singular articulation of what counts as legitimate knowledge, the Eurocentric university erases the importance of 'connected histories' (Subrahmanyam, 2004) and global knowledges that the Enlightenment was built on (Andrews, 2021). Such gross erasures have material consequences for racialised people and students who experience alienation, unworthiness and shame at being denied the opportunity to express their ways of knowing and being in the world. These issues can only begin to be addressed when we prioritise racial justice activism within the academy by bringing insurgent knowledges produced in social movements at the intersections of different axes of inequality, including race, class and gender (Balachandran, 2021).

Questions to Reflect Upon

- How can we connect the calls for racial justice to the question of epistemic justice?
- How can we not reduce demands for decolonisation to half-hearted diversity initiatives while not compromising on the importance of diversification?
- What does it mean to be 'doing the work of diversity' (Chakravarty, Feldman, & Penney, 2020)?

Further Reading

Bhambra, G. K., & Holmwood, J. (2021). *Colonialism and modern social theory.* Cambridge: Polity Press (This text re-examines the bedrocks of 'modern' social theory, highlighting how discussions of colonialism are absent from or present within the writing of sociology's 'founding texts'. This is a critical work given that these European/Western thinkers were writing either during or in the immediate aftermath of a key point in the European colonial project.)

Delgado, R., & Stefancic, J. (2017). *Critical race theory: An introduction* (3rd ed.). New York, NY: New York University Press (This book provides an overview of the core arguments of Critical Race Theory (CRT). As CRT may be new to you, it is important to use overview texts such as this to get a clear grasp of central theoretical debates.)

Kehinde, A. (2021). *The New Age of Empire: How racism and colonialism still rule the world.* Great Britain: Allen Lane (This comprehensive social historical analysis traces the persistent dominance of the Global North/West. It highlights the intersection of colonial dominance, knowledge and ideas of development and progress. This text is particularly useful as it traces how colonial matrices of power have been reinforced and sustained by the (Western) image of what development and progress look like.)

References

Ahmed, A. K. (2019). *The rise of fallism: #RhodesMustFall and the movement to decolonize the university.* PhD thesis, Colombia University. Retrieved from https://academiccommons.columbia.edu/doi/10.7916/d8-n7n3-e372

Ahmed, S. (2021). *Complaint!* Durham and London: Duke University Press.

Andrews, K. (2021). *The New Age of Empire: How racism and colonialism still rule the world.* Great Britain: Allen Lane. Retrieved 2 March 2021, from https://www.amazon.co.uk/New-Age-Empire-Racism-Colonialism-ebook/dp/B08NB9J9KW/ref=nav_ya_signin?_encoding=UTF8&qid=&sr=&

Balachandran, G. (2021). *Decolonising the curriculum and racism in academia by Kehinde Andrews [Online Event], Gender Centre and Black Conversations*. Geneva: Graduate Institute of International and Development Studies. 1 March.

Bell, D. A. (1995). Who's afraid of critical race theory? *University of Illinois Law Review, 1995*(4), 893–910.

Bhambra, G.K. (2007). *Rethinking modernity: Postcolonialism and the sociological imagination*. Basingstoke: Palgrave.

Bhambra, G. K., Gebrial, D., & Nişancıoğlu, K. (2018). *Decolonising the university*. London: Pluto Press.

Bhambra, G. K., & Holmwood, J. (2021). *Colonialism and modern social theory*. Cambridge: Polity Press.

Bhopal, K. (2018). *White privilege: The myth of a post-racial society*. Bristol: Policy Press.

Bonilla-Silva, E. (2015). The structure of racism in color-blind, "Post-racial" America. *American Behavioural Scientist, 59*(11), 1358–1376.

Burke, P. (2015). Widening participation in higher education: Racialised inequalities and misrecognitions. In C. Alexander & J. Arday (Eds.), *Aiming higher: Race, inequality and diversity in higher education*. London: Runnymede, pp. 21–24.

Chakravarty, D., Feldman, A., & Penney, E. (2020). Analysing contemporary women's movements for bodily autonomy, pluriversalizing the feminist scholarship on the politics of respectability. *Journal of International Women's Studies, 21*(7), 170–188.

Cotton, J. W. (2018). *The ivory tower must fall: Exploring the decolonisation of higher education at Cambridge university in theory and practice*. MPhil thesis. University of Cambridge.

Crenshaw, K. (2011). Twenty years of critical race theory: Looking back to move forward. *Connecticut Law Review, 43*(5, July), 1253–1352.

Delgado, R. (1990). When a story is just a story: Does voice really matter? *Virginia Law Review, 76*(1), 95–111.

Delgado, R., & Stefancic, J. (2017). *Critical race theory: An introduction* (3rd ed.). New York, NY: New York University Press. Retrieved 18 February 2021, from https://www.amazon.co.uk/Critical-Race-Theory-Third-Introduction

de Sousa Santos, B. (Ed.). (2007). *Cognitive justice in a global world: Prudent knowledges for a decent life*. Lexington Books.

Du Bois, W. E. B. (1967 [1899]). *The Philadelphia Negro: A social study*. New York, NY: Schocken Books.

Du Bois, W. E. B. (1994 [1903]). *The souls of black folk*. New York, NY: Dover Publication.

Eiland, S. (2021). *African scholars association protests UCD 'Writing black' module taught by White Professor*. College Tribune, 13 March. Retrieved 20th April 2022, from https://collegetribune.ie/african-scholars-association-protests-ucd-writing-black-module-taught-by-white-professor/

Essed, P., & Goldberg, D. T. (Eds.). (2002). *Race critical theories: Text and context*. Oxford and Malden: Blackwell Publishing.

Fanon, F. (2008 [1952]). *Black skin, white masks* (R. Philcox, Trans.). New York, NY: Grove Press.

Feldman. (2020). Knowledge justice as global justice: Epistemicide, decolonising the university, and the struggle for planetary survival. In B. O'Toole, E. Joseph, & D. Nyaluke

(Eds.), *Challenging perceptions of Africa in schools: Critical approaches to global justice education* (pp. 141–159). London and New York, NY: Routledge.

Friedman, J. R. (1951). Review of principles and methods of colonial administration. *The British Journal of Sociology*, *2*(4), 377.

Goldberg, D. T. (2009). Racial comparisons, relational racisms: Some thoughts on method. *Ethnic and Racial Studies*, *32*(7), 1271–1282.

Goldberg, D. T. (2015). Racial comparisons, relational racisms: Some thoughts on method. In K. Murji & J. Solomos (Eds.), *Theories of race and ethnicity: Contemporary debates and perspectives*. Cambridge: Cambridge University Press, pp. 251–262.

Hall, S. (1992). The west and the rest: Discourse and power. In S. Hall & B. Gieben (Eds.), *Formations of modernity*. Cambridge: Polity and Open University.

Hall, S. (2019 [1980]). Race, articulation and societies structured in dominance. In D. Morley (Ed.), *Essential essays volume 1: Foundations of cultural studies, Stuart Hall*. Durham and London: Duke University Press.

Harris, A. P. (1994). Foreword: The jurisprudence of reconstruction. *California Law Review*, *82*(4), 741–786.

Heleta, S. (2016). Decolonisation of higher education: Dismantling epistemic violence and Eurocentrism in South Africa. *Transformation in Higher Education*, *1*(1), 1–8.

Henriques, F. (1951). Colour values in Jamaican society. *The British Journal of Sociology*, *2*(2), 115–121.

Kipling, R. (1929 [1899]). *The white Man's burden: The United States & The Philippine Islands, 1899*. Rudyard Kipling's verse: Definitive edition. Garden City, New York, NY: Doubleday.

Kuper, L. (1953). The background to passive resistance (South Africa, 1952). *The British Journal of Sociology*, *4*(3), 243–256.

Kurasawa, F. (2013). The Durkheimian School and colonialism: Exploring the constitutive paradox. In G. Steinmetz (Ed.), *Sociology and empire: The imperial entanglements of a discipline* (pp. 188–209). Durham and London: Duke University Press.

Leach, E. R. (1953). Review of survey of marriage and family life, by Arthur Phillips, L. P. Mair and Lydon Harries. *The British Journal of Sociology*, *4*(3), 286–288.

Lentin, A. (2018). Race. In W. Outhwaite & S. P. Turner (Eds.), *The Sage handbook of political sociology* (Vol. *1*). London, Thousand Oaks, New Delhi and Singapore: SAGE.

Lentin, A. (2020). *Why race still matters*. Cambridge: Polity Press.

Lewis, L. A. (2012). *Chocolate and corn flour: History, race, and place in the making of 'Black' Mexico*. Durham, NC: Duke University Press.

Maldonado-Torres, N. (2004). The topology of being and the geopolitics of knowledge. *City*, *8*(1), 29–56.

McKittrick, K. (2015). *Sylvia Wynter: On being human as Praxis*. Durham and London: Duke University Press.

Meghji, A. (2021). *Decolonizing sociology: An introduction*. Cambridge: Polity Press.

Mignolo, W. D. (2012). Coloniality at large: Time and the colonial difference. In S. Dube (Ed.), *In enchantment of modernity: Empire, nation, globalization*. London: Routledge, pp. 62–95.

Mignolo, W. D., & Walsh, C. E. (2018). *On decoloniality: Concepts, analytics, Praxis*. Durham and London: Duke University Press.

Mills, C. W. (1997). *The racial contract*. Ithaca and London: Cornell University Press.

Mills, C. (2007). White ignorance. In S. Sullivan & N. Tuana (Eds.), *Race and epistemologies of ignorance* (pp. 13–38). Albany: State University of New York Press.

Moller, V. (2019). *The map of knowledge: How classical ideas were lost and found: A history in seven cities*. London: Picador.

Mudimbe, V. Y. (1989). *The invention of Africa*. Bloomington, IN: Indiana University Press.

Ngũgĩ, T. (1986). *Decolonising the mind: The politics of language in African literature*. London: J. Currey.

Nyamnjoh, F. B. (2012). 'Potted plants in greenhouses': A critical reflection on the resilience of colonial education in Africa. *Journal of Asian and African Studies*, *47*(2), 129–154.

Omi, M., & Winant, H. (1994). *Racial formation in the United States: From the 1960s to the 1990s*. New York, NY: Routledge.

Puwar, N. (2004) *Space invaders: Race, gender and bodies out of place*. Oxford and New York: Berg.

Santos, B. D. S. (Ed.). (2007). *Cognitive justice in a global world: Prudent knowledges for a decent life*. Lanham: Lexington Books.

Shilliam, R. (2018). *Race and the undeserving poor: From abolition to brexit*. Newcastle upon Tyne: Agenda Publishing Limited.

Sofer, C. & Ros, R. (1951). Some characteristics of an East African European population. *The British Journal of Sociology*, *2*(4), 315–327.

Stoler, A. L. (1995). *Race and the education of desire: Foucault's history of sexuality and the colonial order of things*. USA: Duke University Press. London.

Subrahmanyam, S. (2004). *Explorations in connected history: From Tagus to the Ganges*. Delhi: Oxford University Press.

Valluvan, S. (2019). *The Clamour of nationalism: Race and nation in twenty-first-century Britain*. Manchester: Manchester University Press.

Weheliye, A. (2014). *Habeas viscus*. Durham, NC: Duke University Press.

Wynter, S. (2003). Unsettling the coloniality of being/power/truth/freedom: Towards the human, after man, its overrepresentation – an argument. *CR: The New Centennial Review*, *3*(3), 257–337.

Young, R. J. C. (1995). *Colonial desire: Hybridity in theory, culture and race*. London: Routledge.

4

GENDER

Peace Kiguwa

━━━━━━━━━━ Learning objectives ━━━━━━━━━━

- To explore how feminism can help understand gender inequalities
- To engage with feminist arguments on the structural and social bases of gender inequalities
- To become familiar with intersectional feminism decolonial and Afro-feminist thought
- To reflect on case studies outlining (i) gendered disparities and HIV and (ii) gender-based violence

━━━━━━━━━━ Framing questions ━━━━━━━━━━

- Why are gendered inequalities so hard to address?
- How have decolonial and Global South theorists contributed to feminism?
- Is there a difference between White/Global North/Eurocentric feminist and African/Global South feminist perspectives?

Introduction

This chapter considers the place of feminism in making sense of gender inequalities in society. It begins by demonstrating how gender is present in multiple and diverse situations of social inequality in different contexts. In flagging this presence of gender, I argue that gender largely remains an invisible factor in the formation and practice of social inequality. It is further precisely because of this invisibility that gendered inequality remains so recalcitrant in effect and practice. Put differently, taking gender for granted in how social inequalities take shape may often mean that relations of inequality will remain. Secondly, interventions aimed at reducing social inequality may prove resistant to change precisely because these interventions are incomplete in their understandings of gendered power dynamics. It is therefore imperative that we make gender visible in terms of how it configures in society and cultures. Thus, the chapter engages the importance of feminist theories that have enabled us to analyse gender in social inequalities. As a key point of departure and anchor, the chapter highlights the role of feminist theories from the margins – Afro Feminisms, Latin American Feminisms and Black Feminisms – that have provided key conceptual and epistemological insights into how gender appears and unfolds in social inequality. In particular, the contribution of intersectionality as an analytic lens through which to read convergences and divergences of privilege and oppression is discussed.

Social Inequality: How Does Gender Matter?

Gendered disparity in HIV infection rate in sub-Saharan Africa

Consider the following: according to UNAIDS, the scourge of HIV infection in Africa continues to be borne by many women and young girls. In sub-Saharan Africa, it is reported that 'young women are twice as likely to become infected with HIV as their male counterparts. And in sub-Saharan Africa, three out of four new HIV infections among 15–19-year-olds are among young women, and seven out of 10 young women do not have comprehensive knowledge about HIV. Approximately 6900 adolescent girls and young women aged 15–24 years are newly infected with HIV every week around the world' (https://www.unaids.org/sites/default/files/media_asset/women_girls_hiv_en.pdf). These infection rates are especially significant because they highlight the gendered disparities not only in terms of HIV infection but also relative to access to health, education, and sexual and reproductive rights for many women living in Africa. Put differently, social issues of access to health, education and other structural and cultural issues that impact the general well-being of the individual are not gender neutral. They are invariably inflected with the gendered configurations of a society. These configurations include matrices of power that include intersections of class, race, geography, education and so on.

Interrogating why women and young women are twice as likely to become infected with HIV, for example, begins to unravel some of these complexities. What access to employment opportunities exist for women and young girls? What access to sexual and reproductive health care and education? How does structural violence impact women differently from their male counterparts? How does cultural normative practices influence how many women may navigate their sexual and reproductive health concerns? What of gender-based violence and its enabling economies of fear that affect restrictions of movement and security for many women and young girls? These questions demonstrate that tackling gender inequalities must engage an intersecting politics that challenges the tendency towards single-issue problematisations and interventions that undermine gender's role in social inequality. To this end, a continued problematisation of gender as concept, identity category, practice and ideology is necessary.

Gender's continued and largely taken-for-granted status in much social and everyday contexts often means that many people do not consider the intricate ways that this supposedly meaningless and neutral concept is deeply entrenched in their lives, daily practices, social and personal interactions, sense of self and material, institutional, relational and even temporal imaginations. This taken-for-granted nature of gender and the way that gender configures in society also means that we are not always attentive to the ways that relations and networks of power and social inequalities take on gendered forms and are configured in gendered dynamics. Indeed, it is quite ironic that while we may unconsciously take gender for granted, we are, in the words of West and Zimmerman (1987, p. 125), continually 'doing gender'. Therefore, this dilemma of gender's common-sense role in our lives means that we must continually seek to theorise and analyse the meaning of gender as it is configured in our society. This is essential if we are to attempt an understanding of gendered inequalities and their intersections across different contexts. In so doing, the chapter seeks to demonstrate the efficacy of a critical theorisation of gender and social inequalities that attends to the nuances, complexities and intersections of gender in people's lives. Drawing on the contributions of Black feminisms, African feminisms, Latin American feminisms, the chapter engages the intersections of struggle that contribute to and are part of gendered inequalities in society. Such an engagement implicitly calls for a critique of much traditional feminist theorisations of gender that do not address fully these intersections of social class, gender, race, religion, culture, among others. The chapter posits that understanding gendered inequalities requires an exploration of the different axes of privilege and oppression that all humans embody and occupy as social position, including among women.

Feminist Re(imaginations): Looking Back and Looking Forward

Feminism, as social movement, and philosophy, has a particular interest in social inequalities. This is expected given social inequalities' inflection with gendered social orders. Its diverse and multiple forms notwithstanding, feminism, as a social and philosophical movement is tied to the idea that women as a social political group are deserving of human dignity and equal access to resources that promote their well-being as much as their male counterparts (Lorber, 2010). Traditions of feminist theorising has enabled us to understand some of the structural, political, economic and cultural influences of women's continued minority status in society. In flagging the role of structural factors in women's unequal status in society for example, Marxist and Liberal Feminism has provided significant insights into the failings of social, economic and political orders that re/produce gendered hierarchies between men and women in society. These hierarchies cut across multiple and different spheres of influence that include the workplace, health care, the domestic home context, schooling and education, intimate relationships and so on. At the heart of these feminist contributions to understanding gender inequality in society is the notion that the problem is primarily women's lack of access to resources and in the same vein, addressing these inequalities through better access for women (Lorber, 2010). Discriminatory practices – rooted in patriarchy – that re/produce women's minority status are of interest in tackling some of these structural and institutional practices of inequality

(Kiguwa, 2004). These approaches to feminist understandings of inequality are useful in their pinpointing of inequality as an issue that is rooted in the social order of a society that denies women access to resources and not in the personal attributes or failings of individuals per se. This is very important given the potential to undermine gender transformation strategies via recourse to individualised and pathologising of individuals.

Yet, the exclusive emphasis on structural roots of women's oppression remains a limiting lens through which to understand gender inequality in society. Aiming for equality without a critical interrogation of the social order to begin with, merely lets patriarchal systems and practice off the hook. These scholars have observed that patriarchy – an ideology of gender superiority that favours men over women, and which is inflected in heteronormative and cultural and social systems of practice, institutions and relationships – is inherently a problem and cannot be redeemed in any way. The very function of such an order is the re/production of hierarchies of gender as well as reproduction of distorted meanings of gender and difference that reinforce structural and interpersonal inequalities. A strategy of fighting for equality within such an order is therefore not only fruitless but also undesirable. These scholars propose that attention be given to the practices, the beliefs and value systems that reinforce patriarchal systems. In so doing they highlight the role that is played by institutions in society, such as the role of socialisation in culture, in religion, etc., in promoting beliefs about gender inequalities. Feminist critiques in this tradition have contributed to an understanding of how some modes of being and relating take on gendered attributes but also come to be devalued and pathologised. For example, the undermining of emotion and other effects in women as problematic and evidence of irrationality. Other scholars demonstrate the way that emotions of shame, for example, have been deployed in ways that reinforce women's marginalised status in society and so engage the necessity for reclaiming these affective economies as part of gender resistance (Fischer, 2018).

Other key strands of feminist theorising of inequality include the deconstruction of gender as a social category to engage its social constructed nature as well as critically reflecting on the role of language in the re/production of gender. Social constructionist approaches to the analysis of gender have been insightful in their elaboration of how gender is constructed and re/produced via discursive rhetoric and practice that constructs subjects as gendered. These studies have illustrated how experiences of gender are mediated via different resources that include cultural understandings of gender and/or representations of gender that serve to construct gender as natural and stable. Social constructionist approaches to gender highlight the taken-for-granted status of gender categories in our lives and challenge understandings of gender that are apolitical in form. Therefore, feminist social constructionist approaches to gender and sexuality aim for a political critique that attests to these markers of social embodiment as both function and effect of power matrices. And yet, can such a focused emphasis on power intricacies still be limited in analytic scope? And if so, how do we move beyond this impasse? Scholars have pointed out that the exclusive reliance on constructionist readings of social and political matters presents a danger of reducing or ignoring altogether the affective, material, bodily dimensions of human experiences of inequality and oppression in society (Hook, 2006). This is to say that constructionist readings tend to favour analysis at the level of the discursive to the detriment of material embodied and other dimensions of structural inequalities in society. So that such readings might entail a critical deconstruction of discursive constructs and rhetoric but fail to engage the pre-discursive, the material lived meanings of inequality and the complex ways that these experiences of structural inequality come to be embodied in our very being and relationships with others. Aileen Douglas frames it succinctly when she asserts 'if you prick a socially constructed body, it still bleeds' (p. xxii).

Nonetheless, much of mainstream feminist engagements – even in their attention to structural issues of access, undermining of women's standpoint and subjective contributions to everyday contexts, and/or social constructed nature of gender as a category – have demonstrated several limitations that include a lack of critical reflection on intersectional matrices of gendered inequality, particularly as these affect women of colour and sexual and gender minorities. Black Feminist scholarship has flagged this significant omission arguing that a conceptualisation of gender and gendered inequalities that does not attend to intersecting issues of race, class and other categories of differentiation in society is limiting (Collins, 1986; Nayak, 2015, among others). For example, in addressing gender-based violence in South Africa, Melanie Judge (2021) notes that:

> Women in rural areas are further confined by their primary role in the domestic sphere (including the unpaid work of childrearing, cooking and cleaning), and by unequal access to employment, education, healthcare, property, and financial and other services (ILO, 2019, p. 2). These structural inequalities enable harassment and violence, which then further undermine the right to equality and dignity, and cause physical, psychological and/or sexual harm. As such, inaccessibility to land, education, social and political capital, and employment, are all key to understanding the constraints women face in rural settings. Moreover, conditions of poverty exacerbate vulnerability to GBV and limit the choices available in how violence can be responded to – resulting in women bearing the brunt of gendered role divisions that drive and sustain patriarchal social relations. (p. 11)

Kimberlé Crenshaw's work on intersectionality – with roots in Black Feminism and Critical Race Theory – (Carbado, Crenshaw, Mays, & Tomlinson, 2013; refs here) has been instrumental in the analyses of gender in society that attends to its multiple intersections of privilege and discrimination. Both an orientation and method, intersectionality as a framework for analysing gender inequalities in society has spanned a body of work that has traversed disciplines and different contexts of engagement. In her flagship essay titled 'Demarginalizing the Intersection of Race and Sex: A Black Feminist Critique of Antidiscrimination Doctrine, Feminist Theory and Antiracist Politics', Crenshaw (1991) introduced the term to analyse gender inequality as these pertain to Black women. Her analysis, further developed in her famous (1991) essay

'Mapping the Margins: Intersectionality, Identity Politics, and Violence Against Women of Color', aimed to critique Black women's positions and status as lesser than with focused attention to intersections of gender, race, class. Her analysis addressed itself not only to discrimination within the context of the law but also within feminist and antiracist theory and practice. The significance of Crenshaw's critique is illustrated in her evaluation of both supposedly progress movements such as feminism and antiracist movements as embodying core fault lines in their engagements with both gender and race. Willoughby-Herard (2021) has however noted the limits of Black Feminism within current strategies of mainstreaming within North American universities. She argues that the danger of such co-option into mainstream academe is that once radical orientations and methodologies, such as intersectionality, may inadvertently be rendered apolitical and meaningless. This critique has also been noted by other scholars (Bilge, 2013; Brah & Phoenix, 2004; Davis, 2008; McCall, 2005; Phoenix, 2017; Yuval-Davis, 2006 among others) concerned with approaches to intersectionality that adopt merely additive layers of identity categories without any real analysis of their intersections – both in terms of lived experiences as well as matrices of privilege and marginalisation. Indeed, for Willoughby-Herard (2021), contemporary younger activism has extended Black Feminist theorising to reflect what she refers to as a 'liberatory queer Black transfeminism' (p. x) that aims to honour these intersections. This locating of a transfeminism that challenges rigidly identitarian politics is not recent. Audre Lorde's oeuvre of work (see Nayak, 2015 for a succinct overview) is especially critical for contemporary feminism movements precisely because she engages these nuances and complexities of social struggle and inequalities. Lorde's contribution to gender and feminist activism provides us with conceptual, theoretical, and methodological tools for analyses. In *A Burst of Light and Other Essays* (1988) and *Sister Outsider and Other Essays* (1984), Lorde challenges the universalising agendas of mainstream feminist theory that does not engage seriously differences between women in society.

Case study

Intersecting economies of gender violence

In March 2002, a 30-year-old young woman, Amina Lawal, was convicted of the crime *Zina*[1] under Northern Nigeria's Sharia Law. Under this law, illicit sexual relations between men and women were not only forbidden but also punishable by death. Lawal, according to the law, had conceived a child outside of wedlock and sentenced to death by stoning. The man she would identify as the father of her child was not found guilty and deemed innocent by the law. Following international outcry and through the concerted campaign efforts of women's rights groups and lawyers in Nigeria, the sentence was overturned in the Appeals Court and Amina was a free woman.

(Continued)

[1] Islamic legal term referring to unlawful sexual intercourse that may include rape, sodomy, adultery, sex before marriage, incest, homosexuality amongst others.

In 2020 at the early height of the COVID-19 pandemic lockdown, citizens across the globe and on the continent were under strict regulations to remain at home as nations struggled to cope with the steadily increasing numbers of COVID-related deaths and infections. In South Africa and elsewhere across the region, the economic and other losses of lockdown was not the only specter hanging over the nation. According to Amnesty International 'During the COVID-19 lockdowns imposed by Southern African countries, some homes across the region became enclaves of cruelty, rape and violence for women and girls trapped with abusive family members and nowhere to report or escape the danger'. Furthermore, in South Africa, 'In the first week of the lockdown, the South African Police Service (SAPS) reported receiving 2,300 calls for help related to gender-based violence' (https://www.amnesty.org/en/latest/news/2021/02/southern-africa-homes-become-dangerous-place-for-women-and-girls-during-covid19-lockdown/). According to this report, South Africa, Mozambique and Zimbabwe stand out as the countries that especially did not consider women's and young girls' safety in their responses to the pandemic and lockdown. In Mozambique, women nurses without adequate transportation (public transport was very limited due to the lockdown) were at risk of abductions and sexual assault. And in Zimbabwe, 'an organization that offers protection for women survivors of domestic violence, had documented 764 cases of gender-based violence in the first 11 days of the national lockdown. By 13 June 2020, the number was 2,768' (https://www.amnesty.org/en/latest/news/2021/02/southern-africa-homes-become-dangerous-place-for-women-and-girls-during-covid19-lockdown/). The loss of employment for many women also meant that care for family was severely impacted.

What are we to make of these increased incidences of violence against women? In keeping with an intersectional analytic framing, the increase in gender-based violence against women during the lockdown must be read in tandem with the broader social, economic, and cultural inequalities that exist in society. Several issues are at stake here: in the case of Lawal, a clear gendered disparity in access to dignity and safety, whereby women are more likely to be punished for social and cultural infractions than their male counterparts. More than this, the clear need for constitutional reform that does not discriminate against and marginalise already marginalised sexual and gender population groups. The harmful gender stereotypes and cultural norms that are part of this marginalisation and discrimination must also be addressed. In addition, feminists have consistently argued against the simplistic separation of so-called private and public spheres of practice and embodiment, arguing that these two spheres are intimately connected and affect each other. As bell hooks, the Black Feminist scholar succinctly observes:

> The public reality and institutional structures of domination make the private space for oppression and exploitation concrete . . . . I think it is crucial to talk about the points where the public and private meet, to connect the two. (bell hooks, 1989)

Put simply, personal experience cannot be read as separate from larger structural and political influences in society. One only need consider a woman's sexual and reproductive health – which is considered by many to be a matter of personal concern – as intricately intertwined with policies, regulations and even social and cultural norms that dictate and influence how she may exercise decisions affecting her body and reproductive choices. Citing Jato (2004, p. 4), Judge (2021, p. 11) further notes that:

> Gender inequality diminishes women's access to and control over assets and household income. In resource-deprived settings this is compounded, given that 'women are more vulnerable to poverty, because of inequalities in access to productive resources, lack of control over their own labour and earned income, gender biases in labour markets and the exclusion that women experience in a variety of economic, social and political institutions'.

In flagging the special vulnerabilities that women are exposed to during contexts of emergency – whether health, security and otherwise – it is also critical to remember that these heightened moments of emergency and crisis emerge within already contested and unequal contexts of governance and relating that impact well-being more generally. For this reason, that Indian author and critical scholar Arundhati Roy lamented that the COVID-19 pandemic 'will be dealt with, with all the prevailing prejudices of religion, caste and class completely in place' (Roy, 2020). Gender inequalities exist in tandem with other social inequalities that are in turn inflected with racial, class, and other formations. Intersectional analyses are therefore necessary if we are to further our understandings of gendered configurations of inequality.

Attention to marginalised social groups that include women, young girls and children is not the only concern when we speak about gender inequality. Consider this: In South Africa, while women and girls may be at highest risk of sexual violence in the country, men constitute the most at risk group for homicide and violent crime. More specifically, men are simultaneously majority perpetrators of violent crime as well as victims of violent crime. According to Bruce (2019), 'official figures are that men, including male children, account for 85% of victims of murder, upwards of 80% of victims of attempted murder, and more than 70% of victims of assault with grievous bodily harm'. The Critical Masculine Studies scholar, Kopano Ratele, has also noted that 'South African male homicide is approximately seven to eight higher than female homicide, with young black and coloured men bearing the burden of homicidal violence' (Ratele, 2013; Vetten & Ratele, 2013, p. 5). Clearly then, violence in the country, as elsewhere, takes on differentials (that include gender, race, class etc.) and relative to forms of violence. According to the United Nations, 'while the vast majority of homicide victims are men, killed by strangers, women are far more likely to die at the hands of someone they know' (UNODC, 2018). Reading the gendered formations of risk and vulnerability to different forms of violence necessitates the need to understand both structural and symbolic influences and meanings of gender. Thus, in addition to critical analysis of structural factors, such as material poverty and geographical vulnerabilities that influence risk to violence, we would also need to consider the gendered affective and symbolic economies that are part of a society.

These gendered affective and symbolic economies include an understanding of con-structs of masculinity, the affective economies of shame and fear that are part of these formations of masculinity and femininity. The South African feminist scholar Pumla Gqola (2015, 2021) for example engages the notion of a 'female fear factory' to refer to those affective economies that govern and police how women and girls navigate their immediate environments through fear of being violated. Female fear is 'manufactured' (2021, p. 44) in the service of patriarchal oppression and control that dictates how many women and girls exist in a state of perpetual looking over one's shoulders and being ever mindful of potential violation against their bodies. Such affective economies are intrinsic to reinforcing and sustaining patriarchal systems in society. Other affective economies may include shame, evidenced in the reluctance demonstrated by many women to report instances of sexual violation and intimate partner abuse. Shaming cultures function to further render women powerless in the face of their unequal access to protection and dignity. And yet, we in considering the reach of patriarchy to also include a governance of men, we may also consider affective economies that are functional in sustaining hege-monic patriarchal masculinities. In *The Will to Change: Men, Masculinity, and Love* (2004) bell hooks makes a plea for a critical analysis of patriarchy that includes recognition of men's victimisation within patriarchy in addition to women's victimisation. And so, what affective economies underlie practices of hegemonic masculinities in society? Research shows that a culture of shame may also be inherent to how many young boys and men express vulnerabilities and insecurities, whether in the face of unemployment, sexual violation, fatherhood etc. (Javaid, 2018; Langa, 2010; Mensah, 2021). Gendered affective economies are in turn inflected with racial affective economies among others. It is for this reason that Gqola (2020) and Coetzee and Du Toit (2018) argue that any readings of gendered violence must contend with the racialised and other histories of a society. In her analysis of sexual and reproductive inequalities in South Africa and across the Southern African region, Nduna (2020) similarly argues for an intersectional reading that attends to the historical, racial and classed influences and how these impact current gendered inequalities regarding access and rights.

Building on from Black Feminist theorising, contributions of feminists from the Global South have posed further critical questions about the social order of gender in the world and its effects. These contributions engage an approach to feminist theorising that has been categorised as Decolonial in orientation and method. Although couched within an overarching philosophy that has been labelled 'Decolonial', it should be noted that Decolonial philosophy and Decolonial Feminisms encompass a myriad of approaches or strands to engaging decoloniality. These include Latin American feminisms, Afro-Feminisms, among others. It is to these contributions that we now turn.

Decolonial and Afro-Feminisms: What Relevance for Engaging Gender Inequalities?

Critical scholars from the Global South have been prominent in the recent calls for decolonisation as part of a re-imagining of a world that is free from social and political inequalities. The veteran Decolonial Studies scholar, Walter D. Mignolo, provides a useful explication of decolonisation that is worth noting. For Mignolo, given that coloniality is 'the logic of oppression and exploitation' (2007, p. 162) that is also at the heart of modernity and capitalism, decoloniality must therefore entail a practice and process of 'epistemic delinking' (Mignolo, 2007, p. 450) from modes of governance and relations that continue to sustain and reinforce these logics of oppression and exploitation. These logics include '…control of economy and authority, of gender and sexuality of knowledge and subjectivity' (2007, p. 162). Epistemic delinking further entails a strategy of critique that starts from sources that are not Eurocentred in origin and orientation. A decolonial shift, for Mignolo, entails a delinking from such sites of knowledge as the centre from which to view and understand the world. It embraces engagements with other sites of knowledge that have been marginalised and often rendered invisible. These sites of knowledge traverse domains of knowledge, political economies, subjectivity, gendered ordering of the world and ethics among other issues. For example, honoring indigenous knowledges enables us to understand the lives of a people from their point of view and lived realities. Such facilitated understanding in turn fosters practices of working together to transform people's lives for the better. Thus, in challenging the tendency towards universal thinking and centering:

> de-linking presupposes to move toward a geo- and body politics of knowledge that on the one hand denounces the pretended universality of a particular ethnicity (body politics), located in a specific part of the planet (geo-politics), that is, Europe where capitalism accumulated as a consequence of colonialism. (2007, p. 453)

David Everatt (2019) echoes this importance of delinking to fostering more democratic governance within a Global South context. He argues that 'without a genuine rupture at the point of decolonisation, without an attempt to find a new national identity, voice and set of values and newly designed institutions, that in Mignolo's terminology are 'delinked' from the colony, decolonisation birthed a post-colonial local and global structure of power, institutions and violence' (p. 5). Mbembe (2001, p. 102) goes further to assert that postcolonial inheritance of colonialism includes 'regimes of violence' that both reinforce and invent new sites and contexts of power in society. Similarly, the Ugandan feminist scholar, Sylvia Tamale (2021, p. 20) states that 'the prefix "de-"' in the terms 'decolonisation' and 'decoloniality' connotes an active action of undoing or reversal.

To tackle then, gender regimes of violence within the Global South context, a multi-level process of delinking that attends to both macro and micro politics of power is needed. To address the gaps in methodological clarity concerning feminist intersectional work, Winker and Degele (2011) engage a multi-level intersectional analyses to demonstrate the intricate ways that inequality manifests in society. They take up McCall's (2005) three-tiered complexities of intersectionality as follows: *Anticategorical Complexity* – concerned with deconstruction of analytic categories such as gender and race. Interest is in exploring how identity categories are constructed and to what end. This level of analysis is largely deconstructive and focused on the meaning of terms and concepts and not based on empirical research; *Intracategorical Complexity* – concerned with micro level analysis of identity and how identities are constructed in the everyday. This is empirical focused and concerned with the ways that people live their lives via multiple intersecting identities; *Intercategorical Complexity* – concerned with the relationship between social groups. This level of analysis is concerned with the structural and other group dynamic aspects of relationships. For example, researchers may be concerned with exploring inequalities between social groups based on set criteria. Such a multi-level approach to exploring inequality through intersectional lens would thus entail engaging issues of representation (in terms of how gender is constructed within contexts and deployed to what ends), identity exploration (that attends to how people in society navigate and create lives and livelihoods via their embodied identities and the intricate ways that these may intersect and at times even contradict each other) and lastly, by focusing on differential group dynamics and inequalities that exist in society, whether in terms of unemployment, vulnerability to sexual violence, access to education and health care and so on.

Maldonado-Torres (2007) further elucidates the reference to 'coloniality' when he points out that a coloniality of being signals those dimensions of the effects of colonialism, not only on the mind, but also on the lived experiences of colonised peoples. This is what he refers to as a 'coloniality of being' (p. 242) to draw attention to the ways that very modes of being-in-the-world and being-in-relation-to-each-other have been influenced by colonial relations of power. In line with Mignolo, such a reach for Torres also extends to areas of knowledge, gender and sexuality, political and cultural economies etc. And so, for example, our knowledge of gender and sexuality in the world and the political and social ordering of gendered bodies is far from a neutral practice. Rather, such practice and processes must be read relative to the histories and political and other economies that configure gender in particular ways in society. This is one of the ways that coloniality survives colonialism. It is part of the way people come to relate to themselves and to others in their communities and societies and even more broadly. It is also part of what comes to be understood as common sense thinking that may for example include conceiving of being in binaried and rigid ways. This includes how gender and sexuality come to take on such common sensical characteristics. Across the African continent, for example, non-heteronormative sexualities are disciplined and punished (that includes death sentencing in some countries) in many parts of the continent as 'un-African' and unnatural. Additionally, the status of women is inflected with these commonsense understandings of gender and very often informs policies on women's rights and bodily integrity. Sabelo Gatsheni's (2014) provoking question 'Can Africans create African futures within a modern world system structured by global coloniality?' (p. 181) also underscores this continued influence of global coloniality on relations and sites of agency and power within the continent. The goal towards a future that embraces diversity both as ethic and practice is one that Gatsheni (2014) considers to be possible but constrained within this global coloniality of power.

Tamale (2021) further describes 'decolonisation' as referring to 'various processes of deconstructing colonial interpretations and analyses of the social world' (p. 2). Noting the masculinist bias in much decolonial theorising she flags the necessity of deconstructing the ideals of freedom and equality that attend to gender regimes of power. This masculinist bias in decolonial thought has also been flagged by African feminist scholars such as Desiree Lewis and Gabeba Baderon (2021) in their recent edited work *Surfacing: On Being Black and Feminist in South Africa*. They rightly point out that much decolonial critique related to sites of power and violence (knowledge, economic systems, environmental and ecological systems) have for a long time been concerns addressed by Global South feminisms, particularly in their intersectional work and critique.

The prominent Latin American decolonial scholar, Marìa Lugones, in her essay 'Toward a Decolonial Feminism' (2010) proposes a decolonial feminist orientation that encompasses a reading of capitalist modernity that attends to gender regimes in an intersectional lens. Such a reading for Lugones includes engaging with colonial gender impositions that 'cuts across questions of ecology, economics, government, relations with the spirit world, and knowledge, as well as across everyday practices that either habituate us to take care of the world or to destroy it' (p. 742). Lewis and Baderoon (2021) also point out the dominance of North American feminist theorising over voices and perspectives from the Global South. A similar concern that Ratele (2019) and Kessi and Boonzaier (2018) raise in their expansions of African and decolonial feminist-oriented perspectives as a centring orientation to understanding lived realities and well-being from the Global South, with particular attention to African contexts. In challenging the dominant emphasis on race as the organising category for subjugation and inequity within the post-colony, Tamale (2021) reminds us that gender bears a similar and equally weighty effect in the ongoing inequities that characterise colonial and post-colonial relations across the continent. This is a similar assertion that both the Nigerian scholar Oyeronke Oyewumi (1997) and Maria Lugones (2010) point out in their respective works. These scholars highlight that separation of racial and gendered categories is not in the service of women especially as it makes invisible the nature and impacts of the inequities that they experience. This further resonates in Audre Lorde's (1984) activist politics advocating for a multi-pronged approach to addressing social inequalities. In the words of Lorde: 'There is no such thing as a single-issue struggle because we do not lead single-issue lives' (p. 183). The Kenyan environmentalist Wangari Maathai's ecological activism also encompassed a struggle for women's rights more generally, addressing this necessity for a holistic redress that engages the intersecting and multiple ways that gender inequalities are sustained (Musila, 2020).

For Lewis (2009), African feminism must also encompass a struggle against language and the intricate ways that it robs many women of access to rights and agency. The skepticism that this struggle against language entails includes awareness of how words such as 'development' may be deployed and used by governments in supposedly progressive and equitable ways but in practice fail to engage the nuances of what development means, especially for women. In addressing such ambiguities of gender equality,

Lewis asserts that nations may adopt a language of women's rights as part of their constitutional self-imaging – what may be termed as 'gender mainstreaming' (p. 207) but in reality may not be as gender-sensitive as may seem. She urges a concerted focus on the shifting ways that power takes shape relative to the information-age and other digital arenas – arenas that facilitate the representation through language of a nation as gender sensitive. In considering Lewis' caution, it is also important to consider the ways that feminism within some African context continues to be sidelined altogether or tolerated in others in ways that render real change meaningless. For scholars such as Charmaine Pereira (2004) and Lewis (2009) this struggle must therefore include constant vigilance of the shifting effects and function of gendered inequalities that are produced within neoliberal, global and local contexts.

■■■■■■■■ Chapter summary ■■■■■■■■

This chapter provides an overview of feminism and feminist theory and includes:

- An outline of gender-based social inequalities and explains how exploring gendered power relations deepen our understandings.
- Emphasises Afro-feminist thought and decolonial feminist theories.
- Uses case studies related to HIV infection and gender-based violence to highlight issues

Conclusion

This chapter has discussed feminist contributions to understanding gender inequalities within a Global South context. The chapter presented a critique of mainstream feminist approaches to inequality that tend to universalise women's experiences of gender. The argument is made that attention to contextual matters is important if issues of gender inequalities are to be adequately addressed. Focusing on the Global South that includes contributions from African and Decolonial feminisms, the chapter elucidates some of the key principles of these orientations, making the argument that addressing effects of coloniality on women's experiences of gender in these contexts remains an important aspect in engaging inequality and women's rights and access.

Questions to Reflect Upon

1   Decolonial and African feminist scholars accounts of power and violence in women's lives differs significantly from the emphasis of much Western and Eurocentric feminism. List these differences, reflecting on how these orientations may further our insights in thinking about gender inequalities today.

2   Discuss the notion of the coloniality of power. In what ways do you think such a concept may enhance our thinking of the ways that power takes effect in society? Sylvia Tamale's notion of Afro-Feminism may be a useful example to consider the

effects of coloniality of power and how we may challenge this effect. Revisit her definition of Afro-Feminism. What does she highlight as central to 'de-linking' from matrices of power? Why do you think she flags gender as central to this de-linking?

3 Why is gender inequality so resistant to change? What reasons can you think of why this might be so?

Further Reading

Ampofo, A. A., & Arnfred, S. (2009). *African feminist politics of knowledge: Tensions, challenges, possibilities*. Nordiska Afrikainstitutet. (This important book outlines the challenges and tensions facing feminist and decolonial academics and researchers. It emphasises how Global North institutions – universities, bureaucracies, donor organisations – limit the work of African feminist scholars. This is an important work as it offers a Global South critique based on the experiences of Global South scholars.)

Lugones, M. (2010). Toward a decolonial feminism. *Hypatia*, *25*(4), 742–759. (This critical intervention outlines ways of organizing that are, to use Lugones' term, 'un-modern'. By this Lugones means ways of being that are not shaped by colonial capitalist modernity. The paper is useful as it presents an alternative perspective on social relations.)

Tamale, S. (2021). *Decolonization and Afro-feminism*. Ottawa: Daraja Press. (Tamale's book provides an expansive, detailed overview of key decolonial and Afro-feminist debates. It includes theoretical discussions about Pan Africanism, decolonialism, and Global South feminisms alongside illustrative examples of colonial power relations. You may find this text useful in trying to understand the arguments from the chapter on race.)

References

Bilge, S. (2013). Intersectionality undone. *Du Bois Review: Social Science Research on Race*, *10*(02), 405–424.

Brah, A., & Phoenix, A. (2004). Ain't I a woman? Revisiting intersectionality. *Journal of International Women's Studies*, *5*(3), 75–86.

Bruce, D. (2019). *Ignore male victims at society's peril*. https://mg.co.za/article/2019-09-19-ignore-male-victims-at-societys-peril/

Carbado, D. W., Crenshaw, K. W., Mays, V. M., & Tomlinson, B. (2013). Intersectionality: Mapping the movements of a theory. *Du Bois Review: Social Science Research on Race*, *10*(2), 303–312.

Coetzee, A., & Du Toit, L. (2018). Facing the sexual demon of colonial power: Decolonising sexual violence in South Africa. *European Journal of Women's Studies*, *25*(2), 214–227.

Collins, P. H. (1986). Learning from the outsider within: The sociological significance of Black feminist thought. *Social Problems*, *33*(6), s14–s32.

Crenshaw, K. (1991). Mapping the margins: Intersectionality, identity politics, and violence against women of color. *Stanford Law Review*, *43*(6), 1241–1299.

Davis, K. (2008). Intersectionality as buzzword: A sociology of science perspective on what makes a feminist theory successful. *Feminist Theory*, *9*(1), 67–85.

Douglas, A. (1995). *Uneasy sensations: Smollett and the body*. Chicago: University of Chicago Press.

Everatt, D. (Ed.). (2019). *Governance and the postcolony: Views from Africa*. Johannesburg: Wits University Press.

Fischer, C. (2018). Gender and the politics of shame: A twenty-first-century feminist shame theory. *Hypatia, 33*(3), 371–383.

Gqola, P. D. (2015). *Rape: A South African nightmare*. Cape Town: MF Press.

Gqola, P. D. (2020). *Patriarchal violence and the inadequacy of condemnations*. Tambo Foundation 10-Year Anniversary Lecture Series. https://www.tambofoundation.org.za/event/prof-pumla-dineo-gqola/

Gqola, P. D. (2021). *Female fear factory*. Cape Town: MF Press.

hooks, b. (1989). *Talking back: Thinking feminist, thinking black* (Vol. 10). Boston, MA: South End Press.

hooks, b. (2004). *The will to change: Men, masculinity, and love*. Hillsboro, OR: Beyond Words/Atria Books.

Hook, D. (2006). 'Pre-discursive' racism. *Journal of Community & Applied Social Psychology, 16*(3), 207–232.

Jato, M. N. (2004). *Gender- Responsive programming for poverty reduction*. Technical Report. Addis Ababa: UNFPA.

Javaid, A. (2018). Hegemonic masculinity, heteronormativity, and male rape. In *Male rape, masculinities, and sexualities* (pp. 155–193). Cham: Palgrave Macmillan.

Judge, M. (2021). *'Finish this Elephant': Rural community organisations' strategic approaches to addressing gender-based violence*. Research Report. Cape Town: Social Change Assistance Trust.

Kessi, S., & Boonzaier, F. (2018). Centre/ing decolonial feminist psychology in Africa. *South African Journal of Psychology, 48*(3), 299–309.

Kiguwa, P. (2004). Feminist critical psychology in South Africa. In D. Hook (Ed.). *Critical psychology* (pp. 278–315). Landsdowne: UCT Press.

Langa, M. (2010). Contested multiple voices of young masculinities amongst adolescent boys in Alexandra Township, South Africa. *Journal of Child and Adolescent Mental Health, 22*(1), 1–13.

Lewis, D., & Baderoon, G. (Eds.). (2021). *Surfacing: On being black and feminist in South Africa*. Johannesburg: Wits University Press. Johannesburg, South Africa.

Lorber, J. (2010). *Gender inequality: Feminist theory and politics* (4th ed.). New York, NY: Oxford University Press.

Lorde, A. (1984). *Sister outsider: Essays and speeches, 1984*. Berkeley, CA: Crossing Press.

Lorde, A. (1988). *A burst of light*. New York, NY: Ixia Press.

Lugones, M. (2010). Toward a decolonial feminism. *Hypatia, 25*(4), 742–759.

Maldonado-Torres, N. (2007). On the coloniality of being: Contributions to the development of a concept. *Cultural Studies, 21*(2–3), 240–270.

Mbembe, A. (2001). *On the postcolony*. Berkeley, CA: University of California Press.

McCall, L. (2005). The complexity of intersectionality. *Signs, 30*(3), 1771–1800.

Mensah, E. O. (2021). To be a man is not a day's job: The discursive construction of hegemonic masculinity by rural youth in Nigeria. *Gender Issues, 38*(4), 438–460.

Mignolo, W. D. (2007). Introduction: Coloniality of power and de-colonial thinking. *Cultural Studies, 21*(2–3), 155–167.

Musila, G. A. (2020). *Voices of liberation: Wangari Maathai's registers of freedom*. Cape Town: HSRC Press.

Nayak, S. (2015). *Race, gender and the activism of black feminist theory: Working with Audre Lorde*. New York, NY: Routledge.

Ndlovu-Gatsheni, S. J. (2014). Global coloniality and the challenges of creating African futures. *The Strategic Review for Southern Africa, 36*(2), 181–202.

Nduna, M. (2020). *A magnifying glass and a fine-tooth comb: Understanding girls' and young women's sexual vulnerability*. Pretoria: CSA&G Press, Centre for Sexualities, AIDS and Gender, University of Pretoria.

Oyewumi, O. (1997). *The invention of women: Making African sense of western discourses*. Minneapolis: University of Minnesota Press.

Pereira, C. (2004). *Understanding women's experiences of citizenship in Nigeria. Gender, Economies and Entitlements in Africa, Council for the Development of Social Science Research in Africa, Dakar, Senegal, 87*.

Phoenix, A. (2017). Unsettling intersectional identities: Historicizing embodied boundaries and border crossings. *Ethnic and Racial Studies, 40*(8), 1312–1319.

Ratele, K. (2013). Subordinate black South African men without fear. *Cahiers D'études Africaines, 53*(209–210), 247–268.

Ratele, K. (2019). *The world looks like this from here: Thoughts on African psychology*. Johannesburg: Wits University Press.

Roy, A. (2020). *The pandemic is a portal*. https://www.ft.com/content/10d8f5e8-74eb-11ea-95fe-fcd274e920ca

Tamale, S. (2021). *Decolonization and Afro-feminism*. Ottawa: Daraja Press.

UNODC (2018). *Global study on homicide gender-related killing of women and girls*. https://www.unodc.org/documents/data-and-analysis/GSH2018/GSH18_Gender-related_killing_of_women_and_girls.pdf

Vetten, L., & Ratele, K. (2013). Men and violence. *Agenda, 27*(1), 4–11.

West, C., & Zimmerman, D. (1987). Doing gender. *Gender and Society, 1*, 125–151.

Willoughby-Herard, T. (2021). Which black feminism? In D. Marco, T. Willoughby-Herard, & Z. Zegeye (Eds.), Sasinda Futhi Siselapha: Black feminist approaches to cultural studies in South Africa's twenty-Five years since 1994 (pp. x–1). Cape Town: Africa World Press.

Winker, G., & Degele, N. (2011). Intersectionality as multi-level analysis: Dealing with social inequality. *European Journal of Women's Studies, 18*(1), 51–66.

Yuval-Davis, N. (2006). Intersectionality and feminist politics. *European Journal of Women's Studies, 13*(3), 193–209.

5

SEXUALITY

Lee Gregory

═══════════ Learning objectives ═══════════

- To discuss key theories explaining homosexuality in contemporary society
- To investigate the impact of heteronormativity on the development of welfare systems
- To outline ongoing discrimination experienced by LGBTQ+ people
- To illustrate the relevance of intersectionality to LGBTQ+ identities

═══════════ Framing questions ═══════════

- What factors have created a heteronormative society?
- Has full equality been attained for LGBTQ+ citizens?
- How does queer theory challenge assumptions regarding welfare provision?

Introduction

At the time of writing there is considerable global debate around issues of sexuality which remain prominent in political debates. While nations, such as Canada, have banned conversion therapy, a pseudoscientific practice of attempting to change an individual's sexual orientation from homosexual or bisexual to heterosexual, other nations, such as the UK, have delayed their public consultation on the topic. High profile debates around trans identities and rights have dominated in the global West with celebrities and a range of academics coming out against trans recognition (attracting the acronym TERF – trans-exclusionary radical feminist). This is within a global context death penalty remains in effect within 6 countries and possible within 5 for same sex sexual acts and can result in 8–10 years to life in prison within a further 57 countries. In contrast 81 countries offer employment protection, 57 offer broad protection and 11 constitutional protections against discrimination based on sexual orientation. In the UK, after the referendum to leave the European Union, there was a reported 147% increase in homophobic hate crimes in the three months that followed the result. As illustrated in Figure 5.1 there has been an increase in hate crimes against people in relation to their sexual orientation and for being transgender (the data also show increases in hate crimes towards BAME and

Numbers and percentages						England and Wales % change 2019/20 to 2020/21
Hate crime strand	2016/17	2017/18	2018/19	2019/20	2020/21	
Race	58,294	64,829	72,051	76,158	85,268	12
Religion	5,184	7,103	7,202	6,856	5,627	−18
Sexual orientation	**8,569**	**10,670**	**13,311**	**15,972**	**17,135**	**7**
Disability	5,254	6,787	7,786	8,465	9,208	9
Transgender	**1,195**	**1,615**	**2,185**	**2,542**	**2,630**	**3**
Total number of motivating factors	78,496	91,004	102,535	109,993	119,868	9
Total number of offences	74,967	86,254	97,474	105,362	114,958	9

Figure 5.1 Hate Crimes Recorded by the Police
Source: Home Office (2021) – emphasis added.

disabled people, as discussed in Chapters 3 and 7 of this book). Additionally, trans people are experiencing higher levels of hate crime and discrimination, with some of the findings from the Trans Lives Survey (TransActual, 2021) indicating that 40% of respondents experienced transphobia when seeking housing, 27% experienced homelessness, 63% experienced transphobia and 85% of trans women reported transphobic harassment from strangers in the street (71% for trans men and 73% for non-binary people). Despite a broader context of equality, there are significant challenges to address to ensure LGBTQ+ citizens are able to live safe, harassment-free lives.

This chapter examines the emergence of the term homosexuality and how it was established as a 'deviant other' against the heterosexual lifestyles. Providing insight into the power of discourse and social construction theory this leads into a discussion of homophobia and heterosexism and how discourses of homosexuality come to be reinforced through the wider structure of, and institutions within, societies: using the example of welfare provision to illustrate these points. The final parts of the chapter broaden out the discussion to consider intersectionality with class and race/ethnicity prior to a brief consideration of the critique of the equality agenda for adopting an assimilationist approach.

The Social Construction of 'Homosexuality'

Developing from feminist analysis, theoretical work stated to suggest that sexuality plays an integral part in everyone's life, from heterosexual, homosexual, asexual and all other varieties of sexuality. Although this chapter is focused upon LGBTQ+ citizens, experiences and debates, we must recognise that sexuality is much broader and resides in a variety of forms across *all* citizens. Consequently, calls to rethink citizenship to incorporate the intimate aspects of our lives draw attention to how we live our intimate lives in terms of rights, obligations, recognitions and respect and the choices we make about our intimate lives (Plummer, 2003). Carabine (2004) adds that sexuality is not just who or what we desire, it is also what we do and how we practise our sexuality combined with cultural meaning. Labels used are mediated through cultural understandings which have naturalised heterosexuality and presented homosexuality as a deviation from the 'norm' (see discussion below).

Scott and Jackson (2020) provide a useful starting set of definitions:

- Gender: referring to a specific culturally informed social division between groups of people within society, for example men and women, which now captures a broader range of genders with increasing recognition of trans and non-binary as well as gender fluid identities.
- Sex: erotic activity.
- Sexuality – a broader concept encompassing erotic desire and identities as well as practices.

While in terms of policy debates a definition of *sexual orientation* is utilised, with the World Health Organization incorporating into this term physical, emotional and romantic attraction towards other people (WHO, 2021), this does not reflect broader queer scholarship that has sought to disrupt and complicate such simplistic definitions. Alternatively, the term sexual identity is often used to highlight how labels relating to non-normative sexual identities (homosexuality) are imbued with meaning within society and shape how those labelled view themselves and are viewed. This is an important starting point in the discussion here, for queer theory has sought to illustrate and challenge the normative status of homosexuality in modern society and the way this generates social ordering of both gender and sexuality.

Sullivan (2003, p. 1) has suggested 'sexuality ... is constructed, experienced and understood in culturally and historically specific ways'. Yet early attempts to understand sexualities started with the belief that (hetero)sexuality was a 'pre-social' fact, something given and regulated by social institutions. Significant medical, legal and religious discourse presented non-heterosexuality as a deviation from the norm and, often a condition that could be 'treated'. But it was the development of such thinking that drew a spotlight onto non-heterosexuals explicitly in legal frameworks. Initially the illegality was focused on *acts* rather than people: such as the pre-late 1880s death penalty attached for 'the abominable vice of buggery'. While the pre-1880s was focused on illegality of acts, as noted, there was a shift towards illegality of certain people because of these medical discourses making same-sex relationships illegal. These were about male, same sex relationships as sex was legally defined in relation to penetration. Consequently, female homosexuality 'took much longer than male homosexuality to constitute the basis of a communal, subcultural identity' (Jagose, 1996, p. 13) and later faced increased persecution in Western culture from the 20th century, which Faderman (1985) argues was partly a backlash to the growing Feminist movement. However, these medical assumptions around sexuality were eventually challenged.

Psychological thinking started to challenge the assumptions that non-heterosexual sexualities were a deviation from the norm, such as Hirschfield's suggestion that sexual variability was akin to fingerprints and so could not have a 'normal' and 'abnormal' division in sexuality. The work of Kinsey, and the subsequent Kinsey Scale, demonstrated diversity in sexual activity and how some heterosexual identifying individuals engaged in same sex acts. Problematically this analysis only looked at data from white men and women and did not, until later analysis, start to draw attention to social factors informing sexuality and sexual practices. Yet it is within such research that a challenge to the assumption that sex was simply about procreation was possible, highlighting the importance of pleasure through sex. Importantly, this facilitates recognition of same-sex relations as valid. Weeks (1989), summarising the work of Freud, illustrates that there was a growing suggestion that heterosexuality was *culturally* necessary but not naturally preordained.

Social theorists working within the social constructivist tradition further illustrated the culturally constructed nature of sexuality. The rise in new theories of deviance suggested that 'deviance' was a matter of social definition providing a powerful challenge to earlier biological determinism. Through a series of *sexual scripts* (Gagnon and Simon, cited in Jackson & Scott, 2010) we construct our biographies to align with current identities, roles, situations, and vocabularies. These sexual scripts exist at three levels, although Gagnon and Simon were not necessarily clear from where these scripts came:

1 Cultural scenarios – the cultural narratives around sexuality and institutional guides for sexual conduct;
2 Interpersonal scripting – our everyday interactions negotiating sexual activity;
3 Intrapsychic scripting – the level of individual desires and thoughts, the internal reflexive process of the self.

Such theories influenced wider social thinking, and eventually the *genealogical* approach adopted by Foucault (1990) in his work mapping the history of sexuality shaped wider social thinking, especially later queer theory. Exploring the power of discourse Foucault demonstrated that homosexuality was constructed a distinct identity and a medical defect in the 1870s creating a clear distinction to such acts within societies across the globe and human history. For Foucault, this reflected a concern with maintaining male primogeniture (Foucault, 1990). Further, Sullivan (2003, p. 14) suggests that medical writers and social commentators sought to maintain existing cultural hierarchies in relation to class and race differences to maintain the privileged position of white, middle/upper-class heterosexual masculinity. This intentionally obscured any other views and interpretations of social life that challenged the status quo.

Such views have influenced not only social theory but social actions, liberation campaigns to change the law and ensure equal rights for LGBTQ+ people. Despite slow progress these efforts have accumulated in contemporary laws such as equal marriage and sexual orientation being a protected characteristic in the Equality Act 2010. However, many of these earlier discourses still dominate: such as the ongoing debate around trans identities and rights, debates about 'conversation therapy' facilitating a continued narrative in some parts of society that homosexuality is 'curable' to continued efforts to tackle discrimination despite the existence of the 2010 Act.

Heteronormative Assumptions and Welfare Provision

Within society heterosexuality is presented as an unproblematic state, privileging this one sexuality over all others, and creating a context of heterosexism – the establishment of prejudice and discriminating attitudes towards LGBTQ+ people by homosexuals. Historic processes have created a context heteronormativity (Jackson, 2007): the privileging of heterosexual identities and lives and an implicit assumption that all people are heterosexual. Heteronormativity flows through every day social life. It captures all social practices and forms of social regulation which equates 'normal' sexuality with heterosexuality and establishes a form of 'compulsory heterosexuality' to suggest that heterosexuality is imposed on us rather than being freely chosen.

However, it was these same processes of urbanisation and industrial capitalism facilitated greater ability to live as an individual and independently of wider kinship networks via wage labour. People no longer relied on the family unit (D'Emilio, 1992), allowing homosexual desire to become a central aspect of identity in a way that was not previously possible. Katz (1983) suggests that this historic emergence implied heterosexuality is somehow more natural and implicit within social life, when in fact the term heterosexuality emerges only because of the concept of homosexuality was established first.

This heteronormative assumption extends into the development of welfare systems and institutions as these emerge with industrialisation. With industrialisation there was a growing concern with 'social issues'. Emerging from this concern was social science investigation which identified structural causes of poverty and social problems, an approach which became associated with a group called the Fabians. This sets a tradition for what would later become Social Policy conducting research into and policy suggestion for the development of welfare systems. Yet this Fabian tradition embedded the assumed heterosexuality of the time (see Gregory and Matthews, forthcoming) and will present heteronormative assumption of family and intimate lives. Furthermore, Weeks (1989) has suggested that Fabian thinking retained eugenicist ideas which sought to promote policy which produced the 'right sort' of people. State intervention, therefore, explicitly sought to promote appropriate forms of motherhood, family, citizen conduct and implicit assumptions about the nation. Thus, while sexuality was at the heart of much policy intervention and the regulatory activity of the state, it was heteronormative in its intent. As Richardson (2017) noted, Social Policy has developed limited theorising about the relationship between sexuality and social policy with Gregory and Matthews (forthcoming) suggesting that the discipline fails to appreciate the broader experience of non-heterosexuals and non-cisgender people.

It is important to also recognise the significance of gender in many of these debates. Cisgender, a term in academic usage since the 1990s, is used to refer to people whose gender identity aligns with the gender assigned at birth. Thus, it is possible to be a cis-heterosexual, a cis-gay man, cis-lesbian, etc. The alternative to a cis identity is a *trans* identity, referring to a gender that is different to that which was assigned at birth. As such, it is possible to be assigned male at birth and identify as heterosexual but to transition to become a trans-woman who is still sexually attracted to women. As noted earlier there is also greater diversity of gender identities to include non-binary and fluid identities, none of which would conform to the assumed cisgender identities that dominate in society. Heteronormative assumptions will also assume cis identities, which is another implicit assumption within welfare state development.

Recent debate therefore critiques the collectivist endeavour of welfare systems as being built upon 'false universalism'. Welfare systems have perpetuated a white, male, able-bodied, heterosexual image of a citizenship and failed to recognise the diversity and difference that exists across citizens within any given society (Lister, 1998). An early attempt to illustrate the tension between citizenship and LGBTQ+ people, utilised the concept of social exclusion to argue for a new model of social welfare provision which engages and responds more clearly to the needs of LGBTQ+ people and communities (Concannon, 2008). In just over a decade since this argument, however, a range of policy changes has occurred in the UK (equal marriage rights, the Equality Act 2010 and the rise in prominence of trans debates) and have superseded much of this analysis, but the broader point and some of the wider challenges remain.

Yet a persisting challenge of heteronormative assumptions has disrupted social science investigations. We have limited data on LGBTQ+ citizens, as survey tools have only recently been modified to start 'counting' variety in sexuality and gender. Thus we have a longer trend of data around LGB people, but trans identities are a recent inclusion. However, there remains critique that the terminology used is often imposed by wider heterosexual society, and for some there are active efforts to lobby against the inclusion of such questions so that LGBTQ+ are *not* counted (Guyan, 2021). Furthermore, despite significant advances in equality legislation a complex picture of discrimination persists. Research suggests that while lesbians are likely to earn more than heterosexual women they have greater incidence of work-based anxiety. Gay men, however, do not seem to have an earning impact because of their sexual identity while bisexuals have lower wellbeing compared to other groups. LGB people are less likely to be homeowners compared to heterosexuals and often have higher rates of poor health. Matthews and Besemer (2015) also demonstrate that LGBTQ+ people are more likely to live in deprived communities compared to heterosexuals. LGBTQ+ people tend to have higher levels of homelessness, and these can quite often impact on younger people because of 'coming out' to family (Valentine, Skelton, & Butler, 2003). Generally, we see a complex picture for non-heterosexual and non-cisgender individuals suggesting a wider interplay of intersectional disadvantages (and at times advantages) in relation to welfare support and interventions.

Despite advances, recent history also contains examples where policy activity, or inactivity, has been intentionally pursued causing subsequent harm to LGBTQ+ communities. For example, in relation to education policy the introduction of section 28 of the Local Government Act 1988 which prohibited the intentional promotion or teaching of homosexuality in schools. The legislation referred to homosexuality as a 'pretend family relationship' and was not repealed until 2000 (in Scotland) and 2003 (in England and Wales). The legislation prevented many LGBTQ+ teaching from 'being out', prohibited teaching of LGBTQ+ relationships and sexual health and even prevented schools from tackling homophobic bullying. Quite often the fear of prosecution under the law dissuaded many teachers from offering support and counselling to students. Similarly, under the same government, the emergence of the HIV/AIDS epidemic resulted in homophobic attitudes within government resisting efforts to develop education and public health campaigns for 'fear' of the message this would be sending and a 'concern' that this would expose children and young people to inappropriate message around sex (despite the need for safe sex message).

It might be easy to assume that since the Equality Act 2010 and a more progressive shift in public attitudes would prevent such policy practices from occurring. But one need only look at the delay in banning conversion therapy and the culture war around trans identities to see that many of these discriminatory attitudes persist. But it need not always manifest so boldly as the examples above. While the assumptions around compulsory heterosexuality are normalised into service delivery this also occurs at the local level, where services are delivered. Such developments potentially reflect a form of everyday homophobia. For example, within homelessness legislation in England local authorities must support families and households who are experiencing unintentional homelessness. But this provision is based upon a concept of 'priority need', and this is often a category that does not include single-person households. As such there is potential for indirect discrimination against LGBTQ+ people who are more likely to be single and thus a bureaucratic barrier develops which can be used to limit the support given to LGBTQ+ people. Additionally, as Matthews and Poyner (2020) illustrate how housing associations reinforced heterosexuality through their equality and diversity tools because they did not offer tenants an opportunity to declare that their sexual and gender identity was not heterosexual and cisgendered. The key point here is that even when progressive policies are established, implementation will not always result in intended outcomes. For example, Brown (2011) analysis of benefit claiming applications processes after the Civil Partnership Act.

Browne maps the various ways local authorities in England did, and did not, modify their application forms to recognise civil partnerships. While some authorities did integrate options to inform agencies of being in a civil partnership while other local authorities did not. Some provided information and guidance around how to apply for benefits when in a civil partnership, others had no information about civil partnerships on their websites at all. Consequently, across England, there was an initial variety in practice in which depending on where one lived it was possible to declare you were in a civil partnership, or you had no option to do so. For claimants there was the risk of making fraudulent claims because they did not declare their civil partnership (couples have a reduced claim to benefit) but also, as Brown (2011) notes, the heterosexual structure of the benefits system puts certain, heterosexual family types, under scrutiny and potentially impacts on the value of benefits, and tax exemptions, they can claim. This contrasts to those who are defined as 'single' who experience no reduction in what they can claim despite the potential of being in a same-sex relationship. In being unrecognised and ignored through the heterosexual lens LGBTQ+ claimants, assessed as a single person, may benefit from a higher level of benefit income. Such advantages are rarely just beneficial, however. As noted, this not only generates a risk of being accused of fraud, but LGBTQ+ partners may need to continue to live outside the boundaries of a 'couple' to retain their incomes, homes and other provisions which have been a key part to securing their wellbeing, but might otherwise be at risk from couple status.

Homophobia, Transphobia and the 21st Century

The gradual fight for LGBTQ+ equality has seen a gradual and incomplete move from illegality and punishment by death to one of growing acceptance and recognition of rights. This does not, however, suggest that discrimination and hate attacks against LGBTQ+ people have vanished. In fact, the move from a denial of civil and social rights has not easily removed the stigmatised treatment and assumptions around LGBTQ+ people, perhaps most clearly illustrated in the contemporary UK context, at the time of writing, whereby trans people have also become the focus of contemporary 'culture wars', resulting in societal abjection and rising moral panics, putting them in an even more invidious position.

The analysis published in 2018 of a UK government survey exploring the lives of LGBT people provides some insight into the experience of LGBTQ+ people in the 21st century.

* Two in five respondents had experienced verbal harassment or physical violence because of their sexuality.
* More than nine in ten of the most serious incidents went unreported.
* 20% had accessed mental health services and this figure varied across respondents (30% for trans women, 40% for trans men, 37% for non-binary people and 29% for cisgender bisexual people).
* 77% of respondents indicated that the sexuality and gender orientation had never been discussed in school although there was as age influence here as this figure was 54% for 16–17-year-olds.
* 21% experienced disclosure of the LGBT status without permission.
* 21% had experienced verbal harassment.
* 6% had faced exclusion from events/activities.
* Sexual and physical harassment had been experienced by 2% and 2% respectively.
* 46% of cisgender respondents never discussed their sexual orientation with health professionals, as they felt it was irrelevant – this figure was 67% for bisexual people compared to 36% for lesbian/gay respondents (GEO, 2018).

Around the same time as the government analysis the LGBT rights campaign organisation, Stonewall (2018) had its own data showing that 14% of LGBT people avoid seeking treatment for fear of discrimination while 5% reported they had felt pressure to question/change their sexual orientation when accessing health services.

The subsequent development of the LGBT Action Plan by the UK government was applauded as the first, comprehensive, cross-departmental plan to address LGBTQ+ inequality. Yet, the discourse of the plan continues to reflect heteronormative ideology. As Lawrence and Taylor (2020) outline, the use of language continues to portray LGBTQ+ people as the 'other' which implicitly reinforces heteronormative and cis-normative assumptions and social practices. The Action Plan appears to accept LGB lives when presented within a socially conservative and neoliberal framework (furthering the concerns of some around assimilationist attitudes) while offering opaque support for trans* and gender-non-confirming citizens. Acceptance and recognition of queer lives remain, at best, marginal.

Assimilation through Equality?

This Action Plan is part of an ongoing history of LGBTQ+ rights and equality which has seen a very gradual move from illegality punishable by death to the eventual decriminalisation and moves to provide equal marriage more recently. Some of the key legal and equality debates in UK history include the following:

- The Buggery Act of 1533 made anal sex an offence punishable by hanging.
- Offences Against the Person Act 1861 removed the death penalty but male homosexual acts remained illegal.
- In 1885, the law was extended to include any kind of sexual activity between males, illustrated by the high-profile case of Oscar Wilde.
- During the 1950s, the police actively pursued and prosecuted gay men, illustrated again by another high-profile case of Alan Turing (a famous mathematician and war-time code breaker), who was chemically castrated as an alternative to prison (he later committed suicide).
- The Wolfenden Committee was set up in 1950 to consider UK law relating to 'homosexual offences', ultimately suggesting homosexual behaviour between consenting adults should not be considered a criminal offence. It should be noted that lesbians were largely ignored under these legislations and would not feature in legislation until much later.
- After several attempts, the Sexual Offences Act 1967 eventually secured royal assent, decriminalising homosexual acts where these were consensual, had taken place in private, and involved people aged 21 and above (a higher age of consent than that set for heterosexuals).
- The Sexual Offences Act 1967 however only covered England and Wales and Scotland did not align its laws until the 1980s and Northern Ireland in 1982.

- In 1979, there were recommendations to further lower the age of consent to 18 – although the age of consent was eventually changed in the mid-1990s.
- In 1999, the age of consent equalised to 16 despite continued protests by some policy makers that such changes posed health risks to young people.
- In 2000 – the Scottish Parliament repelled section 28, the Westminster government attempt was blocked by the House of Lords and would not be repelled until 2003.
- In 2005, the Civil Partnership Act offered legal recognition to same sex relationships and granted most (but not all) the same rights and responsibilities as civil marriage.
- In 2010, the Equality Act made sexual identity and gender reassignment protected characteristics.
- In 2013 – Equal Marriage in England and Wales.
- In 2014 – Equal Marriage in Scotland.
- In 2019 – Equal Marriage in Northern Ireland was granted. This legislation took five votes to finally secure a slim majority only to be vetoed by the Democratic Unionist Party. It later became legal for same sex couples in Northern Ireland to marry in 2020 only after an indecisive election in 2017 resulting in no formation of a Northern Ireland Executive. In 2019, triggered by a return to power of the UK Parliament, same sex marriage regulations were then signed off by the Secretary of State for Northern Ireland.

The development of these rights however did not just emerge organically, creating a greater context of equality. They have been hard fought for by LGBTQ+ activists, organisations and their allies. Essentially however a tension has arisen within the LGBTQ+ community as to the purpose of this campaign activity. For many, the move towards liberation has been a key part in securing social rights and protecting LGB people – it is still debateable to extent to which trans people are afforded protections. But a counter narrative has developed which suggest that this is equality through 'assimilation'. For some this equality reflects the privilege of cis-gendered, wealthy middle and upper class LGB people and marginalises the broader diversity of the LGBTQ+ community. Broadly, assimilationist approaches to equality reframe LGBT people in a heteronormative way to secure protection, rather than seeking equality demonstrating sameness and hiding the difference, rather than securing equality which recognises and protects the diversity of the community.

Despite the progress however there remain issues to be resolved. Especially in relation to trans rights we see not only resistance within governments to granting and supporting the rights of these individuals/groups, but also parts of the LGB community also voicing opposition to the inclusion of trans identities and community. Even some of the campaign organisations have been called out for failing to be as vocal on trans issues. Many of these debates however echo the attitudes towards and claims about LGB people several decades ago. Additionally, as mentioned above, the slow response by the UK government to ban conversion therapy indicates a reluctance to fully support LGBTQ+ rights. To illustrate the point, governments would in no way support efforts to 'convert' straight people to different sexualities but seems willing at present to let this pseudoscientific practice continue when targeted at non-heterosexuals. It cannot yet be assumed that a context of equality has been attained with regards the wider LGBTQ+ community. There are ongoing debates and challenges which have yet to be resolved.

Intersectionality With Class and Race

A concern with diversity of citizens, as discussed above, has been further illustrated through the work regarding intersectionality. Crenshaw (1989) writing from a critical race legal perspective argued for the need to identify the overlapping identities that people hold. Fundamentally, everyone has unique experiences of discrimination and oppression which vary by gender, race, class, sexual orientation, physical ability etc. More broadly we can consider a whole series of factors which can be a source of marginalisation for people, not just the characteristics linked above but a whole range of other religious, cultural, age, language and other aspects of human nature which can confer advantage on some but discriminate/oppress others. Fundamentally, it offers a framework for revealing the intersections to challenge unidimensional and exclusionary analysis of oppression and discrimination. Thus, while this chapter is about LGBTQ+ sexuality, these sexualities are just one of several intersectional identities that people will hold.

Subsequently consideration of the intersectional lives of LGBTQ+ people will illustrate some of the themes we have already examined and how they are patterned across many aspects of social life. Here the hegemonic nature of heterosexuality which prescribes certain gender roles will likely be reinforced across several intersectional identities (gender, class, ethnicity, religion to name a few). For example, Jewell and Morrison (2012) illustrate how the perception of gay men breaking 'traditional' male roles creates unfavourable views of gay men. Combined with discomfort that some men take the 'women's position' in a relationship establishes a firmer negative view held by both men and women. Such views in turn reinforce hegemonic masculinity and the higher status given to heterosexuality over homosexuality and establish a social expectation for all men to act in heterosexual, masculine ways. The source of these social expectations is varied and generated by the wider pervasive heteronormativity that exists throughout society and how it will cut through in notions of class, gender, ethnicity, religion, language and so many other constituent parts of social life.

Class is predominately a missing dynamic in many of these debates, becoming an under-investigated aspect in sexuality studies. In part this relates to Foucault's neglect of class and state power. Whereas Drucker (2014) argues that the importance of the power of capital and the state, of men over women and of white over non-white people cannot be underestimated. In accepting Foucault at the micro level, therefore, it is important to not forget the macro level of social structures. The slippage of account of class, however, cannot be laid solely at the feet of Foucault. As Richardson (2017) notes, the language of sexual citizenship is one of individual rights, citizenship, choice and privacy which do not align with the language of class. Thus, progress to create more equal contexts often disguises rather than challenges the role of social structures in sustaining inequalities as a focus on individual rather than collective rights comes to dominate.

This reflects developments in social theory. Debates in the late 20th century argue that Western society could no longer be adequately summed up with the label of modernity which characterised the early industrial period and subsequent social change. Suggestions that a period of late modernity had arrived through the process of globalisation were observed in the work of sociologists such as Giddens (1992) and Beck and Beck-Gernsheim (2002). This gave rise to individualisation theories which suggested that traditional class characteristics and influences no longer held sway other people's lives. Rather, citizens had increased fluidity, choice and greater agency over their lives, including their intimate relationships. Class, in the words of Beck and Beck-Gernshiem, had become a 'zombie category'. The phrasing of a zombie category suggesting that while the idea (in this case class identity) lives on, the reality to which this idea relates has died.

Such claims, however, have not gone unchallenged. A number of studies have sought to demonstrate the ongoing relevance of class. Often these studies indicate that class patterned inequalities continue to shape all aspects of life, including sexual life. One key issue to arise from efforts to examine the intersection of class and sexuality has been to question whose accounts of sexual and intimate life are being drawn upon to develop an understanding of sexuality. The significance of class is that it not only draws attention to differences in material wealth and economic security but because it also shapes social life in terms of the relationships, practices and experiences that we have and the value we attach to such aspects of social life. It also effects how others value us and respond to us, with significant research into issues of stigma and the harms of class identities demonstrating how working-class identities are often demonised and critiqued from within a dominant upper class value system. Combine this with the derogatory treatment of certain sexualities and we can see how the intersection of class and sexuality may create complex patterns of discrimination and stigmatisation. Furthermore, debates around social class and sexuality draw attention to how both culture and the economy play significant roles in social life and how patterns of economic inequality and exchange play out in cultural struggles (Skeggs, 2004).

Concerns about class do however encapsulate just one potential intersection within a range of possible intersectional identities, and as noted above we are likely discussing multiple intersectional characteristics held by any one individual. A focus on class should not dispense with additional attention to the dynamics of gender or race, for example, within these constellations of identity. As such the work of Maskovsky (2002) is useful in illustrating the material condition of poor, working class, African American queer people to critique the focus of sexuality studies on consumption spaces and for paying limited attention to labour practices within the commercial scene. Thus, studies obscure economic disadvantage and inequalities within the LGBTQ+ community.

A focus on ethnicity has also examined the intersections of LGBTQ+ identities with ethnicity and religion. Particular attention has been given to South Asian identities which successfully demonstrate the broader intersectional point established here. The research illustrates the challenges that face LGBTQ+ South Asian people as they often have competing pressures to navigate. On the one hand, the expectations of their ethnic community, religion and the expectations and social norms this imbues. LGBTQ+ Muslims, for example, face negative perceptions of gay and lesbian sexualities reinforced through Islam which gives hegemonic status to heterosexuality (Yip, 2004; in Jaspal & Cinnirella, 2012). Thus, the heteronormative pressures are experienced in a complex web of intersectional identities impacting on the wellbeing of these individuals.

Navigating these pressures often requires, in this example, British Muslims to modify existing social representations of homosexuality within ethno-religious contexts. As Adur and Purkayastha (2017) illustrate this often requires, on the one hand, utilising language and cultural symbols to open up discourse within ethnic communities about non-heteronormative identities. On the other, there is a need to draw upon these ethnic and religious traditions to challenge dominant Western values and representations of the LGBTQ+ community. But as Jaspal (2017) demonstrates the intersections can vary. Thus, for British Indian LGBTQ+ people the central aspects of their identity draw upon sexuality and ethnicity, while for British Pakistani LGBTQ+ people this is a mix of their sexuality and religion. For the former, Jaspal finds that it is primarily social obstacles for the development of interpersonal and intergroup relationships; while for the latter this can cause social and psychological challenges in securing their wellbeing. How intersectionality is experienced varies the social and individual consequences. Jaspal further illustrates this challenge with analysis demonstrating how British South Asian gay men experience multiple layers of rejection. Not only the ethno-religious homophobia of their own community but also the wider racism and homophobia of the general population *and* racism from White British gay men. Consequently LGBTQ+ people from ethnic minority groups may find that they have few sources of social support across various communities within wider society creating negative impacts on their social and psychological wellbeing and identify formation.

■■■■■■■■ Chapter summary ■■■■■■■■■■■

This chapter has explored the ongoing challenges experienced by the LGBTQ+ community, and included the following:

- The social construction of homosexuality
- Heteronormative assumptions and welfare provision
- Homophobia, transphobia and the 21st century
- Assimilation through equality
- Key legal and equality debates in UK history
- Intersectionality with class and race

Conclusion

The key aims of this chapter have been to introduce some of the central debates in relation to sexuality, and specifically the sexuality of non-heterosexual people. Attention has been given to the discursive framing of gay and lesbian people a deviation from the norm and the development of regulatory practices, both medical and legal, which have created a context of discrimination and disadvantage for LGBTQ+ people historically in the UK. The development of this heteronormative framework has informed a vast array of social norms, practices and institutions, including the development of the welfare state. Predominately, through the construction of citizenship, there is a limited awareness of diverse sexualities, and genders, within social policy and wider welfare provisions. Consequently, in most cases, this results in disadvantaging and discriminating LGBTQ+ people. More broadly, despite shifts in public attitudes and changes in the wider legal framework, LGBTQ+ people still have a varied experience of homophobia in a range of guises, from physical and verbal hate crimes to bureaucratic discrimination through welfare practices. The chapter has sought to provide some insight into the continued challenges faced by LGBTQ+ people despite an agenda for equality recognising some of the ongoing tensions between liberation and assimilationist debates with regards equality but also the complexity of intersectional identities which fracture and diversify experiences of social life and discrimination within the LGBTQ+ community.

Questions to Reflect Upon

- How might 'homosexuality' be presented as a deviation from the norm in your society?
- Do you think equality has been through assimilation with LGB people seeking to adopt 'heterosexual lifestyles'?
- In what ways might we claim the welfare state is a heteronormative institution?
- Can you list examples of discrimination against LGBTQ+ people might still experience?

Further Reading

Carabine, J. (2004). Sexualities, personal lives and social policy. In J. Carabine (Ed.), *Sexualities: Personal lives and social policy* (pp. 2–48). Bristol: Policy Press. (This chapter provides an orientation to key issues and debates regarding LGBT+ personal lives and the interaction with welfare debates. It sets out a number of key issues and themes which have been explored in wider research and offers a useful orientation to key debates for those seeking to explore this topic in greater detail.)

Gregory, L., & Matthews, P. (2022). Social policy and queer lives: Coming out of the closet?. *Journal of Social Policy*. Cambridge University Press, pp. 1–15. doi:10.1017/ S0047279422000198. (This article suggests that the discipline of Social Policy needs to better engage with the experience of LGBT+ people in relation to welfare provision. It introduces the concept of 'cishet-izenship' as a way of illustrating how Social Policy debates maintain a heteronormative account of citizenship which fails to recognise LGBT+ as full citizens. Additionally, it critiques heteronormative assumptions which informs the development of welfare provision.)

Richardson, D. (2017). Rethinking sexual citizenship. *Sociology*, 51(2), 208–24. (This article is an important contribution to citizenship and sexuality debates. It offers an updated account of earlier worth by Richardson and others in the 1990s and suggests that we need to de-centre a 'western-centric' focus in sexuality debates to adopt theoretical frameworks that resonate with the global North and South.)

Weeks, J. (1989). *Sex, politics and society: The regulation of sexuality since 1800* (2nd ed.). London: Longman. (This book offers a useful historic analysis of social life in relation to sexuality and the intersection between personal life, politics and social life. It reviews a range of theoretical developments and policy/legal debates around sexual identity which are pertinent to understanding ongoing tensions and debates today.)

References

Adur, S., & Purkayastha, B. (2017). (Re)Telling traditions: The language of social identity among queer South Asians in the United States. *South Asian Diaspora*, *9*(1), 1–16.

Beck, U., & Beck-Gernsheim, E. (2002). *Individualization: Institutionalized individualism and its social and political consequences*. London: SAGE.

Brown, K. (2011). By partner we mean...: Alternative geographies of 'gay marriage'. *Sexualities*, *14*(1), 100–122.

Carabine, J. (2004). Sexualities, personal lives and social policy. In J. Carabine (Ed.), *Sexualities: Personal lives and social policy* (pp. 2–48). Bristol: Policy Press.

Concannon, L. (2008). Citizenship, sexual identity and social exclusion: Exploring issues in British and American social policy. *International Journal of Sociology and Social Policy*, *28*(9–10), 326–339.

Crenshaw, K. (1989). *Demarginalizing the intersection of race and sex: A black feminist critique of antidiscrimination doctrine, feminist theory, and antiracist politics*, University of Chicago Legal Forum, 139.

D'Emilio, J. (1992). *Making trouble: Essays on gay history, politics and the University*. New York, NY: Routledge.

Drucker, P. (2014). *Warped: Gay normality and queer anticapitalism*. Chicago, IL: Haymarket Books.

Faderman, L. (1985). *Surpassing the love of men: Romantic friendship and love between women from the renaissance to the present*. London: The Women's Press.

Foucault, M. (1990). The history of sexuality. In R. Hurley (Ed.), *An introduction* (Vol. 1). New York, NY: Vintage Books.

GEO. (2018). *National LGBT survey: Research report*. Retrieved from https://www.gov.uk/government/publications/national-lgbt-survey-summary-report

Giddens, A. (1992). The transformation of intimacy sexuality, love, and eroticism in modern societies. *Contemporary Sociology*, *22*, 845–846.

Guyan, K. (2021). Constructing a queer population? Asking about sexual orientation in Scotland's 2022 census. *Journal of Gender Studies*, 1–11.

Home Office. (2021). *Hate crime, England and Wales, 2020 to 2021*. Retrieved from https://www.gov.uk/government/statistics/hate-crime-england-and-wales-2020-to-2021/hate-crime-england-and-wales-2020-to-2021

Jackson, S. (2007). Heterosexuality, heteronormativity and gender hierarchy: Some reflections on recent debates. In J. Weeks, J. Holland, & M. Waites (Eds.), *Sexualities and society: A reader* (pp. 69–83). Cambridge: Polity.

Jackson, S., & Scott, S. (2010). *Theorizing sexuality*. Maidenhead: McGraw-Hill Education.

Jagose, A. (1996). *Queer theory: An introduction*. New York, NY: New York University Press.

Jaspal, R. (2017). Coping with perceived ethnic prejudice on the gay scene. *Journal of LGBT Youth*, *14*(2), 172–190.

Jaspal, R., & Cinnirella, M. (2012). Identity processes, threat, and interpersonal relations: Accounts from British Muslim gay men. *Journal of Homosexuality*, *59*(2), 215–240.

Jewell, L. M., & Morrison, M. A. (2012). Making sense of homonegativity: Heterosexual men and women's understanding of their own prejudice and discrimination toward gay men. *Qualitative Research in Psychology*, *9*(4), 351–370.

Katz, J. (1983). *Gay/lesbian almanac: A new documentary*. New York, NY: Harper and Row.

Lawrence, M., & Taylor, Y. (2020). The UK government LGBT action plan: Discourses of progress, enduring stasis, and LGBTQI+ lives 'getting better'. *Critical Social Policy*, *40*(4), 586–607.

Lister, R. (1998). Vocabularies of citizenship and gender: The UK. *Critical Social Policy*, *18*(56), 309–331.

Maskovsky, J. (2002). 'Do we all reek of the commodity?' Consumption and the erasure of poverty in lesbian and gay studies. In E. Lewin & W. L. Leap (Eds.), *Out in theory: The emergence of lesbian and gay anthroplopgy* (pp. 264–289). Urbana and Chicago, IL: University of Illinois Press.

Matthews, P., & Besemer, K. (2015). The 'pink pound' in the 'gaybourhood'? Neighbourhood deprivation and sexual orientation in Scotland. *Housing, Theory and Society*, *32*(1), 94–111.

Matthews, P., & Poyner, C. (2020). Achieving equality in progressive contexts: Queer(y)ing public administration. *Public Administration Quarterly*, *44*(4), 545–577.

Plummer, K. (2003). *Intimate citizenship: Private decisions and public dialogues*. Seattle, WA: University of Washington Press.

Richardson, D. (2017). Rethinking sexual citizenship. *Sociology*, *51*(2), 208–224.

Scott, S., & Jackson, S. (2020). Sexualities. In G. Payne & E. Harrison (Eds.), *Social divisions: Inequality and diversity in Britain* (4th ed.). Bristol: Policy Press.

Skeggs, B. (2004). *Class, self, culture*. London: Routledge.

Stonewall. (2018). *LGBT in Britain – Health*. London: Stonewall.

Sullivan, N. (2003). *A critical introduction to queer theory*. Edinburgh: Edinburgh University Press.

TransActual. (2021). *Trans lives survey 2021: Enduring the UK's hostile environment*. Retrieved from https://static1.squarespace.com/static/5e8a0a6bb02c73725b24dc9d/t/6152eac81e0b0109491dc518/1632824024793/Trans+Lives+Survey+2021.pdf

Valentine, G., Skelton, T., & Butler, R. (2003). Coming out and outcomes: Negotiating lesbian and gay identities with, and in, the family. *Environment and Planning D: Society and Space*, *21*(4), 479–499.

Weeks, J. (1989). *Sex, politics and society: The regulation of sexuality since 1800* (2nd ed.). London: Longman.

World Health Organization. (2021). *Gender and human rights*. Retrieved from https://www.who.int/reproductivehealth/topics/gender_rights/sexual_health/en/

Yip, A. K. (2004). Embracing Allah and sexuality? South-Asian non-heterosexual muslims in Britain. *In South Asians in the diaspora* (pp. 294–310). Brill.

6

AGEING

Anya Ahmed, Lorna Chesterton and Sarah Campbell

=== Learning objectives ===

- To understand the constructs and theories around ageing across different cultures and contexts
- To understand how social inequalities across the life-course affect experiences of ageing
- To understand how inequalities across the life-course impact on health outcomes in later life
- To understand why and how Western experiences of ageing have been privileged in discourse, research and policy

=== Framing questions ===

- Why do you think that ageing is perceived and experienced differently according to culture and context?
- What impact do you think that social inequalities across the life-course have on people's experiences of ageing?
- Why do you think that Western experiences of ageing have been privileged in research and policy?

Introduction

In this chapter, students will be introduced to different ways that ageing is experienced and conceptualised across societal, policy and political contexts. Presenting a critical discussion of ageing and the impacts of post-colonial thinking, it focuses on how various positionalities, or social locations, intersect with age. Throughout the chapter, there will be a consideration of the cross-cultural conceptions of ageing, and how these align – or not – with Western approaches, such as successful and positive ageing. It will also examine the narrative around ageing and explore why this has taken a predominantly white affluent focus, which neglects minoritised groups, and invariably the oldest old (fourth age) in our society. The chapter will also examine how socioeconomic and political factors intersect with ethnicity, gender, sexuality and social class to result in poor health and social outcomes for older people in the United Kingdom (UK), highlighting that the materiality of older age can be different according to bodily inscription.

Constructions of Ageing

Age can be understood as a social construct, meaning that ageing is viewed differently across cultures (Fry, 2017). While we cannot escape the reality that ageing is a biological process, different cultures ascribe different meanings and values to youth and older age (Eagly & Koenig, 2021). In this way, how a person's chronological age is perceived – and ageing in general – is shaped by cultural, geographical and societal norms. This in turn affects attitudes towards age and ageing and expectations of how people of a particular age should act (Barken, 2019). Furthermore, constructions of older age and perceptions of older people are shaped by theories of ageing, bio-medical and political constructs, and also by ageist assumptions (Phelan, 2011). Ageism is broadly defined as any discrimination based upon age, which is often portrayed in the stereotypical construction of certain age groups such as old people (Ayalon & Tesch-Römer, 2018). Culturally, there are different perceptions of old age and the social roles and value afforded to older people (North & Fiske, 2015) often underpinned by belief systems which influence attitudes towards providing care to elders (Voss, Kornadt, Rothermund, Hess, & Fung, 2018). An example of this would be in some Eastern cultures, which adopt Confucian values of reciprocity and filial piety, holding elders in high regard within families and society (Ng, Phillips, & Lee, 2002). However, urbanisation, modernisation, migration and poverty have significantly changed the dynamics of families and communities in many countries, eroding traditional care systems (Apt, 2002; Cheung & Kwan, 2009). Alongside this, in countries which historically relied on families caring for their elders, there are often limited formal infrastructures to provide long term care for older people (Lloyd-Sherlock, Ebrahim, Geffen, & McKee, 2020). Consequently, elders who were once seen as wise and respected members of the family and community are now living in poverty and isolation (Apt, 2002).

Rajan-Rankin (2018) along with Zubair and Norris (2015) provide understandings of how mainstream theories about ageing act to 'other' experiences that are outside of Westernised norms. These dominant and pervasive norms form the lens through which ageing bodies are viewed, that of the 'white, youthful, masculine gaze' (Rajan-Rankin, 2018, p. 32). This viewpoint then denigrates and 'others' those whose ageing experiences deviate from the representation of successful or positive ageing that seek to perpetuate youth. Rajan-Rankin (2018) notes how age, like race and ethnicity, is visible through the body, and as such, the body has been 'weaponised' in order to 'other' ageing bodies through the creation of abject feelings in visualising the performance of wrinkly, leaky bodies of the old, particularly those that are in deep old age (Rajan-Rankin, 2018). Hence, the abjectification of the fourth age (Gilleard & Higgs, 2009). This weaponisation of old bodies mirrors how whiteness is used to weaponise against those bodies that are not white (Rajan-Rankin, 2018). Further to this 'othering' of those bodies which do not fit the ideals of the hegemonic gaze there is a homoge-nisation of different ageing bodies. Bodies of colour, minority ethnic older people are then grouped together in these categories that do not explore the nuance and diversity within and between them (Rajan-Rankin, 2018).

Ageing Well

In recent decades, theories and approaches to ageing have been dominated by perspec-tives that challenge discourses focusing on the physical and cognitive decline associated with older age. Instead, there has been the development of more positive approaches to 'ageing well' encompassing notions of 'healthy ageing', 'active ageing' and 'successful ageing' to name a few (Bowling, 1993). These approaches have been advanced by social gerontologists who have contributed to perspectives on ageing which premise that greater levels of individual agency and choice are involved in the ageing experience (Settersten, 2021). However, although representing a more positive approach to the conceptualisation of ageing, such models do not recognise the complexity and diversity of circumstances and experiences within which ageing takes place. The World Health Organization's (hereafter WHO) campaign: 'a decade of healthy ageing', promotes the idea that we need to 'add life to years', rather than simply adding 'years to life' (WHO, 2020). The WHO recognises the value of a life-course approach which acknowledge how different life experiences and social inequities contribute to the experience of later life (WHO, 2020), and that health inequalities in later life are linked to broader structural inequalities. Similarly, accounts of positive ageing have contributed to ideas of ageing that have been in opposition to notions of decline but have attempted to think more inclusively around ageing well to promote ways for older adults to remain active agents in their own lives and in their own positive self-narrative (Ahmed, Ormandy, & Seekles, 2019; Phoenix & Sparkes, 2009). While the concept of positive ageing offers a more inclusive approach to ageing, it is nonetheless a Western-centric perspective, neglecting accounts of ageing from different cultures and contexts (Liang & Luo, 2012).

Successful ageing – a term popularised by Rowe and Kahn (1987) as a method for measuring life satisfaction of growing older – has been highly influential within geron-tology (Katz & Calasanti, 2015) and in contributing to the development of ageing policy, particularly through the affiliated terms 'positive ageing' and 'healthy ageing'. Essentially 'successful ageing' has evolved from Rowe and Kahn's (1987) notion of ageing that defines success as ageing without disease and illness, and where older people are able to resemble the capabilities, physiological and psychological of younger people (Torres, 2015). Ideas of successful ageing tend to denote an ageing experience that is about achievement, life satisfaction and adaptability (Torres, 1999) and the maintenance of independence (Annele, Satu, & Timo, 2019). These aspects of life then determine the quality of older life that can be attained (Annele et al., 2019). As Torres (2015) suggests, a number of assumptions are made through this theoretical framework which originates from a particular Western philosophical and ideological standpoint: one that privileges cultural value orientations from the United States.

Successful ageing and these related concepts create an image of ageing that allows for the ongoing pursuit of goals and engagement in activity. McGuire (2020) unpacks the emergence of the new cultural symbol of 'zoomer' within Canadian culture that symbolises a new type of older person who remains economically productive as well as youthful, mobile, physical and social. McGuire (2020) relates this new phenomenon as having growing influence on the direction of social ageing policy and legislation within Canada. 'Boomers' who previously represented the aspirations of successful ageing, have since become associated with fears of economic burden, as these large numbers of older people move from the third age into a period of dependency within the fourth age (oldest old) and have associated financial implications due to their developing needs and health and social care concerns (McGuire, 2020). The 'boomer' has become associated with intergenerational division, and 'zoomers' are represented as no threat to the economy as they continue to be youthful, energised, productive and contributing to the economy as they continue to work. Marshall and Rahman (2015) liken 'zoomers' to glamorously ageless ageing celebrities, and inevitably these representations are of White, middle-class and able-bodied older people, who portray the image of vibrant ageing (McGuire, 2020). This newer even brighter version of the successfully ageing older person further exacerbates division between those who are not able to age so well.

Transnational Experiences of Ageing

The impact of globalisation on the experiences of cross-cultural ageing have been immense according to Torres (1999, 2013) who highlights the need to develop research exploring transnational experiences of ageing. This, notes Torres (2013), will enable more insight into how cultural value orientations on ageing are shaped by host nations and how they are balanced with cultural value orientations of the home culture. For older migrants there are some real challenges of ageing 'out of place' with many barriers preventing the older migrant from accessing the same ageing experience of the majority population (Kobayashi & Khan, 2021). Such experiences will depend on many factors, such as the reason for migration, and the ability to form connections in the new place. Lack of language skills can create a barrier for the older migrant in terms of accessing support, and a lack of connections to friends, and social engagement which all act to contribute to a challenging ageing experience and often economic and social disenfranchisement (Kobayashi & Khan, 2021). Many older migrants will not have access to, or understand, their rights to claim financial aid or pensions within the new host country and may have used their savings (if they had any) to migrate. Older migrants will also be in a category of people, over 50, who will find it hard to access work, with the compounding issues of not knowing the employment system or speaking the native language. Hence, these older migrants are completely excluded from notions of successful and positive ageing, despite their own coping strategies and agency in everyday life. Often practicing faiths, maintaining family obligations and making connections within their cultural communities can act as 'buffers' but do not completely offset the challenges of institutional and structural exclusion (Kobayashi & Khan, 2021, p. 121).

The impact of systemic racism and discrimination has a deeply damaging impact on individual lives, often manifesting as 'othering' as the systems of the host country develops a notion of 'us' and 'them', portraying immigrants as threats to security, employment, and lifestyle (Joffe, 2007). Many older migrants find themselves living in difficult circumstances in host countries, despite migrating to seek a 'better life' and often leaving an economically more secure lifestyle behind (Kobayashi & Khan, 2021). This is certainly the experience for the post-colonial migrant population, some of whom were encouraged to travel to countries to fulfil particular job roles such as the African-Caribbean Windrush generation in the UK (Cummings, 2020). The Windrush scandal, as it became known, exposed how the UK used criminal law in immigration policy to deport countless people who were unable to provide documentation of their immigration status (Hewitt, 2020). This illustrated the kind of precarity experienced by migrants within systems that are not built to support them (Hewitt, 2020). The following case study illustrates the experience of an older women managing the complexities of transnationalism across geographical locations to find opportunities for a positive later life. Exploring the transnational experience provides important insights into the immigrant experience, and the precarity involved.

■■■■■■■■■■■■■ **Case study 1** ■■■■■■■■■■■■■

Delores' story

Dolores is 73 years old; she was born in Jamaica where she lived until the late 1960s when she migrated to the UK at 18 years old, as part of what has been labelled 'the Windrush generation'. In the UK, she trained as a nurse, got married and had a family, and spent the next 35 years working within the NHS, retiring from full time work when she was 65. Although she has lived in the UK longer than anywhere else, she still has strong ties to Jamaica, where some of her siblings still live. Dolores and her husband divorced many years earlier, and since then, she has created a good life in Britain, despite having recollections of raising her children in an environment of racism and discrimination. When she retired from full-time work she decided to return to Jamaica where two of her sisters lived in order to enjoy the climate and benefit from a more positive experience of being an older person there. She had dual citizenship to the UK and returned a couple of times a year to visit her son and daughter and their families. During her time back in the UK she also worked part-time as an agency nurse for fixed periods to top up her income and savings. While her savings, her pension and continued earnings go further in Jamaica, healthcare is expensive there and she worries about what would happen if she became unwell. Also, the cost of travelling back and forth is expensive and may eventually be constrained by a deterioration in health and mobility. She misses her children and their families, who were all born in the UK and would not consider migrating to Jamaica.

The reality of becoming a transnational migrant is seen here for Dolores who constantly lives apart from a section of her family and is forced to work for longer than she might have wanted to. However, her future remains uncertain due to the precarity of the economic and healthcare systems in Jamaica, and her longing to be with her children in the UK. The challenge of successful ageing for transnational migrants relies on bodily wellbeing and the ability to continue to exercise mobility between the host country and country of origin. This denotes to some extent initially successful mobility and independence, but this is only possible for those people with a degree of financial power and the continued ability to work. However, as noted by Hepburn and Coloma (2019), the longer-term impact of this for older migrants means that the future remains uncertain regarding where they can remain in their later old age.

Calasanti (2010) notes that gender also influences the experience of ageing, and women are more likely to be poor whether in the global South or North. Many older people around the world do not have access to a pension and this is worse for women because pensions are tied to wages and particular types of employment (Calasanti, 2010). There are also more women who are living in widowhood than men, and this too is likely to contribute to their experience of poverty in later life (Calasanti, 2010). The following case study represents the experience of an older women, still working at 67 in a demanding role that requires her to travel great distances to run a food stall with her sisters. The earnings then have to be distributed to an extended family, and there is no prospect of retirement for her.

━━━━━━━━━━━━ Case study 2 ━━━━━━━━━━━━

Margarita's story

Margarita is a 67-year-old woman, living in Mexico. She runs a quesadillas and tlacoyos stall with her two younger sisters. They take it in turns to travel from their village to the 'megacity' of Juarez. They start preparing their wares at 4.30 a.m. and the journey to the city takes 90 minutes. The stall supports all three sisters and their families. Making tortillas is a female tradition, passed from mother to daughter, and Margarita had helped her mother make tortillas in the village. Women tend to operate stalls during daytime hours only because it is dangerous at night in the city. Margarita packs up her stall late afternoon to make the journey back home. Margarita is widowed with three children, who are all sons and hence do not work on the stall but instead, work in farming in the rural village they are from. Margarita's husband was also a farm worker but was killed five years ago in a serious road accident. The income from the tortilla stall is vitally important and provides the necessary finance for the whole family. Margarita's health is beginning to deteriorate, and she has high blood pressure and thyroid issues. However, because she has no pension, she will have to rely on her family to support her when she is physically unable to work.

As the case study demonstrates, there are many more older people working for longer in less developed parts of the world, where access to pensions is limited. For people like Margarita who have not worked within the formal labour market, they have no access to a pension (Calasanti, 2010). The next case study depicts a middle-aged woman, forced to migrate to the UK because of war, to seek safety for herself and children. While the UK has granted asylum, Aveen still faces immense challenges accessing the labour market, housing market and welfare services, creating financial precarity, which further impact upon her mental wellbeing.

■■■■■■■ **Case study 3** ■■■■■■■

Aveen's story

Aveen is a 55-year-old Kurdish Iraqi who escaped from Iraq 8 years ago with her children who are now 18 and 21. Her husband was killed in military action in Iraq fighting against the Government. In Iraq she did not work and looked after her children. In the UK, she was given residency after 8 years of being an Asylum Seeker. During this time, her mental health deteriorated, and she was hospitalised for clinical depression. She spent three months within a psychiatric unit, during which time her eldest child who was 18 at the time, provided care to the younger child. Aveen lives in Manchester in a council flat, with both her children. Her eldest child has just completed a degree and the younger child has completed 6th form college. For Aveen she hopes that both her children will be able to find work which will help bring more finance into the family home. They currently live on a very low income, Aveen has been unable to find work since gaining permanent status and her English language skills are limited.

Aveen's situation highlights the point made by Kobayashi and Khan (2021) that those migrating in later life are already facing the challenges of a discriminatory labour market, where older workers struggle to find employment. Aveen situation is further exacerbated by the language barriers and her mental health problems. The trauma that Aveen has faced that had forced her into a situation of seeking asylum in another country has been made far worse by the inhospitable welcome she has received in that country. The asylum process has led to her worsening mental health, and she has lost confidence, and is socially isolated. For Phillipson, Greiner and Settersten (2021) viewing the experience of ageing through the lens of precarity enables a better understanding of the types of challenges facing older people that lead to such insecurity and risk in later life. Although Aveen is still only in her 50s her experiences across the life-course have meant that she is already in an insecure position and her future later life is currently looking extremely uncertain.

An Intersectional Perspective on Ageing

The case studies have been used to show some of the complex challenges facing people as they grow old, often with limited resources, and compounded by structural inequalities. Taking an intersectional perspective allows identification of the multiple and intersecting forms of inequality which often work together and compound each other and are contextually affected by social, historical and political factors. Intersectionality is an analytical framework, first introduced by Crenshaw (1989, p. 139) and focuses on how discrimination works, how individuals experience it, and how society responds to it. The multi-dimensional layers of discrimination intersect across gender, race, religion, culture, caste, sexuality, age, class, disability, and immigration status to increase disadvantage and inequality, factors which are both socially constructed and bodily inscribed. Systems of power and forms of discrimination operate and impact greatly on marginalised communities, resulting in layer upon layer of disadvantage, which erode personal agency and opportunity while negatively influencing health and wellbeing. Such disadvantage and discrimination operate across a person's life, from birth to death, continually impacting the quality of life for people as they age.

Raising Awareness of Inequalities and Their Impacts Upon Ageing

Earlier in the chapter, we looked at the concepts of positive and healthy ageing, used to describe the process of optimising opportunities for health, participation and safety as ways to increase a person's quality of life (WHO, 2020). However, in order to 'develop and maintain good functional ability that enables well-being in older age' there must be consideration of the multi-dimensional factors which can influence a person's health (WHO, 2015). The WHO assert that the social determinants of health can be conceived as the conditions in which people are born, work, live, and age in, which are influenced by the political and social policies, social norms and systems in the country they live in (WHO, 2021) which in turn shape individual's opportunities to grow older in good health (Marmot, 2020). Table 6.1 presents factors that influence health.

The case studies in this chapter reference individual's health, which may have been caused by or exacerbated by their social and economic situations, which are referred to as health inequalities. The term health inequalities describes the disparities experienced in the health of people 'occupying unequal positions in society' (Graham, 2009, p. 3). These differences in health are socially constructed and as Williams, Buck and Babalola (2020) note, avoidable and unfair.

Ageing in a Migration Context

Observing the nexus between the two complex dimensions of ageing and migration highlights the interdependency and resulting vulnerability that can ensue as migrants grow old in their host country (Kristiansen, Razum, Tezcan-Güntekin, & Krasnik, 2016). The WHO (2017) note that ageing in a migration context is shaped by multiple factors

Table 6.1 Factors Influence Health

Factors Influencing Health
Health status, such as prevalence of health conditions
Socioeconomic factors such as income, housing, neighbourhood, crime rates
Lifestyle/behavioural choices such as diet and smoking
Access to appropriate health and social care services, welfare support
The presence of societal and structural discrimination

across the life-course, at micro, macro and meso levels. In the UK, 14.4% of the population identify as being from Black and minoritised backgrounds (Uberoi & Lees, 2020) with evidence showing that older people from these backgrounds are more likely to live in poorer health in old age and have lower life expectancy (Marmot, 2020) due to the health inequalities that they are exposed to across the life-course (Kings Fund, 2020). Bhopal (2014) further notes that the health inequalities faced by older people from Black and minoritised communities are compounded by discrimination, marginalisation and social exclusion.

Against this backdrop, there is a critical need to address the multiple inequalities that impact health (Marmot, 2020), and ensure that this vulnerable population group engages with services across the life-course. However, the literature shows that Black and minoritised populations are under-represented across all areas of health care, including preventative care, chronic health management and palliative care (Gardiner, Abraham, Clymer, Rao, & Gnani, 2021; Haque, Choudry, & George, 2020) resulting in unmet needs, reduced quality of life and loss of opportunities for treatment (Cookson, Propper, Asaria, & Raine, 2016). Reasons for not accessing healthcare are complex and include: difficulty navigating services and accessing information (Markham, Islam, & Faull, 2014); limited language or literacy skills (Memon et al., 2016); lack of interpreters (Hossain & Khan, 2020); poor translation of information (Dixon, King, Matosevic, Clark, & Knapp, 2018), cultural and religious values which include familism, collectivism, and emotionalism (Hossain & Khan, 2020); difficulty in accessing same sex healthcare professionals (Hassan, Leavey, Rooney, & Puthussery, 2020); and not being allowed to access services because they have no recourse to public funds (Kang, Tomkow, & Farrington, 2019). Other explanations for such poor access to services is around previous negative experiences of care (Public Health England, 2020a, 2020b). This includes receiving sub-optimal care from health professionals who have exhibited racially discriminatory behaviour (Public Health England, 2020a) and the existence of false stereotyping (Hoffman, Trawalter, Axt, & Oliver, 2016; Majedi et al., 2019; Samulowitz, Gremyr, Eriksson, & Hensing, 2018). Challenges at the intersection of ageing and migration therefore must be reflected in health and social policy to provide appropriate services.

■■■■■■■■■■ Chapter summary ■■■■■■■■■■

This chapter provides students with a discussion on ageing, and looks at key theories alongside societal and political influences which include the following:

- Constructions of ageing
- Theories and approaches to ageing
- Transnational experiences of ageing
- An intersectional perspective on ageing
- The impact of inequalities on ageing
- Ageing in a migration context

Conclusion

The chapter has explored the complex challenges of ageing in different environments for people from different cultures and backgrounds. Using case studies, we have described the precarity and uncertainty that is faced by many people as they approach old age, when their functional ability to work decreases and their dependency increases. The chapter has taken an analytical approach to some theories of ageing, and the extent to which these exclude individuals who are not affluent and white. Decolonising the ageing narrative to reflect the diversity of older migrants and their challenging life-course journey can generate new insights and perspectives (Torres, 2013) destabilising the Western-centric bias which has dominated societal thinking about ageing (Hepburn and Sintos-Coloma (2019)). The chapter also introduces students to intersectionality, which shows how systems of power and forms of discrimination operate across gender, class, sexuality and culture etc., resulting in multiple disadvantage and inequality. The chapter concludes by highlighting the avoidable inequalities which are visible in the UK, and the impacts which these have upon people's lives as they age.

Questions to Reflect Upon

- Reflecting upon the case studies and reading this chapter, consider how gender can impact upon the experience of ageing.
- Consider how older people are represented in the media, and the potential impact of these stereotypes.
- We have looked at some theories about ageing. Consider how these theories exclude experiences outside of Westernised norms and the impact of doing so.
- Consider returning to the case studies presented in this chapter, reappraising your perspective using an intersectional approach, and knowledge gained from this chapter.

Further Reading

Bhopal, R. S. (2014). *Migration, ethnicity, race, and health in multicultural societies*. Oxford: Oxford University Press. (In this book, Raj Bhopal explores the challenges faced by Health Care Practitioners, policymakers and other stakeholders from globalisation, international travel, and migration. In exploring the complex issues of race, ethnicity and migration, the book aims to raise awareness of the often unethical and atheoretical ways which have been used to study ethnicity in the past.)

Crenshaw, K. (1989). Demarginalizing the intersection of race and sex: A black feminist critique of antidiscrimination doctrine, feminist theory and antiracist politics. u. Chi. Legal f., 139. (Generally acknowledged as a landmark essay, Kimberlé Crenshaw introduces the concept and analytical framework of 'intersectionality' to address the marginalisation of Black women. Crenshaw provides a Black feminist critique on antidiscrimination law, feminist theory and antiracist theory and politics, and highlights how these processes can further marginalise Black women.)

Marmot, M., Patel, C., North, F., Head, J., et al. (2010). *Fair society, healthy lives: Strategic review of health inequalities in England post 2010*. London: University College London. (The Marmot review in 2010 offered policy makers a solution focused approach to reducing the health inequalities in the UK. Proposing six policy objectives, he highlighted the need to improve access to health services, education, and employment, to improve people's quality of life, communities and opportunities from childhood to old age.)

Marmot, M. (2020). Health equity in England: The Marmot review 10 years on. *British Medical Journal*, 368. (The second Marmot review in 2020 offers students a chance to see the changes which policy makers had enacted since the original report. One decade later, the impact of austerity measures showed the increasing disparity between rich and poor, with life expectancy falling and people experiencing poorer health in older age in deprived communities across England.)

Torres, S. (2013). Transnationalism and the study of ageing and old age. In C. Phellas (Ed.), *Aging in European societies: Healthy aging in Europe* (pp. 267–281). New York, NY: Springer. (In this chapter Sandra Torres explores the concept of transnationalism and presents research findings from transnational studies, underlining its importance to social gerontology. Torres also looks at the future implications of transnationalism to old age policy and practice.)

References

Ahmed, A., Ormandy, P., & Seekles, M. L. (2019). An examination of how the 'household model' of care can contribute to positive ageing for residents in the 'Fourth Age'. *OBM Geriatrics*, *3*(1), 24.

Annele, U., Satu, K. J., & Timo, E. S. (2019). Definitions of successful ageing: A brief review of a multidimensional concept. *Acta Bio Medica: Atenei Parmensis*, *90*(2), 359.

Apt, N. A. (2002). Ageing and the changing role of the family and the community: An African perspective. *International Social Security Review*, *55*(1), 39–47.

Ayalon, L., & Tesch-Römer, C. (2018). Introduction to the section: Ageism—concept and origins. In L. Ayalon & C. Tesch-Römer (Eds.), *Contemporary perspectives on ageism* (pp. 1–10). Cham: Springer.

Barken, R. (2019). 'Old age' as a social location: Theorizing institutional processes, cultural expectations, and interactional practices. *Sociology Compass*, *13*(4), e12673.

Bhopal, R. S. (2014). *Migration, ethnicity, race, and health in multicultural societies*. Oxford: Oxford University Press.

Bowling, A. (1993). The concepts of successful and positive ageing. *Family Practice*, *10*(4), 449–453.

Calasanti, T. (2010). Gender and ageing in the context of globalization. In D. Dannefer & C. Phillipson (Eds.), *The SAGE handbook of social gerontology* (pp. 137–149). London: SAGE Publications Ltd.

Cheung, C. K., & Kwan, A. Y. (2009). The erosion of filial piety by modernisation in Chinese cities. *Ageing and Society*, *29*, 179–198. doi:10.1017/S0144686X08007836

Cookson, R., Propper, C., Asaria, M., & Raine, R. (2016). Socio-economic inequalities in health care in England. *Fiscal Studies*, *37*(3–4), 371–403.

Crenshaw, K. (1989). *Demarginalizing the intersection of race and sex: A black feminist critique of antidiscrimination doctrine, feminist theory and antiracist politics.* u. Chi. Legal f., 139.

Cummings, R. (2020). Ain't no black in the (Brexit) union Jack? Race and empire in the era of Brexit and the Windrush scandal. *Journal of Postcolonial Writing, 56*(5), 593–606.

Dixon, J., King, D., Matosevic, T., Clark, M., & Knapp, M. (2018). *Equity in the provision of palliative care in the UK: Review of evidence.* Personal Social Services Research Unit: London School of Economics. 2015.

Eagly, A. H., & Koenig, A. M. (2021). The vicious cycle linking stereotypes and social roles. *Current Directions in Psychological Science, 30*(4), 343–350.

Fry, C. L. (2017). The social construction of age and the experience of aging in the late twentieth century. *New Dynamics in Old Age, 2,* 11–24.

Gardiner, T., Abraham, S., Clymer, O., Rao, M., & Gnani, S. (2021). Racial and ethnic health disparities in healthcare settings. *British Medical Journal, 372,* n605. doi:10.1136/bmj.n605

Gilleard, C., & Higgs, P. (2009). The power of silver: Age and identity politics in the 21st century. *Journal of Aging & Social Policy, 21*(3), 277–295.

Graham, H. (2009). *Understanding health inequalities.* London: McGraw-Hill Education.

Haque, E. U., Choudry, B., & George, R. E. (2020). How can we improve health and healthcare experiences of black, Asian and minority ethnic (BAME) communities? In J. Matheson, J. Patterson, & L. Neilson (Eds.), *Tackling causes and consequences of health inequalities* (pp. 233–244). Boca Raton, FL: CRC Press.

Hassan, S. M., Leavey, C., Rooney, J. S., & Puthussery, S. (2020). A qualitative study of healthcare professionals' experiences of providing maternity care for Muslim women in the UK. *BMC Pregnancy and Childbirth, 20*(1), 1–10.

Hepburn, S., & Coloma, R. S. (2019). Ageing transmigrants and the decolonisation of life course. *International Journal of Lifelong Education, 38*(1), 48–66.

Hewitt, G. (2020). The Windrush scandal: An insider's reflection. *Caribbean Quarterly, 66*(1), 108–128.

Hoffman, K. M., Trawalter, S., Axt, J. R., & Oliver, M. N. (2016). Racial bias in pain assessment and treatment recommendations, and false beliefs about biological differences between blacks and whites. *Proceedings of the National Academy of Sciences, 113*(16), 4296–4301.

Hossain, M. Z., & Khan, H. T. (2020). Barriers to access and ways to improve dementia services for a minority ethnic group in England. *Journal of Evaluation in Clinical Practice, 26*(6), 1629–1637.

Joffe, H. (2007). Anxiety, mass crisis and 'the other'. In P. Perri, S. Radstone, C. Squire, A. Treacher, & A. T. Kabesh (Eds.), *Public emotions* (pp. 105–118). London: Palgrave Macmillan.

Kang, C., Tomkow, L., & Farrington, R. (2019). Access to primary health care for asylum seekers and refugees: A qualitative study of service user experiences in the UK. *British Journal of General Practice, 69*(685), e537–e545.

Katz, S., & Calasanti, T. (2015). Critical perspectives on successful aging: Does it 'appeal more than it illuminates'? *The Gerontologist, 55*(1), 26–33.

Kingsfund. (2020). *Ethnic minority deaths and covid-19: What are we to do?* Retrieved 20 August 2020, from https://www.kingsfund.org.uk/blog/2020/04/ethnic-minority-deaths-covid-19

Kobayashi, K. M., & Khan, M. M. (2021). Health promotion practices for immigrant older adults. *Promoting the Health of Older Adults: The Canadian Experience, 266,* 203–219.

Kristiansen, M., Razum, O., Tezcan-Güntekin, H., & Krasnik, A. (2016). Aging and health among migrants in a European perspective. *Public Health Reviews*, *37*, 20.

Liang, J., & Luo, B. (2012). Toward a discourse shift in social gerontology: From successful aging to harmonious aging. *Journal of Aging Studies*, *26*(3), 327–334.

Lloyd-Sherlock, P., Ebrahim, S., Geffen, L., & McKee, M. (2020). Bearing the brunt of Covid-19: Older people in low and middle income countries, *British Medical Journal*, *368*, m1052. doi:10.1136/bmj.m1052

Majedi, H., Dehghani, S., Soleyman-jahi, S., Tafakhori, A., Emami, S., Mireskandari, M., & Hosseini, S. M. (2019). Assessment of factors predicting inadequate pain management in chronic pain patients. *Anesthesia and Pain Medicine*, *9*, e97229.

Markham, S., Islam, Z., & Faull, C. (2014). I never knew that! Why do people from black and Asian minority ethnic groups in Leicester access hospice services less than other groups? A discussion with community groups. *Diversity & Equality in Health & Care*, *11*, 237–245.

Marmot, M. (2020). Health equity in England: The Marmot review 10 years on. *British Medical Journal*, *368*, 1–4. doi:10.1136/bmj.m693

Marmot, M., Patel, C., North, F., Head, J., et al. (2010). *Fair society, healthy lives: Strategic review of health inequalities in England post 2010*. London: University College London.

Marshall, B. L., & Rahman, M. (2015). Celebrity, ageing and the construction of 'third age' identities. *International Journal of Cultural Studies*, *18*(6), 577–593.

McGuire, A. (2020). From boomer to zoomer: Aging with vitality under neoliberal capitalism. In K. Aubrecht, C. Kelly & C. Rice (Eds.), *The ageing-disability nexus (disability, culture, politics)* (pp. 180–199). Vancouver, BC; Toronto, ON: UBC Press.

Memon, A., Taylor, K., Mohebati, L. M., Sundin, J., Cooper, M., Scanlon, T., & de Visser, R. (2016). Perceived barriers to accessing mental health services among black and minority ethnic (BME) communities: A qualitative study in Southeast England. *BMJ Open*, *6*(11), e012337.

Ng, A. C. Y., Phillips, D. R., & Lee, W. K. M. (2002). Persistence and challenges to filial piety and informal support of older persons in a modern Chinese society: A case study in Tuen Mun, Hong Kong. *Journal of Aging Studies*, *16*(2), 135–153.

North, M. S., & Fiske, S. T. (2015). Modern attitudes toward older adults in the aging world: A cross-cultural meta-analysis. *Psychological Bulletin*, *141*, 993–1021. doi:10.1037/a0039469

Phelan, A. (2011). Socially constructing older people: Examining discourses which can shape nurses' understanding and practice. *Journal of Advanced Nursing*, *67*(4), 893–903.

Phillipson, C., Greiner, A., & Settersten Jr., R. A. (2021). Conclusion: Precarity and ageing in the 21st century. In A. Grenier, C. Phillipson & R. A. Settersten Jr. (Eds.), *Precarity and ageing: Understanding insecurity and risk in later life. Ageing in a global context* (pp. 237–246). Bristol: Policy Press.

Phoenix, C., & Sparkes, A. C. (2009). Being fred: Big stories, small stories and the accomplishment of a positive ageing identity. *Qualitative Research*, *9*(2), 219–236.

Public Health England. (2020a). *Beyond the data: Understanding the impact of COVID-19 on BAME groups*. London: Public Health England. Retrieved from https://assets.publishing.service.gov.uk/government/uploads/system/uploads/attachment_data/file/892376/COVID_stakeholder_engagement_synthesis_beyond_the_data.pdf

Public Health England. (2020b). *Disparities in the risk and outcomes of COVID-19*. Public Health England.

Rajan-Rankin, S. (2018). Race, embodiment and later life: Re-animating aging bodies of color. *Journal of Aging Studies*, *45*, 32–38.

Rowe, J. W., & Kahn, R. L. (1987). Human aging: Usual and successful. *Science, 237*, 143–149.

Samulowitz, A., Gremyr, I., Eriksson, E., & Hensing, G. (2018). 'Brave men' and 'emotional women': A theory-guided literature review on gender bias in health care and gendered norms towards patients with chronic pain. *Pain Research and Management*. doi:10.1155/2018/6358624

Settersten Jr, R. A. (2021). How life course dynamics matter for precarity in later life. In A. Grenier, C. Phillipson, & R. A. Settersten Jr. (Eds.), *Precarity and ageing: Understanding insecurity and risk in later life. Ageing in a global context* (pp. 19–40). Bristol: Policy Press.

Torres, S. (1999). A culturally-relevant theoretical framework for the study of successful ageing. *Ageing and Society*, *19*(1), 33–51.

Torres, S. (2013). Transnationalism and the study of ageing and old age. In C. Phellas (Ed.), *Aging in European societies: Healthy aging in Europe* (pp. 267–281). New York, NY: Springer.

Torres, S. (2015). Expanding the gerontological imagination on ethnicity: Conceptual and theoretical perspectives. *Ageing & Society*, *35*(5), 935–960.

Uberoi, E., & Lees, R. (2020). Ethnic diversity in politics and public life. House of Commons Library Briefing Paper, CBP, 1156, 22.

Voss, P., Kornadt, A. E., Rothermund, K., Hess, T. M., & Fung, H. L. (2018). A world of difference? Domain-specific views on aging in China, the US, and Germany. *Psychology and Aging*, *33*, 595–606. doi:10.1037/pag0000237

Williams, E., Buck, D., & Babalola, G. (2020). *What are health inequalities?* London: The King's Fund.

World Health Organization. (2015). *World report on ageing and health*. Geneva: World Health Organization. https://apps.who.int/iris/handle/10665/186463

World Health Organization. (2017). *Global strategy and action plan on ageing and health*. Geneva: World Health Organization. Retrieved 3 January 2022, from http://www.who.int/ageing/global-strategy/en/

World Health Organization. (2020). *Decade of healthy ageing: Baseline report*. Geneva: World Health Organization. Retrieved 3 January 2022, from https://www.who.int/publications/i/item/9789240017900

World Health Organization. (2021). *Social determinants of health*. Geneva: World Health Organization. Retrieved 26 January 2022, from https://www.who.int/health-topics/social-determinants-of-health#tab=tab_1

Zubair, M., & Norris, M. (2015). Perspectives on ageing, later life and ethnicity: Ageing research in ethnic minority contexts. *Ageing & Society*, *35*(5), 897–916.

7

DECOLONISING DISABILITY RESEARCH AND DISABLING WAR

Susie Balderston

━━━━━━━━━━ Learning objectives ━━━━━━━━━━

- To explore the relationship between social inequalities experienced by disabled people and colonialism
- To contrast colonial, social and collective models of disability
- To analyse a case study of disability and war, which illuminates the disabling effects of trauma after gendered and racist lived experiences of genocide
- To adopt intersectional framings of disability and peace-building from Global South scholars
- To understand how allies can tackle and prevent war as a cause of disability and enable disabled survivors of war to gain social, economic, and political safety, equality and inclusion

━━━━━━━━━━ Framing questions ━━━━━━━━━━

- Why is important to consider colonialism in the study of disability?
- How do we challenge the Eurocentric dominance in disability policy and studies of war?
- How do collective models of disability encourage collective resistance to inequalities?

Introduction

In this chapter, you will be invited to think about disability through the lens of colonialist criticism. Disability is a significant focus of social inequalities literature. People with disabilities, and their family networks, frequently the group most disadvantaged by unequal social and economic policies (Ryan, 2020). Additionally, leading disability writers and academic activists such as Shakespeare (2006, pp. 197–204) and Oliver (2013) have contended for decades (under the social model of disability and, later, critical disability studies) that people with long-term health conditions, people with impairments, and people with infirmities are 'disabled' by how society is organised. Everything from promotion of self-reliance to the physical layout of streets and buildings disadvantages and 'disables' individuals and communities who do not or cannot mirror a specific, 'able-bodied' way of being and acting. From the late 20th century through to the present, disabled people and activists have emphasised that these disabling experiences are the active, lived outcome of political and legal inequalities. These arguments have been mobilised and articulated through equal rights movements, for example.

Figure 7.1 presents a man in a wheelchair in front of an outdoors staircase. The man's back is to the camera. His head is leant to one side in his hand in a gesture of frustration.

Yet such exclusions are not solely an issue of ensuring equal treatment but of defending the lives of people with disabilities. There are numerous examples of how negative, discriminatory attitudes towards disability – as 'abnormal' or 'less than' – have reinforced arguments for the eradication of disabled persons. In the late 19th and early 20th centuries, these arguments came together under the heading of eugenics. Now we frequently connect eugenics with political fascism, the Nazis in particular. However, the eugenic movement originated in the United Kingdom and the largest branch of the Eugenics Society was based in the United States of America (Klausen & Bashford, 2010, pp. 98–115). There is a persistent history of state-financed eugenic campaigns, including forced sterilisation, against disabled people throughout the 20th century (Hansen & King, 2013).

Discrimination against people with disabilities has been frequently articulated through economic arguments. For example, as the chapter on Health outlined, the arguments of Malthussian and Neo-Malthussian thinkers and public intellectuals problematise economic dependency as a threat to global stability (Hodgson & Watkins, 1997). A focal contention of proponents of these theories was that economic sustainability could be guaranteed by controlling the spread of undesirable populations. This included people with disabilities (Klausen & Bashford, 2010, pp. 98–115). The connection of disability with economic risk is a persistent theme in disability discrimination, dovetailing with challenges to welfarism and the importance of capitalist productivity.

The chapter will introduce you to the arguments around disability and inequality. As in other chapters, the chapter adopts a global perspective. Around one billion people (or 15% of the world's population) have disabilities and over 80% of disabled people live in so-called 'developing countries' (WHO, 2021) or the Global South. Rather than repeat existing literature on critical disability studies, we will centre the connection between disability and colonialism. One of the major and enduring inequalities created by colonialism is disability. When powerful countries go to war, domination and violence create physical, sensory and mental impairments as inevitable collateral damage. Centuries of colonialism have created people with disabilities from conflict (as civilians in war zones and veterans and in generations afterwards), with disabled individuals and their families thrust into displacement, invisibility in humanitarian responses, stigma and poverty.

Religious, charity, medical and development models of disability have been colonially exported and mainstream the stigma, inequality and exclusion of disabled people across the globe. But civil justice campaigners, including women raped systematically in war (Banyanga, Björkqvist, & Österman, 2017) and injured soldiers returning home (Williamson, 2019), have worked for social protections, legal rights, welfare and accessible environments from social justice movements led by disabled people. Today, critical race feminisms, peace and conciliation studies and disabled people's own research destabilise colonial 'natural' constructs about disability that preserve power and privilege (Meekosha, 2011) and set out an alternative future.

This chapter explores two of these frames – *Ubuntu* from South Africa (Berghs, 2017) and the Māori Whānau Hauā (Hickey, 2006). These framings understand disability as a social problem for the whole community to address, offering powerful paths to eradicating war alongside the inequalities, segregation and poverty experienced by disabled people in and after conflict. You are invited to reflect that neither war nor disability are inevitable; by using intersectional framings from Global South scholars, we can destabilise the colonial dependence on war to maintain power (and the disabling consequences of this); there is another way that we can ally collectively towards peace and inclusive community life.

Background

The colonial Global North has successfully exported pathologising and stigmatising disabling inequalities across the world for centuries. As noted above, stigmatising attitudes have developed alongside the political orientations of Global North colonial powers. The emphasis on capitalist productivity has been distinctly problematic, justifying social and structural discrimination as disabled bodies and persons are framed as non-contributors. Moreover, one of the most successful ways that disability is created globally is war; conflict both disables victims (as civilians or combatants in battle zones) and displaces people fleeing war, disproportionately.

In and after war, disabled people are treated as expendable and those who survive experience entrenched collateral damage. People with impairments, including people with learning or physical disabilities were euthanised, sterilised and exterminated under the Nazi T-4 programme, which used disabled people to perfect the gas chamber technology. Experiences of violence related to mental health distress range from the targeted slaughter of psychiatric hospital patients during the Rwandan genocide to the persistent and common depression, suicide attempts and alcohol used as self-medication by civilian populations from war zones and veteran soldiers. These marginalised locations and inequalities are compounded by racist and gendered inequalities, which justify the 'brutality of slavery, colonialism … and the continued exploitation of people of color in contemporary times' (Erevelles, 2011, p. 102).

Disabled people who survive in conflict arenas lose any accessible equipment, benefits, medical treatment and family or State support systems and services they may have had before conflict. Disabled people in segregated institutions can be taken as hostages and used as human shields, or if they can flee with others, despite inaccessible evacuation routes and aid they find refugee camps to be inaccessible and sanitary accommodation unusable. As a disabled man who fled the Venezuelan crisis explained to a disabled researcher in Ecuador, 'We have less chance of running, we have less chance of hiding, we have less chance to hear. We are the people…because of disability, … the first ones that could fall. […] Suddenly it's, "Save whoever you can!" And the person who uses a chair or a person with a prosthesis, will not have the same ability to escape the problem, like a normal person' (Francis, 2019, p. 295).

Disability Legislative and Policy Responses in Relation to War

Legislative and policy responses towards disabled people's equality and social protection are relatively recent and hard won, where they exist at all. Neoliberal and colonial powers seeks to destabilise social movements and their concessions, so steps to equality are often followed by backlash and the removal of protections. Rather than States providing strong welfare social protections for all of their communities, the World Bank and other neoliberal funders try to target failed and inadequate means-tested handouts and pilots to an ever-decreasing group of the 'deserving' poor.

After war, the disability focus of invaders is largely on counting injuries to their own veterans, taking the lead from disabled veterans returning after the Vietnam war who then fought for disability rights, pensions and access to the built environment. A nation can assuage its conscience by hailing disabled veterans as returning heroes, though these plaudits are not matched by effective civil, social, political and economic equality. The Americans with Disabilities Act (1990) was built on the work of disabled veterans returning from the Vietnam War, including the Paralyzed Veterans of America, who fought during the 1970s and 1980s for accessible environments and benefit rights. Subsequent laws (such as the Disability Discrimination Act, 1995 in the UK) followed in the Global North.

Disabled people in the Global South do not enjoy legal protections or welfare benefits; colonial models of disability cause unequal impacts and poverty for Indigenous peoples. Many neoliberal classifications and assessments of disability – such as the International Classification of Functioning, Disability and Health (ICF) – do not take account of local cultural, societal, nutrition, mental health understandings, welfare or sanitation requirements, disabling people with impairments even further and stripping them of appropriate support and resources.

With regard to disabled people in war and conflict zones, there are international human rights instruments which attempt to protect and acknowledge the need to address disabling inequalities. For example, the United Nations Security Council Resolution 1325 builds on the Convention of Rights of People with Disabilities, calling on Member States to ensure accessible humanitarian responses and the representation of people with disabilities (United Nations, 2019). However, these supra-national responses are critiqued as unhelpful universalism (Clarke, 2004) and often fail to have an intersectional lens, or a State-wide social welfare redistributive frame that enhances the collective empowerment and political engagement of the poor. Indeed, the United Nations, World Bank and other supra-national bodies can be seen to be hegemonically recreating colonial universalism through their control of funding and political supremacy.

Some intersectional progress has arguably been made, in the UN Resolution 2475 (2019), which acknowledges the 'disproportionate impact that armed conflict has on persons with disabilities, including abandonment, violence, and lack of access to basic services'. It stresses the protection and assistance needs of persons with disabilities in humanitarian response, healthcare and recognition of disabled people's organisations in peace-building resolution, but stops short of requiring full civil, political, social, economic and cultural rights. It is non-binding and does not enjoy support or adoption from all United Nations Member States. Kuzmin, representing Russia's objection to the Resolution 2475, saying that the, 'Specific needs of one category of population should not come at the cost of and with prejudice to another category…Do not get too preoccupied with devising new categories of individuals who should need specific protection under the international humanitarian law'. Yet people with disabilities are not 'new categories of individuals'. Specific, intersectional provision, going further than human rights models can offer, is critical to ensure the safety and security of people harmed disproportionally in and after war.

The recent report (2021) of the Special Rapporteur for the Resolution, Gerard Quinn, recognises intersectional needs of disabled people (including on the grounds of religion and for children) and the impact of trauma. The report highlights the needs of people with disabilities to have collective voice and inclusion in peace-building, to purge paternalism from protection and acknowledge human agency, linked to the goals of inclusion and development. It identifies more to be done, in terms of accessible early warning, evacuation procedures and victim assistance after land mine impairment. However, the needs of disabled women and girls for sexual health, menstrual and abortion support, particularly in relation to fleeing violence or having been subject to rape in war zones, is absent. Quinn states concern about the use of disabled people as human shields and hostages in war and the lack of remedy through criminal law for disablement of victims (both as ex-combatants and civilians). He asks for further research and data about the extent and impact of disabled people in war. Before understanding the research, it is important to understand how disability is conceptualised in societies.

Colonial Models of Disability

This section outlines and critiques several dominant models which have informed how disabled people are treated in society. These are:

- The religious model of disability
- The charity model of disability
- The medical model of disability
- The development model of disability

Models are ways of viewing and representing systems to explain societal norms, so models of disability are important in helping us to understand stigma and social inequalities experienced by people with disabilities. Do you feel sorry for someone who becomes disabled? Do you see wheelchair users as handicapped, 'sick', unable to work or having lost 'normal' functioning? Did you attend an inclusive school with disabled people in your class, or were they segregated in a 'special' school reliant on charity funding or unable to access education because of months or years in hospital? For millennia, religious, medical and charity models of disability have been exported around the world by colonial powers and these create the stigma, poverty and inequality experienced by disabled people. Importantly, this discrimination became more, not less, entrenched as the imperial project led by European countries receded in the early 20th century and was replaced by neo-colonialist, development agendas. These seemingly 'natural' responses which locate disability as a site of individual shame, pity and loss of value are not 'natural' at all.

In the dominant religious model of disability, stigma was created and reinforced by Christian religious framings of disability. Disability has been seen for centuries as being a result of sins of the fathers, or as an evil which must be cast out of bodies by exorcism (particularly prevalent for people with epilepsy or schizo-affective conditions). If disability remained, pity was shown by praying for disabled people or miracles were required to end impairment. Still today, disabled children are taken on pilgrimages to Lourdes and other religious sites or statues, to take healing waters or receive miracles that will cure them.

The pervasive charity model of disability is building on religious narratives of personal tragedy and pity. Rather than social protections at community and State level, disabled people were subjects of philanthropy which allows church goers and rich and powerful privileged classes to assuage their guilt and redeem souls with donations. Highly profitable charities such as Leonard Cheshire in the UK began to create segregated homes for injured veterans returning from war who were expected to be grateful, with landowners avoiding taxes on their estates, while helpfully assuaging the need for State admission of their role in disablement. The charity model of disability locates disabled people as passive subjects who must be grateful for charitable resources and giving by people who pity them, preventing disabled people from having dignity and enjoying equal life chances. The charities rarely share the power and resources equitably for disabled people and are often staffed and led by non-disabled people, who do not share the lived experience of impairment. Such charities and the charity model have been colonially exported across the world and many charities run for, not by, disabled people are central in human rights aid across the globe, while simultaneously massing millions of pounds of profit.

Individual model constructions of disability focus on the person's impairment being the problem, with medical intervention and rehabilitation being the cure or intervention used to classify and attempt to normalise function for people with impairments. The World Health Organization is often critiqued for perpetuating this model globally, particularly in its use of the International Classification of Functioning, Disability and Health (ICF) since 2001; this model is culturally inappropriate for Indigenous peoples and damaging in the aftermath of war. For example, PTSD is commonly researched and diagnosed in African populations after war by Global North organisations. However, this can be understood as a pseudo-diagnosis which medicalises the understandable social consequences of war and which leads to inappropriate neoliberal and colonial treatment models and medication being exported to the Global South (Summerfield, 1999). These framings leads to more shame, pain and stigma, including for disabled veterans who are not 'supercrips' (Hunt, Swartz, Rohleder, Carew, & Hellum Braathen, 2018), those of us who do not overcome their disabilities by demonstrating super human feats of endurance in sport, or contorting our bodies through surgery to pass as 'normal'. In the USA and Europe, these individual and cultural models dominate, but these can be futile and irrelevant with regard to people with disabilities living with entrenched material inequalities in the Global South (Meekosha, 2011).

The colonised fear, stigma, exclusion and invisibility that are created and perpetuated in religious, charity and medical models effectively banish disabled people from mainstream society. From leper colonies (seclusion to protect the masses, which, despite vaccines, have been maintained for centuries) to residential institutions and the stigma and hostility visited on people with HIV+ status, disabled people are segregated from mainstream society, with 'social death' that renders people with impairments invisible. This is maintained colonially across the globe in ways that are largely unsupported for black people after the ending of apartheid in South Africa and Jim Crow laws in the USA were overturned. This segregation prevents mainstream inclusion in work, housing and relationships for most disabled people in all societies.

The development model of disability underpins disability-focused policies designed and financed by supra-national bodies such as the United Nations, NATO and the World Bank. They are presented as inherently preferable and are mobilised through aid and development agendas. While disabled voices are frequently, if not wholly, absent from development policy (Webhi, Elin, & El-Lahib, 2010), the global development agenda has significant implications for the lives of people with disabilities. Proponents of development argue that it resolves and addresses the colonial harms through enabling colonised governments to support those living in poverty and establish institutional infrastructures (e.g. hospitals, education systems) which will result in colonised countries sustainable geopolitical and economic participation.

The development agenda envisaged by the World Bank and UN has been heavily criticised. As Moyo (2010) explains, overreliance on aid has trapped African states in a vicious circle of aid dependency, corruption, market distortion, and further poverty, leaving them with nothing but the 'need' for more aid. Far from a movement away from colonial-era asymmetries of power – where the Global North dominated the Global South – scholars such as Langan (2017) have depicted the aid development agenda has a neocolonialist project. The Global North has retained control through indebtedness and the extraction of resources continues as Global South countries attempt to repay financial aid. Development support through the International Monetary Fund and colonising powers often comes with conditions that worsen rather than ameliorate poverty. For example, colonises aid-recipients may have to maintain exchange and taxation rates that benefit donors, give preferential treatment to Global North corporations, or cede control over trade agreements.

The effect of the development model is an overwhelming emphasis on economic productivity. This has substantial disadvantaging effects on the position and treatment of people with disabilities. Consistent with Neo-Malthussianism, people with disabilities are framed as a cost burden. Furthermore, the ability of governments to invest in infrastructures needed to facilitate universal participation, such as comprehensive welfare systems or architectural adjustments, is heavily constrained. This has effects not just on the lives of people with disabilities living in the Global South in terms of their individual wealth – there is an observable correlation between poverty and disability – but also in terms of their ability to exist. It is telling that development agendas have actively promoted the expansion of contraception and family planning to economically and socially dependent communities. As recently as the 1990s, countries such as Colombia, a key recipient of development relief through the USAID programme, engaged in the coercive and non-consensual sterilisation of undesirable communities including people with disabilities (Guerrero, 2016).

Additionally, the development agenda can entrench discriminatory attitudes in the Global North as independence and responsibility become associated with the absence of governmental, financial support. The journalist and disability activist Frances Ryan has written at length about how UK government agendas targeted at reducing welfare spending have been weaponised against people with disabilities. Ryan highlights how people with disabilities have been treated with suspicion by conservative politicians and media commentators. Despite the passage of the Equality Act 2010 into law, reports of discriminatory attitudes have increased including employers refusing to make reasonable adjustments and workplace bullying as people with disabilities are depicted as 'scroungers'. The receipt of independence payments is contingent on assessments of people with disabilities' capabilities and needs by staff within minimal training who are not in a position to appropriately appreciate disability. The net result of the dominance of development models and understandings of disability underscored by economic productivity is, for some commentators, the increase in stigmatisation, discrimination and harm.

Social and Collective Models of Disability

In contrast, models developed by disabled and Deaf and Indigenous people themselves offer re-framings of disability in social and cultural contexts, challenging individual and paternalistic understandings of disability as well as development framings that problematise the cost burden of disability. The social model of disability, developed from thinking by a union of segregated disabled people in the UK (UPIAS, 1976), locates disability firmly as a social oppression, experienced by people with impairments. This model was explained further by disabled academics and civil rights campaigners (Finkelstein, 1996, pp. 30–6; Oliver & Barnes, 2012), to illuminate how people with impairments are disabled by poverty and social, economic and attitudinal barriers. The social model calls upon society to tackle barriers and create social, economic and political equality for disabled people. Several powerful white male (and often non-disabled) academics have sought to destabilise this model in the last fifteen years, accusing it of a lack of theory and commenting that a historically materialist lens denies agency, while disabled scholars in feminisms have contributed the lived experiences of disabled women to widen the field.

Mindful of Meekosha's (2011) criticism of the futility of individual and cultural pride models for the disabled people living in the Global South and Diaspora populations in Western countries, this chapter develops to argue that collective and relational models of disability are critical to be culturally appropriate and effectively mobilised globally. Mobilised in disability, these critical models which resist the segregation and medical-isation which dominates from colonial damage and also offer more useful principles for community peace-building and voice of people with disabilities who are victims of war.

Ubuntu is an important African model, highly relevant for addressing the European ethnocentrism of both disability and war in Africa. As Berghs (2017) explained, the Ubuntu model of disability is a model of social ethics. It requires all of us to respect the impairments and diversity of others and work together in a shared humanity; only then can we be part of a collective and community. The Zulu term *'umuntu ngumuntu ngabantu'* describes becoming human only through the ways we behave to other human beings; we are all interdependent (ukama), spiritually in the past, present and future and physically with the environment. Oppression, colonisation, exploitation or violence threaten our common humanity, and therefore the shared struggle requires the whole community to tackle it. Ubuntu was applied in South Africa, as central to the work of the Truth and Reconciliation Commission. The apology to the harmed victim and the forgiveness to the perpetrator (in this case for apartheid and violence) was necessary because both were inter-linked and Ubuntu makes the humanness and healing possible for the reintegration of the community.

In Māori framings, Whānau Hauā offers rich and important understandings highly relevant to reconceptualising disability. Te Roopu Waiora, a Māori disability organisation was gifted the term whānau hauä by Donny Rangiahau (Tuhoe) and it recognised, to some degree, in New Zealand policies (Hickey, 2006). Whānau Hauā has parallels with the social model of disability, but goes further, having a cultural basis in which all of the community/ extended family (including ancestors and others with a common purpose) are obligated and responsible to nurture and support the person with a disability as part of the whole, in a collective effort with each other. In this way, a balance can be achieved, but not if the environment is unstable or unwelcoming, has institutional barriers or is segregated. So members of the community can only achieve balance for themselves if these problems for disabled people, which are acknowledged as problems for the whole community, are addressed. This powerful model is not only important for the equality and respect of disabled Indigenous people in New Zealand, but in re-focusing disability studies in the Global North towards a collective responsibility for the whole of society. Furthermore, Whānau Hauā can be mobilised to ensure peace and environmental stewardship brings balance to society, offering a future model for a more sustainable and secure world. Colonial discrimination has brought poverty and exclusion to indigenous peoples and a policy failure to acknowledge the collective necessity of a society not only perpetuates inequality and racist tools which mean Māori people with disabilities are under-assessed and do not gain equal provision, given the poverty visited on them means they cannot afford the aids, adaptations and access needed to have full life chances within society.

While the Global North disability studies should not simply appropriate models of Ubuntu and Whānau Hauā, as our academic fathers have with much Indigenous knowledge, these models offer a way forward collectively to repair the segregation of the past and place the responsibility firmly on the shoulders of non-disabled and disabled, privileged actors who wish to be useful allies to social movements for peace and disability equality.

An Intersectional Perspective: Gender, Ethnicity and Disability in War

An intersectional analysis foregrounds the experiences of disabled women of colour in war, in which gender, disability and ethnicity are always present. Because war is inherently masculine, so gendered violence is inevitable and regard, rape is 'normalised' as an acceptable reward for soldiers, both against combatants and civilians. This leads to a legacy of shame, ongoing pain and the silencing of survivors (Altinay & Pető, 2016). Rape is a highly effective tool for group destruction of an ethnic/religious/community of identity (MacKinnon, 2006), so is systematically used in genocides. For example, the Yugoslav National Army (UNA) Psychological Operations Department in Belgrade developed a plan to drive Muslims out of Bosnia based on an analysis of Muslim behaviour which, 'showed that their morale, desire for battle, and will could be crushed more easily by raping women, especially minors and even children, and by killing members of the Muslim nationality inside their religious facilities' (United Nations, 1994). When people survive or flee war, physical, sensory and mental health impairments remain with them and disable future generations.

History has also obscured the disabling of generations through colonial wars and its policies.

In Bengal, for example, the British colonial policies famine in 1943 killed almost 3 million people from starvation, malaria, a lack of sanitation malnutrition and displacement. Women and children were made homeless and food was priced out of the hands of the people by Churchill's policy of removing resources for the war effort, coupled with war-caused inflation (Mukerjee, 2014). The case study below demonstrates the catastrophic (even if un-intended) effects of racist and colonial policy in Africa more recently.

━━━━━━━━ Case study ━━━━━━━━

Colonial violence – War and famine

Structural violence (Galtung, 1969) waged in India and Africa can be demonstrated clearly in the history of European racist colonial policy.

Belgium's colonial policy and Catholic patriarchy that was responsible for creating the Rwandan genocide, and social science here has a crucial role in decolonising history. Singh explains the Belgian 1933–1934 census had created a system of ethnic identity cards that indicated the Tutsi, Hutu, or Twa 'ethnicity' of each person, based on the 'ethnicity' of their fathers, regardless of the 'ethnicity' of their mothers. This was done despite the fact that Hutu and Tutsi spoke the same language and practiced similar religions and intermarried. Belgian colonial administrators could not distinguish Batutsi from Bahutu, so any man with more than ten head of cattle was classified as Tutsi, and any man with fewer than ten cattle as Hutu or Twa, depending on their profession. After independence from Belgium in 1962, Hutu leaders adopted this identity card classification as 'races' and the seeds of the genocide were sown (Singh, 2016).

Between 1994 and 1996, an estimated 250,000–500,000 Tutsi women were systematically raped in the Rwandan genocide. Semanza understood that rape was a powerful message for the Hutu oppressors and soldiers raped the Tutsi women, then often mounted the victim's genitals on a pole outside the victim's house. When women survived, it was surmised that they would, 'die of sadness' and the reproduction of the Tutsi group would be exterminated.

The International Criminal Tribunal for Rwanda (ICTR) found that the rape of Tutsi women 'constitute[d] genocide in the same way as any other, so long as they were committed with the specific intent to destroy, in whole or in part, a particular group, targeted as such' (Prosecutor v. Akayesu, 1998). The judgement in this case was critical, because it emphasised 'the central elements of the crime of rape cannot be captured in a mechanical description of objects and body parts', and re-defined it as a physical invasion of a sexual nature, committed on a person under circumstances which are coercive (such as in war or detention).

The Rwandan genocide demonstrates that an intersectional viewpoint is critical if we are not to fall into the trap of binary accounts of women or disabled people as a homogeneous group, or minoritised groups that can be ignored, as Kuzmin (2019) stated. This assists researchers to fully understand the disabling and long-lasting consequences of war. For example, interviews with 40 Rwandan Diaspora in Finland, 22 years after the genocide showed that 72.5% were still traumatised, and of these, 37.5% were extremely traumatised. This manifested in sleeping problems, bad dreams and the use of alcohol to deal with the trauma. Half of the women who had been raped became pregnant from the rape and 10% had contracted HIV/AIDS from the rape (Banyanga et al., 2017).

Disability, Colonialism and Peace-Building

Collective models of disability from the Global South and academic Peace and Conflict Studies (PACS), offer an important way forward for justice, in which war and colonial harms can be tackled by survivors, as part of the community linked to the environment. Successful positive peace is not just the absence of war and violence (Barash, 2010), but requires strong community involvement to prevent future conflict and restore justice. For this to be representative of the people who are disproportionately affected by war, efforts in civic and voice building, must include future of Black disabled women and their user-led organisations, being resourced to be meaningfully involved in peace and reconciliation. In this scenario, both veterans and victims of conflict can work together to build secure states with inclusive social policy and adequate welfare protections.

━━━━━━━━━━ **Chapter summary** ━━━━━━━━━━

This chapter has analysed disability using decolonial theory and has included the following:

- A critical reading of how disability is understood and the implications of social attitudes to disability on people with disabilities.
- A global perspective highlighting the effect of global politics on disability, particularly war.
- Alternative ways of thinking about and relating to disability. These ways of thinking stem from indigenous knowledges and Global South theories of society.
- Disability, colonialism and peace-building.

Conclusion

The export of war and the dominance of white, colonial European and American models of disability has perpetrated severe inequalities, with the voices and experiences of African and Asian survivors and scholars with disabilities silenced and ignored. Thus, mainstream ethnocentric disability studies finds itself largely unable to deal with non-ableist intersectional framings which reflect much more lived experience of the world's people impairments than most academics ever can, from a place of privileged, non-disabled lives free from poverty, conflict and displacement.

Having due regard for Global South perspectives is critical in disability studies and social policy, if we are to reflect the body of work and not only the white male cis-gendered ableist contributions we lazily cite again and again. We must work towards eradicating inequalities and creating social justice. And those of us working academia and social policy have a duty to rise to the challenge of confronting our privileges, stop and address colonial approaches to disabled people and recognise our mistakes and erasures.

Questions to Reflect Upon

- What can be done to enable disabled survivors of war to live independently and free from violence and trauma (both as veterans and victims of conflict)?
- What similarities can you see between the effects of colonialism on disability and the effects of colonialism as discussed in other chapters?

Further Reading

Grech, S., & Soldatic, K. (2015). Disability and colonialism: (Dis)encounters and anxious intersectionalities. *Social Identities*, *21*(1), 1–5. (This paper provides a brief overview of the intersections between disability and decolonialist theory. It is important because it recognises that these bodies of writing do not always fit together comfortably, although writers in both fields have used each term as a metaphor for marginalisation and discrimination. The paper will help you navigate decolonial understandings of disability by highlighting how important it is to recognise the historic, social and political differences when using the two fields of thought.)

Berghs, M. (2017). Practices and discourses of Ubuntu: Implications for an African model of disability? *African Journal of Disability*, 6(1), 1–8. Retrieved from https://pubmed.ncbi.nlm.nih.gov/28730067/. (This paper outlines the contribution of Ubuntu to expanding how we understand and relate to disability. The paper will help you further appreciate what an Ubuntu-informed African model of disability looks like and how it is distinct from the medical and social models.)

Haang'andua, P. (2018). Disability policy in embedded cultural-cognitive worldviews: The case of sub-Saharan Africa. *Disability and the Global South*, 5(1), 1292–1314. (This paper highlights the problems of 'transplanting' policy ideas developed in the West/Global North to other parts of the world. It argues that these policies are not always well-suited to the Global South and can be damaging to national- and local-level actors. This paper will help further your understanding of the practical and political benefits of adopting a decolonialist approach.)

References

Altinay, A. G., & Pető, A. (2016). *Gendered wars, gendered memories. Feminist conversations on war, genocide and political violence*. Abingdon: Routledge.

Banyanga, J. D. A., Björkqvist, K., & Österman, K. (2017). The trauma of women who were raped and children who were born as a result of rape during the Rwandan genocide: Cases from the Rwandan diaspora. *Pyrex Journal of African Studies and Development*, 3(4), 31–39.

Barash, D. P. (2010). *Approaches to peace: A reader in peace studies*. New York, NY: Oxford University Press.

Berghs, M. (2017). Practices and discourses of Ubuntu: Implications for an African model of disability? *African Journal of Disability*, 6(1), 1–8.

Clarke, J. (2004). Access for all? The promise and problems of Universalism. *Social Work & Society*, 2(2), 216–224.

Erevelles, N. (2011). *Disability and difference in global contexts: Enabling a transformative body politic*. New York, NY: Palgrave Macmillan.

Finkelstein, V. (1996). *Outside, 'inside out'*. Coalition GMCDP, April 1996.

Francis, R. (2019) Searching for the voice of people with disabilities in peace and conflict research and practice. *Peace & Change*, 44(3), 295–320.

Galtung, J. (1969). Violence, peace, and peace research. *Journal of Peace Research*, 6, 167–191.

Guerrero, N. A. (2016). *The medical discourse and the sterilization of people with disabilities in the United States, Canada and Colombia: From eugenics to the present*. Montreal, QC: McGill University.

Hansen, R., & King, D. (2013). *Sterilized by the state: Eugenics, race, and the population scare in twentieth-century North America*. Cambridge: Cambridge University Press.

Hickey, H. (2006). Replacing medical and social models of disability by a communities-based model of equal access for people of differing abilities: A Maori perspective. *He Puna Korero: Journal of Maori and Pacific Development*, 7(1), 35–47.

Hodgson, D., & Watkins, S. C. (1997). Feminists and neo-Malthusians: Past and present alliances. *Population and Development Review*, 469–523.

Hunt, X., Swartz, L., Rohleder, P., Carew, M., & Hellum Braathen, S. (2018). Withdrawn, strong, kind, but de-gendered: Non-disabled South Africans' stereotypes concerning persons with physical disabilities. *Disability & Society*, *33*(10), 1579–1600.

Klausen, S., & Bashford, A. (2010). Fertility control: Eugenics, neo-malthusianism, and feminism. In A. Bashford & P. Levine (Eds.), *The Oxford handbook of the history of eugenics*. Oxford: Oxford University Press.

Kuzmin, G. (2019). *Statement by deputy permanent representative Gennady Kuzmin at the security Council meeting after security Council vote on draft resolution S/2019/503*. Permanent Mission of the Russian Federation to the United Nations. Retrieved 20 June 2019, from https://russiaun.ru/en/news/scr_2006

Langan, M. (2017). *Neo-colonialism and the poverty of 'development' in Africa*. Cham: Springer.

MacKinnon, C. A. (2006). *Are women human?* Cambridge, MA: The Belknap Press of Harvard University Press.

Meekosha, H. (2011). Decolonising disability: Thinking and acting globally. *Disability & Society*, *26*(6), 667–682.

Moyo, D. (2010). *Dead aid: Why aid is not working and how there is another way for Africa*. London: Penguin.

Mukerjee, M. (2014). Bengal famine of 1943: An appraisal of the famine inquiry commission. *Economic and Political Weekly*, *49*(11), 71–75.

Oliver, M. (2013). The social model of disability: Thirty years on. *Disability & Society*, *28*(7), 1024–1026.

Oliver, M., & Barnes, C. (2012). *The new politics of disablement*. Basingstoke: Palgrave.

Prosecutor v. Akayesu Case No ICTR 96 4 T. (1998), 694, 731.

Ryan, F. (2020). *Crippled: Austerity and the demonization of disabled people*. London: Verso Books.

Shakespeare, T. (2006). *The social model of disability*. *The Disability Studies Reader*, *2*, 197–204.

Singh, A. (2016). Colonial roots of the Rwandese ethnic conflict. *International Journal of Humanities and Social Science Invention*, *5*(5), 2319–7722.

Summerfield, D. (1999). A critique of seven assumptions behind psychological trauma programmes in war-affected areas. *Social Science & Medicine*, *48*, 1449–1462.

United Nations. (1994). *Report of the commission of experts established pursuant to security Council resolution 780 (1992), U.N. SCOR, Annex 1,129, U.N. Doc. S/1994/674*.

United Nations. (2019). *Resolution 2475 on protection of persons with disabilities in conflict*. New York, NY: United Nations.

UPIAS. (1976). *Fundamental principles of disability*. London: Union of the Physically Impaired Against Segregation.

Wehbi, S., Elin, L., & El-Lahib, Y. (2010). Neo-colonial discourse and disability: The case of Canadian international development NGOs. *Community Development Journal*, *45*(4), 404–422.

Williamson, B. (2019). *Accessible America*. New York, NY: New York University Press.

World Health Organization. (2021). *Disability and health: Key facts*. Retrieved from https://www.who.int/en/news-room/fact-sheets/detail/disability-and-health

8

HEALTH

Deirdre Duffy

━━━━━━━━━ **Learning objectives** ━━━━━━━━━

- To understand the 'language' of health policy and inequality.
- To understand the difference between observed and preventable inequalities in health.
- To understand the relevance of decolonial theory to global health debates and programmes.
- To become aware of the problematic histories and logics of health interventions.

━━━━━━━━━ **Framing questions** ━━━━━━━━━

- What is the best way to create a 'healthy' society?
- Who are the targets of programmes to improve population health?
- Is a doctor-led model of 'good health policy' always better? Why do you think so?

Introduction

In this chapter, you will look at health through the lens of social inequalities. Health is a very broad heading and is sometimes approached as being concerned with medicine and medical practice. As the disability chapter discussed, this medical or biomedical focus can divert our attention away from the social aspects of health debates. This chapter positions health as a social issue and will introduce you to issues such as health inequalities, the 'language' of health policy and the problematic histories of health debates. You will also be encouraged to think more critically about the role of health in reinforcing hierarchies of knowledge and its links to the colonial matrix of power (also covered in the chapters on race and gender).

The chapter is intentionally broad, reflecting the range of theoretical and analytic tools you can use to critique health policy in your studies. It will also give you specific case study examples of how to apply a social inequalities perspective to national and global health debates.

The chapter is structured in the following way:

- An overview of how social inequalities appear and impact upon health
- An introduction of the 'language' of health and inequality
- An introduction to some of the critiques of health policy. This will focus on the connections with population health and decolonisation.

Health and Social Inequalities

Health is a key focus of social inequalities literature, both in academic and policy circles. Core concerns include how unequal relations manifest in individuals', communities' and population health. Some of these manifestations are obvious and will be familiar to you – for example higher rates of disease, particularly among infants and vulnerable groups, are accepted as reflecting social inequalities. It is very rare to see a news report that talks about poor health without mentioning broader issues such as poverty or access to education.

But it is important to remember the scope of discussions about health and inequalities. As you engage more with health debates through your studies you will encounter everything from the spread of disease to air and water pollution, and to health insurance. It is not possible to cover all these issues in this chapter, so we will focus on two (connected) areas of discussion – public and population health. The reason why we have chosen to start here is that they connect some of the debates covered so far in this book (e.g. class, the expansion of colonial capitalism, disability). Additionally, when considered at a global scale, these debates show how programmes supposedly intended to address inequalities are both dominated by theories and ideas generated in the Global North and do not always address the best interests of the Global South.

Overall, this chapter should help you understand some of the inconsistences in public and population health narratives, the links between global health projects and colonialism, and how health policy can actually reinforce inequalities.

Understanding the 'Language' of Health and Inequality

The chapter will use some terms (e.g. public health and population health; health inequality and health inequity) so, before moving on, it is important to explain what they mean.

What Is the Difference Between Public Health and Population Health?

Frustratingly, in contemporary writing public health and population health are treated almost synonymously. There is no real agreement over where public health ends and population health begins. The only substantive consensus is that the term public health became popular before the term population health (Kindig & Stoddart, 2003).

The term 'public health' dates back to the early 20th century and is credited to the American physician and bacteriologist Professor C.E.A. Winslow (1920), founder of School of Public Health at Yale University. In a ground-breaking 1925 paper in the journal *Science,* Winslow defined public health as 'the science and art of preventing disease, prolonging life and promotion health and efficiency through organized community effort'. Winslow was trying to do at that point in time was to separate 'health' into the study of disease, the study of bodies and how to treat them, and the study of how to ensure people lived longer. Although disease, treatment, and living longer are connected, for Winslow there was a difference in approaching health as curing sick people and approaching health as a project of trying to (ideally) stop people from getting sick or (at least) stop them from getting sick easily through addressing social, economic, and environmental problems.

These social and ecological problems are now addressed as the social determinants of health (we will return to this term further when we discuss health inequalities and health inequities). You may see the first 'treating sickness' interpretation of what medicine and health does labelled a curative model or a biomedical model because it focuses on cures, biology, and medicine for people who are already sick. The second 'stopping sickness through addressing social determinants' is the public health model because it applies to everyone (the public), is the shared responsibility of public agencies (i.e. governments), and in includes a range of activities like health promotion or vaccination (public health interventions).

The constitution and founding document of the World Health Organization (WHO) combines biomedical and public health models in their definition of health as 'a state of complete physical, mental, and social well-being'. By defining health in this way, the WHO is promoting the purpose of health as making people better and addressing the factors which can either make people unwell directly or make it harder for them to remain well. This concern with achieving complete well-being through good biomedical practice and good public health informed their main projects–specifically reducing the spread of communicable and non-communicable disease, improving life chances in low-and middle-income countries (LMICs; what you may also see labelled as 'third world' 'developing'), and improving sexual and reproductive health programmes. The majority of LMICs are in the Global South.

The popularity of population health is a much more recent. Kindig and Stoddart (2003) argue that it became popular in the United Kingdom and Canada in the late-1980s and early 1990s. Like public health, population health is concerned with social determinants and the health of the whole population (not just sick people). However, population health is sometimes used more descriptively than public health. The term 'population health' will often be used to describe the differences in health across a whole population. For example, a population health debate will talk about issues such as life expectancy and highlight how particular communities live longer than others. Arguably, the different is audience.

Public health – going back to Winslow – is a model of action for health communities or those directly involved in healthcare. Winslow and early adopters of the public health framework were trying to encourage medicine to engage with social issues and circum-stances. The main audience is people involved in health (i.e. doctors, hospital managers). The 'art and science' of public health is represented by vaccination programmes and doctors promoting 'healthy living' in conversations with patients. It was important to 'treat' (in the medical sense) social problems as the diseases and conditions they created. Using the example of 'healthy eating', public health recognises the connection between the opportunity to eat healthily and the effects of unhealthy eating. Interventions and treatments, from a public health perspective, need to 'treat' both.

According to population health commentators, public health emphasises interventions which stop sickness or improve the likelihood of positive health outcomes through improving and expanding the responsibilities of health systems. Population health argues that the starting point for addressing health differences is policy. Health interventions need to be designed alongside interventions intended to tackle social inequalities. In other words, population health argues that policy needs to create space for health. For example, an education programme should talk about health and engage with health effects.

That said, this distinction is not true for all situations where you will encounter the term population health in policy or academic literature. In fact, both public and popu-lation health talk about the same problems in similar ways. For instance, a population health debate considers how opportunities to eat healthily are related to health eating and a public health intervention notes differences in life expectancy across populations. This crossover is not just confusing but reflects the fact that there is no agreement on where public health stops and population health begins. Many authors have pointed out that there is therefore very little difference between the two terms other than the fact population health is more popular now!

Reflection and Reading Task: How Do We Create 'Healthy Societies'? Addressing Obesity and Diet

Obesity and 'unhealthy' diet are frequently referenced as health policy concerns. What we eat has clear, evidenced effects on our 'life chances'. What do you think a good public intervention in this area should look like? What assumptions underpin existing inter-ventions? What are the main narratives?

'Health lifestyle' campaigns are very well-known public health interventions. Examples of public education campaigns include Fit4Life in the UK and the promotion of eating five portions of fruit and vegetables a day. From a public health policy perspective, the key issues are lack of knowledge and problematic behaviour.

Underpinning these campaigns is the argument that diet is an individual decision. The best way to address problems with diet is through health education campaigns and promoting individual steps towards a 'healthier lifestyle'.

However, this public health policy approach has been criticised as ignoring the social determinants of health and the impact of poverty, work, and housing on people's ability to 'live well'. By focusing on individual responsibility, policymakers deflect attention away from the effect of social, economic and policy contexts on health and well-being.

Taking these critiques in mind, read Jane Mulderrig's paper on the UK Fit4Life campaign. The reference for the paper is in the Recommended Reading section below.

Consider the following questions:

- Who does Mulderrig identify as the target of these policies?
- How does Mulderrig connect the Fit4Life campaign with other issues of social inequality?

You may also want to read Mulderrig paper and critique in conjunction with the chapter on class.

Health Inequality and Health Inequity

Two other terms that you will see discussed together are health inequality and health inequity. Like public and population health, these terms refer to similar problems. Both are used to talk about the connection between differences in health and wellbeing and social inequalities. Additionally, it is more common to see both discussed as a plural, i.e. health *inequalities* and health *inequities*. This reflects the fact that multiple inequalities and inequities coexist. For example, communities who are more susceptible to respiratory infections or diseases like asthma are also more likely to die younger.

Broadly, the distinction between health inequalities and health inequities is that the former can be used to describe differences without parsing comment (at least explicitly) on their connection with social and political inequalities. Health inequalities can be used to talk about variations in population health without suggesting what may cause these variations. An example may be the different life expectancies of communities living in one area as opposed to another, or the varying experiences of certain communities with healthcare professionals. We know, for example, that women from Black and Indigenous and People of Colour (BIPOC) backgrounds are more likely to report that their requests for pain relief during pregnancy and childbirth were ignored than women from White backgrounds.

Health inequity, on the contrary, is used to highlight that such variations are unfair, unjust, and connected to social and political systems. Health inequity is a political project to (a) document health inequalities; (b) show their connection with social and political environments; and (c) identify how these social and political environments are unjust. It argues that differences in health are linked to political, social and economic forces. Governance and global power relations negatively impact the health of particular groups, these impacts are caused by systemic problems that could be addressed by are not due to political and/or economic agendas.

Both terms are used frequently, and often synonymously, in writing on health and social inequality. To avoid becoming confused, a basic definition for each is given below:

- Health inequalities are systematic differences in population health. They are observable.
- Health inequities are systemic injustices in population health. They are observable and avoidable.

Health inequity demonstrates how, regardless of the level, 'the lower the socioeconomic position, the worse the health' (WHO Commission). From a decolonialist perspective, the reason why the term 'health inequities' is preferable is because it reorients discussions away from observing difference between communities and towards identifying sources of injustice. As well as this, by using health (in)equity we can highlight how pursuing better health is not just about improving medical treatments. It is about creating a more socially just society. As the WHO Commission of Health Inequities stated in 2020:

> It does not have to be this way and it is not right that it should be like this. Where systematic differences in health are judged to be avoidable by reasonable action they are quite simply, unfair. It is this that we label health inequity. Putting these inequities – the huge and remediable differences in health between and within countries – is a matter of social justice. (WHO, 2020)

In health literature, the sources of health inequity are discussed as the social determinants of health or the social, economic, and political factors shaping lifelong health at an individual and community level. Early literature on the social determinants of health focused on working conditions and income. However, it is important to adopt an intersectional approach. Gender and ethnicity can all shape access to health services, for example, or the ability to afford decent housing.

━━━━ COVID-19 and pharmaceutical health inequity ━━━━

The COVID-19 pandemic highlighted the connection between health and social inequalities in the Global North and Global South in numerous ways. When the pandemic first emerged, the highest transmission and mortality rates were among groups already socially disadvantaged. This persisted throughout the pandemic. Taking a straightforward example, people in 'public-facing' jobs – like those working in transport or retail – were more likely to contract COVID-19 than people who worked in 'white collar' office-based jobs (i.e. financial services, law firms, technology corporations) as the latter could work from home more easily. COVID-19 also showed the importance of discussing health inequities; the organisation of health systems impacted mortality rates. For example, in countries where healthcare access depended on health insurance, people without private health insurance had poor health outcomes. These people were more like to be Black, Indigenous or People of Colour (BIPOC), live in overcrowded housing, and work in poorly paid industries.

COVID-19 also shows how we can use 'health' to examine and question the connections between social injustices and health policies. A pronounced example is policy relating to vaccines. A core strand in the COVID-19 response policy was the development of effective vaccines. But vaccine policies are tied to broader issues such as investment in research and higher education and regulation of pharmaceutical patents. While distributing vaccines globally would undoubtedly help social recovery and limit the spread of disease, distribution can and is limited by the amount pharmaceutical developers charge. Further problems are created by the privatisation of patents–the guides of how to make a vaccine. Even if countries have the facilities to produce enough vaccines for their populations, pharmaceutical companies (who own the 'recipes' for effective vaccines) may refuse to share the information producers need or charge governments for these recipes.

Unsurprisingly, countries in the Global South, who have less money, bear the brunt of this social inequality while companies in the Global North (and the countries they pay taxes to!) benefit. Yet the irony is that, in a global pandemic like COVID-19, universal vaccination programmes are essential to preventing the continued circulation of disease. Borders between countries cannot remain closed indefinitely. Additionally, as we know from COVID-19, viruses mutate and new, more transmissible, variants may emerge and spread quickly if there is no protection.

Challenging Traditional Health(y) Policy
Health and Population Studies

Projects for health equality are, on face value, positive. However, they have been challenged for their connections with population theories which are very problematic, particularly for people living in the Global South. Here it is important to recognise how much of health policy has involved targeting communities seen to be socially problematic. This is most obviously reflected in the work of Thomas Malthus on the effect of 'over-population'. Malthus was an 18th century natural philosopher. His primary contribution was the 1798 work *An Essay on the Principle of Population* in which he argued that the power of population was greater than the power of food production. As such, according to Malthus:

> By that law of our nature which makes food necessary to the life of man, the effects of these two unequal powers must be kept equal. This implies a strong and constantly operating check on population from the difficulty of subsistence. This difficulty must fall somewhere and must necessarily be severely felt by a large portion of mankind. (Malthus, p. 5)

Centrally Malthus contended that to ensure global sustainability we need to actively manage population growth. However, Malthus did not advocate any intervention into sexual desire and concluded that the lack of equilibrium between population growth and food production growth would persist without intervention. This position is known as Malthusianism. By the late 19th century, birth control (mainly through contraception and eugenics) had become positioned as the most effective means of remedying the conflict Malthus identified by the Neo-Malthusians.

Neo-Malthusianism emerged in the US and Europe in the late 19th/early 20th century and expanded Malthus's arguments about the conflict between population growth and sustainability along two lines of debate. Both debates were underpinned by an image of the world as have a finite amount of resources to support 'healthy' lives for all.

The first debate saw the main challenge of over-population as economic – how could we (as a global community) possibly finance and meet the needs of 'unchecked' population growth? Malthus's solution to financial sustainability was that only married men who could financially support themselves should procreate. Neo-Malthusians took this argument to more extreme levels. Dovetailing with the eugenics movement of the late 19th century and early 20th century, Neo-Malthusians advocated for limiting the ability of economically unproductive populations to grow. The most direct strategies to achieve this were, as you will have discussed in Chapter 7 on disability, sterilisation and contraception. Marie Stopes, the seminal birth control writer and advocate, was a passionate Neo-Malthusian and the influence of concerns about population growth (specifically among economically and social unproductive populations) on her activism and campaigning is well-documented.

However, Neo-Malthusian arguments about the need to limit population growth among communities who are positioned as costing more to the economy than contributing also underwrite policies which, while less stark than sterilisation, are no less brutal. This can include a refusal to provide financial aid to lone parents or persistent stigmatising people who have 'more children than they can afford'.

The second debate saw the main challenge of over-population as ecological. This is a much more 20th century debate and focuses, like Malthus, on the environment. But where Malthus spoke about food and farming, ecological Neo-Malthusianism emphasises planetary stability and climate. Over-population is not just a problem because we cannot produce enough food to feed people, but because the planet can only *support* so many people. Ecological Neo-Malthusianism has a plethora of evidence to support these arguments; the rapid rise of urban populations and growth of 'super cities' is directly linked to environmental problems like poor air quality, deforestation, and climate change. Again, there is a resource issues which can be addressed through incentivising birth control among people who live in over-crowded environments. This continues to be one of the main arguments used to support the free and open distribution of contraceptives to the 'urban poor'.

What connects these two strands of Neo-Malthusianism is not just their focus on population and finite resources but their traction within both national and transnational policies framed as supporting collective health and wellbeing. Access to contraception has been supported as a global health priority for decades. With the increased recognition of climate crises, managing population growth is accepted as essential and we are consistently faced by policies which actively connect sustainability and population health to food scarcity.

However, critics of Neo-Malthusianism argue that it frames particular communities– who are already economically and social marginalised – as both wholly problematic and/ or to blame for global ecological or economic challenges. In writing from US-based Neo-Malthusians in the mid-20th century, concerns about population growth were interlaced with social panics about the growth of the black urban poor. Feminist and post-colonialist theorists contend that the concentration of health policy investment in minimising population growth in the Global South is directly linked to Neo-Malthusian logic and the associated narratives of certain populations as a threat to global stability.

Feminist and post-colonial writers argue that global population/public health and development policies implicitly – and sometimes explicitly – reinforce Malthusian and Neo-Malthusian ideologies through connecting the effects of climate change and poverty with over-population. While they do not disagree that overcrowding and food poverty need to be addressed; these commentators argue that health agendas underpinned by population science/controlling populations deflect attention away from the historic and contemporary actions by the Global North/West which have created health inequities and inequalities. These critics outline the connection between global health inequalities and colonial capitalism. They underscore, for instance, how sustainability challenges like food poverty (which Neo-Malthusians and Malthusians link to an inability to control population) have been worsened by unregulated industrialisation and pollution by Global North companies.

In addition, feminist and post-colonial writers highlight how the Neo-Malthusian birth control movement/population control project has been weaponised by colonial powers and white supremacists to strengthen the framing of Black Indigeneous and People of Colour (BIPOC) as threatening (Nandagiri, 2021). Again, global health policies have, critics argue, been active agents in this weaponization by unquestioningly directing investment in birth control at BIPOC communities. From a post-colonial perspective, the key point is that health policy can sanitise some of the brutal interpretations of population debates if not accompanied by a clear recognition that (1) health inequalities are not the result of poorly managed population growth and (2) birth control should not be interpreted simply as a population reduction measure. If it is interpreted in this way, we run the risk of ignoring what populations we – as a global community – are trying to reduce and why.

Challenging Medical Hegemony

A second area of debate relating to the effect of health equality projects is their effect on how 'good health policy' is understood. A central concern for decolonial scholars is how the project of improving public and population health led to biomedical hegemony. This term refers to the interpretation of particular health practices and forms of healthcare as the only solution to public/population health inequalities. Hegemony is a concept first introduced by the Italian political scientist Antonio Gramsci to outline how political elites over populations maintain control when they do not use direct force. Gramsci explained that political elites had reinforced their position through establishing their culture, language, and knowledge as 'normal' and ensuring it was socially dominant. They were a hegemon.

Medical hegemony is an extension of this theory to the context of health and health care. Here the 'normal' mode of healthcare is practiced according to the rules of 'Western medicine' (or allopathic medicine). At its most basic, medical hegemony means that society sees 'good health' as synonymous with the existence of hospital and doctors. The effect of allopathic medicine's hegemonic status – its position as a hegemon in how we understand 'normal' healthcare – has been the marginalisation of any forms of healthcare which is not led by doctors trained in allopathic practices as alternative, traditional and even dangerous.

Social theory has critiqued the hegemonic status of biomedicine for some time. Zola, in 1972, argued that medicine 'is becoming the new repository of truth, the place where absolute and often final judgments are made by supposedly morally neutral and objective experts' (Zola, 1972, p. 487). The emergence of 'Western' understandings of healthcare and medicine as medical hegemon is very much a feature of 20th century health. A straightforward illustration of this is the rapid increase in hospital births managed by doctors in the Global North and the associated positioning of midwifery and home-birth as undesirable. In the United States, between the 1940s and 1970s, the number of women giving birth in hospitals, under the supervision of obstetricians, rose from under 50% to over 98% (Pearse, 1979). Hospital, doctor-led birth became normal even though midwifery had been practised safely and with positive health outcomes for centuries. Indeed, home-birth is still thought of as inherently less safe by US obstetric and medical associations, despite the evidence that safe, patient-centred home birth is both desired and valued by women (Freeze, 2010)!

Medical hegemony by 'Western' medicine both reinforces and creates health inequalities. As doctor-led health practice was increasingly framed as better, investment in hospitals and investment in addressing health inequalities were conflated by governments. This was not associated by a consideration of the general accessibility of hospitals or health centres across the population. While those who could – or wished to – access care in hospital settings benefitted from these strategic investments, communities who could or did not wish to access healthcare in hospitals became increasingly disadvantaged. These disadvantages are most notable in insurance-based healthcare systems where people have to pay for either part or all of the care they receive. You may be aware of the situation in the US where the cost of insurance – and lack of health insurance – has led to millions of people being denied healthcare.

A further effect 'Western' medicine's medical hegemonic status has been the lack of engagement with improving care experiences outside of hospital settings or where patients cannot be 'cured'. This has become a pronounced problem during the COVID-19 pandemic where people with long-term health conditions and older adults who receive care in residential settings or in their own homes and the people who cared for them had higher infection and mortality rates. Because care outside hospital settings is seen as less beneficial to general population health, it did not receive sufficient investment or personal protective equipment to protect staff and those receiving care from COVID-19.

Critics of medical hegemony by the Western clinical approaches and medical elites – specifically doctors working in hospital settings – have also argued that by treating 'good health policy' and 'doctor-led health provision' as synonymous we also ignore the tendency of Western medicine to adopt a fundamentally curative interpretation of healthcare. As Chapter 7 on disability notes, a curative model is highly problematic for long-term conditions and people with disabilities. It also lends itself towards an intensive use of medicines, ignoring that although they may 'cure' specific conditions, their impact on emotional wellbeing of patients and the experience of ill-health can be very negative.

Decolonialist Criticisms of Global Health Policy

The hegemonic position of Global North medicine is closely connected with the colonial matrix of power outlined by post-colonial theorists, particularly Rolando Vázquez (2009). Vázquez's main area of critique relates to the mobilisation of narratives of 'modernity' or 'modern time' by colonising political forces to entrench their superiority over colonised peoples. Like Mignolo, Vazquez describes the multifaceted character of colonisation and its entrenchment through temporalities, materialities and knowledge systems. Vázquez argues that colonialism involves obliterating the histories and knowledges of colonised people in order to legitimise the imposition of Western perspectives on the past and Western ways of knowing. Coloniality is, for Vázquez, a form of temporary discrimination which 'makes invisible all that does not belong to modern temporality' (Vázquez, 2009: np). In the context of health, a decolonialist interpretation suggests that part of the reason why Western clinical approaches dominate is because colonial discourses position these forms of health provision as more clinically and scientifically advanced.

The intersection between biomedical dominance and colonialist ideas of what makes a health system 'modern' is one issue highlighted by decolonial theorists of global health policy. But a more pronounced criticism is based around the ignorance of colonial legacies and their wider health implications. One important area of debate has been around how health interventions against virus and communicable diseases such as Ebola designed in the Global North fail to engage or work with Global South and colonised peoples' histories and cultures. These histories often include experiences of medical testing or coercive public health initiatives (such as forced and non-consensual sterilisation) against colonised and indigenous communities by colonising powers. These experiences have left a pronounced legacy of distrust of clinicians and clinical medicine, a legacy that is reflected in poor health-seeking behaviours and health outcomes. In short, because colonised societies were harmed by medical workers in the past, they are less likely to seek health care, even when it is necessary, free, and available.

To address the reticence to access clinical health care, some countries have engaged in 'task-sharing' initiatives to improve health equity and integrate alternative or traditional health practices with allopathic medicine. For example, the Colombian and New Zealand governments have both piloted projects of 'task sharing' health work with traditional community leaders in indigenous communities. The Indian government has also tried to embed non-allopathic forms of medicine, discriminated against by colonisers, in the broader, allopathic health system as partners in health provision. These ways of working ensure that the health knowledges of colonised groups are respected, and the history of colonial harm recognised, while still pursuing public health goals. At the same time, research of these integration policies indicates that attitudes towards indigenous or traditional medicine among allopathic health workers can remain problematic and underpinned by colonial logics (Josyula et al., 2016).

Global and emergency public health initiatives in response to pandemics can either fail to meaningfully disrupt or ignore entirely the intersection of colonial harms and health. As Gautier, Karambé, Dossou and Mallé Samb (2022) outline, internationally funded and co-ordinated responses to Ebola were not sensitive to the colonial legacies in public health and, in the case of Ebola, did not work with communities. According to Gautier et al.'s (2022) research, from the perspective of communities in the areas where Ebola outbreaks were most acute – the majority in Francophone Africa – the interventions involved 'spacemen' invading and colonising their towns and villages. The messaging from these outsiders involved scare tactics and there was limited recognition of how traditional death and burial practices could be respected. These strategies, while under-taken in the interest of minimising the spread of Ebola, ignored the colonial experience of Francophone Africa. As a result, Gautier et al. (2022) argue, health workers were attacked and the communities who most needed medical support did not wish to access it.

Conceptually, the Ebola strategy fell into a colonial logic trap of working on Global South communities rather than working with them. Applying Mohanty and Vazquez, this speaks to a perception (by Global North/Western health workers and planners) that the reason comprehensive health services do not exist in the Global South is because they are less progressive or skilled. This overlooked the historic and persistent economic exploitation of the Global South by the Global North (impoverishing countries and leaving them with insufficient resources to support comprehensive health care) and the continuing devaluing of health workers trained and practicing in the Global South. Sylvia Tamale (2020) writes on this latter point when she notes how, outside of a limited number of exceptions, academic and professional training from the Global South is seen as less legitimate and of lower quality than academic and professional training from the Global North.

Yet by focusing on providing Global North medics to Global South countries, rather than working with health workers from and in the Global South, public health strategies can directly reinforce global health inequalities. Mistrust of outsiders combined with collective memories of colonial harms in the form of medical mistreatment can damage health-seeking behaviours. It can also leave room for rumours to circulate. In the case of the Ebola response, international co-ordinators did not engage in meaningful dialogue with communities or 'task share' with pre-existing public health community workers. This left communities suspicious of the 'outsiders' intentions and rumours that the 'spacemen' had created Ebola or were the cause of the health crisis spread. The health outcomes of the crisis for these communities were worse.

■■■■■■■■■■ Chapter summary ■■■■■■■■■■

This chapter has provided an overview of how social inequalities impact health and has included the following topics:

- An explanation of how observable health inequalities may be produced by unequal socio-political power relations (or are health *inequities*)
- A challenge traditional health policies

- A challenge to medical hegemony
- A decolonial analysis of health(y) policy, highlighting its connection with problematic theories about race and modernity.

Conclusion

Health is an important arena for examining the complexity of social inequalities. At the most basic level, analysing population-level health and health outcomes shows the impact of social inequalities on different groups. Across all scales – national, transnational and global – people who are already socially, economically, and politically marginalised die younger. They are also more likely to live in conditions and circumstances which could be reasonably described as 'unhealthy'.

Analysing health debates and policies also shows the inequalities/inequities also shows the tensions embedded in health interventions (national and global). It is critical for health policy to remain sensitive to colonial legacies. As students of social policy, decolonial theory and analysis of public health can illustrate the links between seemingly well-meaning programmes – such as investment in family planning or the Ebola virus intervention – have links with problematic and persistent colonial legacies. This includes the targeting of 'problem' communities and devaluing of the skills of health workers in communities.

A Question to Reflect Upon

- 'Vaccine hesitancy' is the term for people's unwillingness to have or distrust of vaccines. What can the experience of poor health-seeking behaviours during the Ebola crisis tell us about the reasons for 'vaccine hesitancy' in the Global South? What strategies should be adopted to address vaccine hesitancy?

Further Reading

Bhatia, R., Sasser, J. S., Ojeda, D., Hendrixson, A., Nadimpally, S., & Foley, E. E. (2020). A feminist exploration of 'populationism': Engaging contemporary forms of population control. *Gender, Place & Culture*, 27(3), 333–350. (This paper provides a useful overview of the different narratives of population control circulating in contemporary global debates. Each of these narratives – which the authors term 'populationisms' – propose different reasons for and ways to intervene in population growth.)

Gautier, L., Karambé, Y., Dossou, J. P., & Mallé Samb, O. (2020). Rethinking development interventions through the lens of decoloniality in sub-Saharan Africa: The case of global health. *Global Public Health*, 1–14. (This paper provides a critical case study of the importance of adopting a decolonialist lens. It focuses on interventions during the Ebola crises in Francophone Africa, illustrating how the 'transplanting' of Western/Global North knowledge without reference to local histories and contexts can worsen a crisis.)

Marmot, M., Friel, S., Bell, R., Houweling, T. A. J., Taylor, S., & Commission on Social Determinants of Health. (2008). Closing the gap in a generation: Health equity through action on the social determinants of health. *The Lancet, 372*(9650), 1661–1669. (This important paper explains how social factors and conditions impact health across the lifecourse. It will help you understand how inequalities can be improved or worsened by policy interventions.)

Mulderrig, J. (2019). The language of 'nudge' in health policy: Pre-empting working class obesity through 'biopedagogy'. *Critical Policy Studies, 13*(1), 101–121.

(In this paper, Mulderrig outlines how policies that aim to improve population health problems emphasise self-control and self-governance through soft, 'nudge' messaging. These policies deflect attention aware from larger structural problems connected with poor health and foreground individualised explanations.)

References

Freeze, R. (2010). Attitudes towards home birth in the USA. *Expert Review of Obstetrics & Gynecology, 5*(3), 283–299.

Gautier, L., Karambé, Y., Dossou, J. P., & Samb, O. M. (2022). Rethinking development interventions through the lens of decoloniality in sub-Saharan Africa: The case of global health. *Global Public Health, 17*(2), 180–193.

Josyula, K. L., Sheikh, K., Nambiar, D., Narayan, V. V., Sathyanarayana, T.N., & Porter, D. H. (2016). 'Getting the water-carrier to light the lamps': Discrepant role perceptions of traditional, complementary, and alternative medical practitioners in government health facilities in India. *Social Science & Medicine, 166*, 214–222.

Kindig, D., & Stoddart, G. (2003) What is population health? *American Journal of Public Health, 93*(3), 380–383.

Nandagiri, R. (2021). What's so troubling about 'voluntary' family planning anyway? A feminist perspective. *Population Studies, 75*(1), 221–234.

Pearse, W. H. (1979). Home birth. *The Journal of the American Medical Association, 241*(10), 1039–1040.

Tamale, S. (2020). *Decolonization and Afro-feminism*. Ottawa: Daraja Press.

Vázquez, R. (2009). Modernity coloniality and visibility: The politics of time. *Sociological Research Online, 14*(4), 109–115.

Winslow, C.-E. A. (1920). The untilled fields of public health. *Science, 51*(1306), 23–33.

World Health Organization. (2020). *Social determinants of health: Key concepts*. Retrieved from https://www.who.int/social_determinants/thecommission/finalreport/ key_concepts/en/

Zola, I. K. (1972). Medicine as an institution of social control. *The Sociological Review, 20*(4), 487–504.

9

UNEQUAL MOBILITIES AND GLOBAL SOCIAL INEQUALITIES

Anya Ahmed, Lorna Chesterton
and Nafhesa Ali

Learning objectives

- To understand the theoretical constructs and disciplines which explore the movement of people, resources, and information
- To understand how mobility and migration are shaped by agency, structure, and context
- To understand the influence of political ideology on migration and immigration policy
- To understand the potential future impact of climate migration

---

Framing questions

- What factors have shaped migration theory over recent decades?
- How will migration patterns change in the future?
- How has UK immigration policy changed and why has it become part of the political agenda?
- What factors have enabled right-wing groups to thrive and impact upon society?

Introduction

This chapter will begin with a brief overview of mobilities and migration research to contextualise the interdisciplinary and theoretical contexts which frame the movement of people, goods and information. We will go onto highlight different forms of migration and discuss how privileged mobilities can be seen in terms of personal agency, as individuals search for lifestyle or economic improvement or contrastingly in forced migration, which occurs as a result of political exile or persecution and will also include climate migration. The chapter also explores how macro structures enable and constrain migration and how geographical and social location shape experiences. Lastly, we will look at the contextual issues apparent in the UK, exploring the rise of right-wing ideologies, which publicise and practice an opposition to immigration and integration, and an alignment to xenophobia, and nationalistic policy. Throughout the chapter will be a number of case studies, allowing students to explore the day-to-day realities of being a migrant, and the challenges they face, often as a result of social, legal and political policy.

Mobilities and Migration

Migration is often viewed as a means towards improving a person's life in one way or another, but an individual's experience will very much depend upon the context with which migration occurs (Ahmed, 2015). Geoffrey and Sibley (2009) contend that there are three types of migration: the voluntary search for economic improvement; pursuing an alternative lifestyle; and forced migration or political exile. Migration is conceptualised by King (2012) as a complex and fluid concept whereby the flow of migration influences the population structure, totals, and settlement patterns. King (2012) uses the structure/ agency debate to demonstrate this, by observing how the use of structuration theory (Giddens, 1986) can explore the interaction between agency and structure alongside the contextual impacts experienced by individual's actions. Massey, Arango, Hugo, Kouaouci and Pellegrino (1998), on the other hand, look at the structural factors facilitating migration and the motivation which individuals experience to migrate. Another migration scholar, O'Reilly (2012), puts forward a 'practice theory' of migration, which focuses on the need to understand the interplay between different structures (external upper/ proximate and internal), practices, habitus and outcomes, ultimately seeking to establish an ontological basis for understanding the connection between structure and agency in a migration context. Indeed, agency and structure when explored through alternative theories can often solely focus on the deterministic role of structures, or the transcendental nature of agency. In contrast, Bakewell (2010) argues that researchers can sometimes acknowledge the interconnectivity of structure and agency yet fail to look at the contextual influences. Bakewell (2010, p. 1703) suggests a hybrid approach, combining the work of Massey et al. (1998) and O'Reilly (2012) with her own work to develop a 'theoretical brick' to elucidate women's search for community and belonging in the context of retirement migration. This approach draws on the different theoretical frameworks from these three researchers, but also their shared aim which is built on the importance of understanding structures, migrant's agency and the intricacies of the shared interactions. Crucially, Bakewell's approach (2010) takes a holistic focus, exploring people, places and time (who moves, where they move to – or not – and when).

What constitutes migration and what does not, leads many to pursue the idea of 'mobilities' instead (Urry, 2012). The term mobilities refers to the movement of people, ideas and information and can include multiple geographical locations. Mobility studies explore the changing characteristics of social life and its interplay with society, space and mobility, all of which are intrinsically and reciprocally linked to social inequality (Ohnmacht et al., 2009). Indeed, the study of mobilities has itself shifted its focus to concentrate on the embodied and practical aspects of movement, communication processes and the underpinning infrastructures which support them (Sheller, 2014). Certainly, as the world changes, and communication processes are enhanced, the crossing of borders enhances mobility for some, and immobilises others (Wood & Graham, 2006). Nagy and Korpela (2013) observe that mobilities should be understood as representing a continuum which encompasses necessity and desire. Adey, Bissell, Hannam, Merriman, and Sheller (2014) suggest that both migration and mobilities research have a responsibility to encompass research from sociology, anthropology, cultural studies, history and geography in order to fulfil the epistemological goal of exploring systems of global movement.

As rapidly growing fields of study, migration and mobilities research encompasses work on several types of migration and migration-related diversity, such as forced migration, economic and lifestyle migration, and their links to personal agency, networks and opportunity. Indeed, underpinning all migration and mobilities research are the social, legal and political policies and ideals of the receiving country, which will exert significant influence on migrants' lives. Following a brief discussion of each concept a case study will be presented, allowing concepts and theories to be contextualised.

Forced Migration

Forced migration refers to the situation whereby individuals are displaced as a result of persecution, conflict, violence or human rights violations (UNHCR, 2020). A distinction here is necessary as the term is also used to describe the involuntary displacement of people caused by natural causes, typically caused by disasters which will be discussed in the next section of this chapter. Forced migration, which is caused by people, needs to be examined as a social process where agency and social networks become important. Indeed, refugees and asylum seekers have become a huge topic for political discussion and changing policy.

The number of people who have been forcibly displaced was estimated to be 79.5 million, of which 45.7 million people were displaced within their countries of origin, and 33.8 million as refugees and asylum-seekers crossing international borders, according to the United Nations High Commissioner for Refugees (2020). For those forcibly displaced there are important implications for their health, citizenship, rights and identity, with many facing increased risk from human traffickers (Foxen, 2021, p. 171). Regarding the repatriation of refugees, the primary consideration is for refugee protection, encompassing voluntariness, safety and sustainability (Crisp & Long, 2016). The law and treaties governing repatriation are contained within 'The International Refugee Regime' (IRR) which was established after the Second World War to provide protection and support to those displaced through the conflict, and proposes three resolutions: 'voluntary repatriation, integration in the first country of asylum or third-country resettlement' (Içduygu & Nimer, 2020, p. 416). However, as the context and content of these three solutions change, countries have sometimes adopted involuntary repatriation to address the refugee crisis. This was seen in 2018 when the Bangladesh and Myanmar governments arranged for the repatriation of the Rohingya people, a Muslim minority community originally from Myanmar who had escaped violence to seek asylum in Bangladesh. The Rohingya refugees were so fearful of returning they fled the Bangladesh refugee camps. The involuntary repatriation deal which was struck by the two governments was condemned by UNHCR (Ellis-Petersen & Azizur-Rahman, 2018).

In the following case study, we see how an individual is subject to the host country's immigration policy, which restricts a person's leave to remain, and then deports them back to country from which they have fled, with no safeguards for the persons safety. The case study also bears witness to another form of forced migration, which is the illegal trafficking of people across international boundaries for exploitation, which thrive because of the strict immigration policies in middle- and high-income countries (Castles, 2003).

━━━━━━━━━━ Case study ━━━━━━━━━━

Bajram's story

Bajram entered the UK from Kosovo as an asylum seeker in 1999 having paid a substantial amount of money to an illegal trafficker in order to flee from the war in his native country. At the UK border he claimed asylum and even though his country was in the middle of a war he was only granted asylum for one year. The armed conflict in Kosovo economically destroyed the country and resulted in displacing huge numbers of the population and widespread loss of life (UNFPA, 2000). In 2000, Bajram was deported back to Kosovo, where there was mass unemployment, poverty, and a severe lack of habitable homes, as most houses were destroyed in the conflict. All Bajram's financial resources had been spent on his escape from Kosovow. His future seems bleak, and his life remains in danger. He was returned to his original village, which is now almost desolate, with only a few old people, trying to forage off the barren land. They urge him to leave, to find somewhere safer to live.

Forced Migration in Response to Climate Change (Climate Migration)

Climate migration can be viewed as adapting one's lifestyle due to the effects of climate change (McLeman & Smit, 2006) and is often signalled by two main causes

(McLeman, 2018). The first is the result of the direct impact of climate change, such as natural catastrophes and extreme weather that can damage and destroy dwellings forcing people from their homes. Rather than being a conscious decision, in this context, migration is forced due to the set of circumstances individuals experience. The second factor is often a consequence of indirect influences such as the environment or societal processes that have a knock-on effect on migration. This may include, for example, governmental changes in regimes but also various other behaviours which may result in lifestyle vulnerabilities (McLeman & Smit, 2006). Evidence suggests that the most socioeconomically poor are worst affected in these circumstances and resort to migration to survive (Rajan & Bhagat, 2017). Migration in these circumstances affects more than the individual who is travelling, with households, families, and communities all affected by the climate change as they 'adjust and adapt to altering climatic conditions' (McLeman, 2018, p. 231). It is important to understand that migration due to climate change is not always forced (Laczko & Piguet, 2014). Yet, often, this is the framing of media and policy where the focus becomes embroiled in 'disasters and displacement' alone (Laczko & Piguet, 2014, p. 2).

How, then, do sending and receiving countries plan for climate migrants? Without addressing climate change – there will be no option, but to receive migrants (internal and external migration). Where climate change and the impact on the environment is less predictable the contrasting movements and mobilities will make migration planning evermore challenging. The response to climate migration, in both sending and receiving countries, can only effectively occur by acknowledging the microstructures and processes involved in the climate movement in addition to analysing the macrostructures involved in climate migration. McLeman (2018) argues that there are three thresholds where climate migration occurs – at the individual, household, and community. By recognising that vulnerable individuals/households move away from risk, such as when flooding or drought occur (Leman & Smith, 2006; Upadhyay & Mohan, 2017) allows greater insight into planning and policymaking. However, some individuals decide not to move away, with Laczko and Piguet (2014) noting that 'environmental factors do not affect all individuals, households and communities equally'. With questions arising for the populations who remain and what this then means for populations who resettle abroad. Both are noteworthy in addressing how unequal and social mobilities impact on both sending and receiving countries, but also how climate migration affects global, regional, and demographic movements, as well as having long-term repercussions on all communities (McLeman, 2018, p. 320).

The decolonisation of climate migration research and its related methodologies are of growing interest (Chen, 2020; Domínguez & Luoma, 2020; Gram-Hanssen, Schafenacker, & Bentz, 2021; Johnson, Parsons, & Fisher, 2021; Ritchie, 2020). Here, the construction of racial hierarchies affiliated to migrants who opt to migrate through privileged mobilities, as opposed to climate migrants who migrate due to vulnerabilities and risk (see also Leman & Smith, 2006; Upadhyay & Mohan, 2017) reidentifies the need to decolonise how migrants are constructed. This will be indispensable to the experiences and field of climate migration, but more importantly will draw attention to social inequalities and how changes in the environment will continue to affect people's lives (Laczko & Piguet, 2014). Indeed, climate research that connects strong conceptual foundations which would help frame debates around significant issues, such as migration (Faist & Schade, 2013); with frameworks adopting more critical thinking – such as critical race theory and decolonial/postcolonial critique would equally be useful in examining the nexus between race, the law and structural inequalities. The following case study tells Sameeia's story, as her family is forced to migrate because of climate change.

◾◾◾◾◾◾ Case study ◾◾◾◾◾◾

'Sameeia's story'

Sameeia is a women in her late sixties, who, with her family has farmed land in Brahmaputra Delta, India for generations. The family have recently been forced to migrate to Sagar Island, in North-Eastern India, after their home, cattle and belongings were destroyed by cyclones. With no possessions the family have tried to rebuild their lives. She observes the increasing intensity of the storms and the diminishing land, which is becoming salinised by the rising sea levels, rending it useless for farming. Sameeia is among the large population in India which are living in regions which are at risk of flooding, cyclones and at the mercy of climate change disasters. The family have an uncertain future, knowing that they will probably have to continue to move to safer environments, but with the prospect of increasing destruction of land by climate change, it is unknown where this will be.

Economic Migration

A recent report from the International Organization for Migration (IOM, 2020) found that 3.5% of the world's population, or around 272 million people, are migrants, with nearly two-thirds of these being labour migrants. These statistics are also accompanied by predictions that this number will accelerate greatly over the next two decades (IOM, 2020). Indeed, evidence suggests that most international migrants move to countries which have higher levels of development than their native country and encompasses both emigration and immigration (exit and entry) according to Song (2018).

Over the years, several theoretical models have been developed to explore the reasons why international migration takes place, with each theory using considerably different approaches and assumptions. King (2012) describes these theories within a chronological context, with neo-classical approaches of the 1960s being based on Ravenstein's (1889) 'laws' of migration, where 'push and pull' factors of choice and labour dominate. In the 1970s there was a lean towards historical structural models, which were heavily influenced by Marxism, political economy models, system and network theories as well as world capitalist systems theories. New economies of migration theories became dominant in the 1980s, and these were superseded in the 1990s by the cultural or transnational turn (King, 2012). The transnational turn challenged the notion that the subject of debate should be the nation, and instead looked at the transnational movement of people, ideas and things which pass across borders (national or defined) epistemologically drawing on post-positivist, post-national and post-structural approaches (King, 2012).

In 1948, there was a mass migratory movement, with people from Africa and the Caribbean entering Britain at the invitation of the British Government. Workers arriving in the UK between 1948 and 1971 from Jamaica, Trinidad and Tobago and other islands, to fill post-war labour shortages were labelled the Windrush generation, in reference to the first ship, MV Empire Windrush. An estimated 500,000 UK residents who were born in a Commonwealth country and arrived before 1971 were given indefinite leave to remain. However, the UK Home Office kept no records and issued no documentation to this effect, and in 2010 it destroyed all landing cards belonging to Windrush migrants, believing them to be British Citizens (since they came from British colonies).

Figure 9.1 presents an image of the *HMT Empire Windrush*, best remembered today for bringing one of the first large groups of post-war migrants from the Caribbean to the United Kingdom, responding to a call for labour.

The subsequent scandal which was uncovered observed how British citizens of African and Caribbean descent were accused of being in the UK illegally and subjected to an abuse of their human rights by denying them access to healthcare, housing, education, employment and legal representation. De Gnova (2002) uses the term 'illegalisation' to describe the impact of law making which directly influences the policing of border practices which illegalise and demonise migrants. De Genova and Roy (2019, p. 360) assert that such practices categorise humans into 'illegal' and 'legal' and in doing so increase their risk of becoming 'stateless, rightless, and utterly disposable'. De Noronha (2019) extends the illegalisation theory by asserting that it is also intersects with race, gender, identity and class. As seen in the Windrush scandal, once people were identified as 'illegal, they also became deportable (De Genova & Roy, 2019). However, this situation was only made possible by the presence of the 'hostile environment', a series of policies introduced by the then Home Secretary Theresa May in 2012. The laws saw accountability pass from the state to ordinary people working in health, housing, education and employers who were all tasked with checking 'immigration status' and thus making every immigrant a suspect until they could prove otherwise (Younge, 2019, p. 10). Younge (2019, p. 10) said of the Windrush scandal:

> it was not a glitch in the system; it was the system (Younge, 2019, p. 10)

The next case study tells John's story and his economic migration for work.

━━━━━━━━━ **Case study** ━━━━━━━━━

John's story

In 1948, John arrived in England after responding to a UK Government recruitment campaign aimed at the former colonies of the British empire, inviting them to help rebuild Britain. Enabling his passage to England was the British Nationality Act of 1948 which permitted free movement of citizens to the United Kingdom from the British colonies. John, a veteran serviceman who fought for Britain in the RAF, in the Second World War saw this as an exciting opportunity to build a new life. However, on arrival into England he was met with hostility and overt racism-seeing signs in boarding house windows saying 'No Blacks, No Irish, No dogs'. Courageously, under such distressing circumstances he found work in the building trade, married and built a life for himself and his family, always putting back into society through voluntary work and civic engagement. However, five years ago, despite all the input that he had given to the UK economy, industry and community, he received orders from the British home office that he had no legal rights to remain in the UK unless he could prove otherwise. Without papers which he did not have he was deported back to a country which he had no ties with and hadn't lived in for over 60 years. The deportation meant that John was separated from his family at a time when he was old, in poor health and extremely vulnerable.

Retirement (Lifestyle) Migration

Research exploring retirement migration has historically been located within the disciplines of population geography, tourism and migration studies (King, 2000) with retirement migration theorises situated in the cultural turn where research becomes broader than concentrating on purely economic rational factors (King, 2002) and situates migration into the global perspective of systems and processes which impact migrants throughout their lives (King, 2012). Retirement migration research has over recent years focused on British retirement migration to European countries such as France (Benson, 2011); Spain (Ahmed, 2015); Portugal (Williams & Patterson, 1998); Malta (Warnes & Patterson, 1998); and Italy (King, 2012). Retirement migration is often motivated by the desire for a better lifestyle (Benson & O'Reilly, 2009) in a more favourable climate which facilitates greater freedom (Gilleard & Higgs, 2005) as is depicted in case study 2. Torres

(2012, p. 39) makes an important differentiation when observing retired migrants and categories them as 'those who migrate early in life and have aged as migrants; and those who migrate in old age'. Retirement migration is often associated with adults reaching the 'third age' (Gilleard & Higgs, 2005) where they are no longer have responsibilities of care-giving or paid work and can embrace 'individualism, consumption practices and experience of travel' (Ahmed, 2015, p. 37). However, such privilege is not afforded to many migrants, who often face social and economic disparity (Repetti, Phillipson, & Calasanti, 2018) Evidence also suggests that retired migrants encounter inequality in choice and constraint (Calasanti, 2003). In the next case study we observe the consequences of being without family ties when people migrate to another country and the decision to adopt legal residency in their host country, which then revokes access to state welfare in their native country. Indeed, research is now emerging of the difficulties facing working class people who have retired abroad. The following case study follows the later lives of two UK-born migrants who moved to Spain in their retirement.

■■■■■■■ Case study ■■■■■■■

Sheila's story

Sheila and her husband Ron both retired at the age of 56, having worked for many years in the hospitality industry. They sold their modest semi-detached house and used the proceeds of the sale to buy a house on the Costa del Sol, on mainland Spain. The couple described their new lifestyle as idyllic, as they enjoyed the warmer climate, cheaper cost of living and greater freedom. As the years advanced however, Ron's health began to deteriorate, and he was diagnosed with dementia. While the couple had enjoyed a good social network in Spain, they needed the security of having family around them, to help care for Ron. A problem presented itself at this point, as they had given up their legal right to residency in the UK some years before and had taken residence in Spain, as they had envisaged that they would live out their lives in Spain. Because of this they were no longer eligible to access UK healthcare or welfare support, facing the decision to return to the UK and pay for any treatment that Ron needs or stay in Spain in which case Sheila would be Ron's sole carer. The couple's financial resources are all tied up in their Spanish property and they now have minimal savings.

The UK Immigration Context

Discussing migration and mobility needs to be placed within a context: in this case within the UK immigration context. In the UK there has been a disturbing rise of right-wing groups, which publicise and practice an opposition to immigration, and engage in xenophobia, and nationalistic behaviour over the past decade. Such electoral and media pressure has been continually stoked by the radical right UKIP party and prompted the Conservative party to introduce new legislation to intentionally create a 'really hostile environment' for migrants (Kirkup & Winnett, 2012). Indeed, politicising immigration became the salient issue in the UK referendum to leave Europe in 2016, publicising the images of refugees crossing the border to access the UK welfare system, reflecting a colonialist stance which could control access to social and political rights through a hierarchical and racialised standpoint.

Following the EU referendum vote the UK saw an increase in hate crime by 15–20% (Carr, Clifton-Sprigg, James, & Vujic, 2020) which while shocking, is likely to be an underestimated figure as typically only half of these crimes are ever reported (Home Office, 2020). Indeed, the hate crime which was acted out on the streets of Britain could also be seen as a reflection of the anti-immigrant state racism which preceded it in the political battle to leave Europe (Burnett, 2016). The reality for migrants, crossing the border into the UK is that they face complex immigration rules, which have the ability to criminalise mobility, indefinitely detain individuals (Goodfellow, 2020) and deport people as criminals, without any judicial conviction (Griffiths, 2017). Deplorably, the Government's campaign called 'Operation Vaken' (Home Office, 2013) saw posters on vans displaying divisive messages stating 'Go home or face arrest' targeting London boroughs which were known to be ethnically diverse (Jones et al., 2017). Discrimination through legislation has also targeted ethnic minority communities through anti-terrorism legislation in the form of the CONTEST strategy (Home Office, 2011, 2018) a framework aimed at preventing radicalisation, but in reality, causing widespread Islamophobia and alienation (Abbas, 2019). Taking such a political stance, promotes the politics of othering and seeks to dehumanise and villainise migrants and particular ethnic groups so that they are seen as unworthy of aid (Looney, 2017).

Chapter summary

This chapter offers a discussion on the theoretical constructs and challenges of migration and mobility as well as highlighting the pressing impact of climate change. It tackles the following topics:

- Understanding mobilities and migration
- Forced migration
- Climate migration
- Economic migration
- Lifestyle migration
- Immigration in a UK context

Conclusion

The chapter has explored the complexities of migration and mobilities research, and the theories which categorise and explain the movement of people, resources and information. Ideas which cut across all types of migration and profoundly affect migrants experience is the rhetoric and popularity of right-wing parties who fuel opposition to immigration (Wodak, 2020). Evidence from the UK showed that when right-wing extremism is cited in conjunction with nationalism, this ideology is accompanied by a political philosophy that declares a doctrine that incites exclusion. This exclusion to refugees, climate migrants, or any other (im)migrant responding to resettlement due to a need, or through choice, becomes cited with nationalistic, racist and xenophobic discourse where exclusion is built through a difference to the nation, state, political system or culture (Carter, 2018). The recent global rise in right-wing extremism has drawn attention to right-wing doctrine which continues to contain racist and xenophobic discourse. Black Lives Matter, the Arab Spring, oppression of Rohingya Muslims and other key events over recent years have highlighted the social inequalities of some groups, but likewise aided the increase in right-wing extremist parties.

The calling for more support in discourse and ideologies that accommodate mobility – particularly in the shared climate crisis (see also Tacoli, 2009) is often founded and championed by groups dedicated to racial and climate issues. These groups reflect movements that bring together key players, individuals and communities, who are devoted to tackling anti-racist discourse, in the field of environmentalism, and are useful in addressing how race and racism fits in with concerns of social cohesion and integration that are linked to contemporary migration. This chapter also highlighted the need to change the migration narrative, decolonising how migrants are portrayed and socially constructed. This approach will draw attention to social inequalities and how environmental change impacts people's lives (Laczko & Piguet, 2014), adopting frameworks and models which take a critical and analytical stance, such as critical race theory.

The chapter has discussed the increasing impact of climate change and the likely affects to population distribution and mobility.While, the climate change agenda has been part of a societal discourse for decades, there has been a more recent focus on social responsibility (Daniels & Endfield, 2009). As an issue of global importance, experts, activists, researchers and policymakers are becoming progressively more concerned with the limited social response and impact (Piguet, Pécoud, & De Guchteneire, 2011; Stehr & Hans von Storch, 1995). Concerns continually rise for the reality and urgency of the global impact and threat of long-term extinction, alongside the effects of forced migration and movement that are a result of these extreme climate changes (Brown, 2008; Piguet et al., 2011). We have also shown how mobility and migration are frequently the consequences of key responses to environmental and non-environmental transformations and pressures (Tacoli, 2009), or as Upadhyay and Mohan (2017) noted earlier they are also key response to reduce the risk of household vulnerability when facing changes in the climate.

Questions to Reflect Upon

- Consider the consequential impacts of UK immigration policy and how this policy aligns (or conflicts) with overarching policies on human rights.
- Consider how and what changes to political policy and planning would have a positive impact on climate change and climate migration.
- How did the UK immigration laws change so radically, to remove citizenship for commonwealth members?

- The case studies portray different migration stories and highlight the challenges which people face. Consider how immigration policy impacts migrant's everyday lives, opportunities and futures.

Further Reading

Ahmed, A. (2015). *Retiring to Spain: Women's narratives of Nostalgia, belonging and community*. Policy Press. (This book offers a critical perspective of retirement migration, allowing the reader to see the practical and emotional challenges as they are experienced by working class women from the UK who retired to Spain.)

Bakewell, O. (2010). Some reflections on structure and agency in migration theory. *Journal of Ethnic and Migration Studies, 36*(10), 1689–1708. (Oliver Bakewell's paper explores migration theory and observes how it fits with the complex relationship between structure and agency. Bakewell highlights the benefits of adopting a critical realism approach which offers a better analysis of structure and agency within the context of migration.)

De Genova, N., & Roy, A. (2019). Practices of illegalization. *Antipode: A Radical Journal of Geography, 52*(2), 352–364. Houston: University of Houston. (This paper provides an historical and contemporary look at how migrants are impacted by the practices of illegalisation. It observes the political and legal landscapes and how such practices are impacting the most vulnerable section of society.)

Piguet, E., & Laczko, F. (Eds.). People on the move in a changing climate. *Global migration issues* (Vol. 2). Dordrecht: Springer (This book's central theme is the impact of environmental change on migration and explores existing research on migration and the environment at the regional level. By doing so Piquet and Laczko offer a different view of climate migration, and allow students to study evidence presented by leading regional experts.)

References

Abbas, T. (2019). Islamophobia as the hidden hand of structural and cultural racism. In I. Zempi & I. Awan (Eds.), *The Routledge international handbook of Islamophobia* (pp. 32–41). London: Routledge.

Adey, P., Bissell, D., Hannam, K., Merriman, P., & Sheller, M. (2014). *The handbook of mobilities*. Routledge.

Ahmed, A. (2015). *Retiring to Spain: Women's narratives of nostalgia, belonging and community*. Policy Press.

Ajzen, I. (1991). The theory of planned behavior. *Organizational Behavior and Human Decision Processes, 50*(2), 179–211.

Bakewell, O. (2010). Some reflections on structure and agency in migration theory. *Journal of Ethnic and Migration Studies, 36*(10), 1689–1708.

Benson, M. (2011). *The British in rural France: Lifestyle migration and the ongoing quest for a better way of life*. Manchester: Manchester University Press.

Benson, M., & O'Reilly, K. (2009). Migration and the search for a better way of life: A critical exploration of lifestyle migration. *The Sociological Review, 57*(4), 608–625.

Brown, O. (2008). *Migration and climate change*. United Nations.

Burnett, J. (2016). *Racial violence and the Brexit state*. London: Institute for Race Relations. Retrieved 22 February 2022 from http://www.irr.org.uk/app/uploads/2016/11/Racial-violence-and-the-Brexit-state-final.pdf

Calasanti, T. (2003). Theorizing age relations. In S. Biggs, A. Lawenstein, & K. Hendricks (Eds.), *The need of theory: Critical approaches to social gerontology* (pp. 199–218). Amitzville, NY: Baywood.

Carr, J., Clifton-Sprigg, J., James, J., & Vujic, S. (2020). *Love thy neighbour? Brexit and hate crime (No. 13902)*. IZA Discussion Papers.

Carter, E. (2018). Right-wing extremism/radicalism: Reconstructing the concept. *Journal of Political Ideologies, 23*(2), 157–182.

Castles, S. (2003). Towards a sociology of forced migration and social transformation. *Sociology, 37*(1), 13–34.

Chen, Y. Y. (2020). Decolonizing methodologies, situated resilience, and country: Insights from Tayal country, Taiwan. *Sustainability, 12*(22), 9751.

Crisp, J., & Long, K. (2016). Safe and voluntary refugee repatriation: From principle to practice. *Journal on Migration and Human Security, 4*(3), 141–147.

Daniels, S., & Endfield, G. H. (2009). Narratives of climate change: Introduction. *Journal of Historical Geography, 35*(2), 215–222.

De Genova (2002). Migrant illegality and deportability in everyday life. *Annual Review of Anthropology* (Vol. 31, pp. 419–447). New York, NY: Columbia University.

De Genova, N., & Roy, A. (2019). Practices of illegalization. *Antipode: A Radical Journal of Geography, 52*(2), 352–264. Houston: University of Houston.

Domínguez, L., & Luoma, C. (2020). Decolonising conservation policy: How colonial land and conservation ideologies persist and perpetuate indigenous injustices at the expense of the environment. *Land, 9*(3), 65.

Ellis- Petersen, H., & Azizur Rahman, S. (2018). *UN criticises Rohingya deal between Myanmar and Bangladesh*. Retrieved from www.theguardian.com/world/2018/oct/31/un-criticisesrohingya-deal-between-myanmar-and-Bangladesh

Faist, T., & Schade, J. (2013). *Disentangling migration and climate change*. Dordrecht: Springer.

Foxen, P. (2021). Forced migration. In D. Bhugra (Ed.), *Oxford textbook of migrant psychiatry* (p. 171). Oxford: Oxford University Press.

Geoffroy, C., & Sibley, R. (Eds.). (2009). *Going abroad: Travel, tourism, and migration. Cross-cultural perspectives on mobility*. Newcastle upon Tyne: Cambridge Scholars Publishing.

Giddens, A. (1989). A reply to my critics. In D. Held & J. B. Thompson (Eds.), *Social theories of modern societies: Anthony Giddens and his critics*. Cambridge: Cambridge University Press.

Gilleard, C., & Higgs, P. (2005). *Contexts of ageing: Class, cohort and community*. Cambridge: Polity Press.

Goodfellow, M. (2020). *Hostile environment: How immigrants became scapegoats*. New York, NY: Verso Books.

Gram-Hanssen, I., Schafenacker, N., & Bentz, J. (2021). Decolonizing transformations through 'right relations'. *Sustainability Science, 7*(2), 673–685.

Griffiths, M. (2017). The changing politics of time in the UK's immigration system. In E. Mavroudi, B. Page, & A. Christou (Eds.), *Timespace and international migration*. Edward Elgar Publishing.

Home Office. (2011). *Contest the United Kingdom's strategy for countering terrorism*. Retrieved 22 February 2022 from https://assets.publishing.service.gov.uk/government/uploads/system/uploads/attachment_data/file/97995/strategy-contest.pdf

Home Office. (2013). *Operation vaken evaluation report October 2013*. London: Home Office. Retrieved 22 February 2022 from https://www.gov.uk/government/uploads/system/uploads/attachment_data/file/254411/Operation_Vaken_Evaluation_Report.pdf

Home Office. (2018). *Contest the United Kingdom's strategy for countering terrorism*. Retrieved 22 February 2022 from https://assets.publishing.service.gov.uk/government/uploads/system/uploads/attachment_data/file/716907/140618_CCS207_CCS0218929798-1_CONTEST_3.0_WEB.pdf

Home Office. (2020). *Hate crime, England and Wales, 2019 to 2020*. Retrieved from https://www.gov.uk/government/statistics/hate-crime-england-and-wales-2019-to-2020/hate-crime-england-and-wales-2019-to-2020

Içduygu, A., & Nimer, M. (2020). The politics of return: Exploring the future of Syrian refugees in Jordan, Lebanon and Turkey. *Third World Quarterly*, *41*(3), 415–433.

International Organization for Migration. (2020). *World migration report 2020*. Retrieved from https://www.un.org/sites/un2.un.org/files/wmr_2020.pdf

Johnson, D. E., Parsons, M., & Fisher, K. (2021). Indigenous climate change adaptation: New directions for emerging scholarship. *Environment and Planning E: Nature and Space*. Doi: 10.1177/25148486211022450.

Jones, H., Gunaratnam, Y., Bhattacharyya, G., Davies, W., Dhaliwal, S., Jackson, E., & Saltus, R. (2017). Living research five: Public anger in research (and social media). In H. Jones, Y. Gunaratnam, G. Bhattacharyya, W. Davies, S. Dhaliwal, K. Forkert ... R. Saltus (Eds.), *Go home?: The politics of immigration controversies* (pp. 141–147). Manchester University Press.

King, R. (2000). Southern Europe in the changing global map of migration. In *Eldorado or fortress? Migration in southern Europe* (pp. 3–26). London: Palgrave Macmillan.

King, R. (2002). Towards a new map of European migration. *International Journal of Population Geography*, *8*(2), 89–106.

King, R. (2012). Geography and migration studies: Retrospect and prospect. *Population, Space and Place*, *18*(2), 134–153.

Kirkup, J., & Winnett, R. (2012). Theresa may interview: 'We're going to give illegal migrants a really hostile reception'. *The Telegraph*, *25*(05). Retrieved from www.telegraph.co.uk/news/uknews/immigration/9291483/Theresa-May-interview-Were-going-to-give-illegalmigrants-a-really-hostile-reception.html

Laczko, F., & Piguet, E. (2014). Regional perspectives on migration, the environment and climate change. In E. Piguet & F. Laczko (Eds.), *People on the move in a changing climate. Global migration issues* (Vol. *2*). Dordrecht: Springer. doi:10.1007/978-94-007-6985-4_1

Looney, S. (2017). *Breaking point? An examination of the politics of othering in Brexit Britain*. An examination of the politics of othering in Brexit Britain (28 April 2017). TLI Think.

Massey, D. S., Arango, J., Hugo, G., Kouaouci, A., & Pellegrino, A. (1998). *Worlds in motion: Understanding international migration at the end of the millennium*. Oxford: Clarendon Press.

McLeman, R. (2018). Thresholds in climate migration. *Population and Environment*, *39*(4), 319–338.

McLeman, R., & Smit, B. (2006). Migration as an adaptation to climate change. *Climatic Change*, *76*(1), 31–53.

Nagy, R., & Korpela, M. (2013). Introduction: Limitations to temporary mobility. *International Review of Social Research*, *3*(1), 1–6.

de Noronha, L. (2019). Deportation, racism and multi-status Britain: Immigration control and the production of race in the present. *Ethnic and Racial Studies*, *42*(14), 2413–2430.

O'Reilly, K. (2012). *International migration and social theory*. London: Macmillan International Higher Education.

Ohnmacht, T., Maksim, H., & Bergman, M. M. (Eds.). (2009). *Mobilities and inequality*. Hampshire: Ashgate Publishing Ltd.

Piguet, E., & Laczko, F. (2014). *People on the move in a changing climate: The regional impact of environmental change on migration*. Springer Netherlands. doi:10.1007/978-94-007-6985-4

Piguet, E., Pécoud, A., & De Guchteneire, P. (2011). Migration and climate change: An overview. *Refugee Survey Quarterly*, *30*(3), 1–23.

Rajan, S. I., & Bhagat, R. B. (Eds.). (2017). *Climate change, vulnerability and migration*. Oxford: Taylor & Francis.

Ravenstein, E. (1889). The laws of migration. *Royal Statistical Society*, *52*, 241–305.

Repetti, M., Phillipson, C., & Calasanti, T. (2018). Retirement migration in Europe: A choice for a better life? *Sociological Research Online*, *23*(4), 780–794.

Ritchie, J. (2020). Movement from the margins to global recognition: Climate change activism by young people and in particular indigenous youth. *International Studies in Sociology of Education*, *30*(1–2), 53–72.

Sheller, M. (2014). The new mobilities paradigm for a live sociology. *Current Sociology*, *62*(6), 789–811.

Song, S. (2018). Political theories of migration. *Annual Review of Political Science*, *21*, 385–402.

Stehr, N., & Von Storch, H. (1995). The social construct of climate and climate change. *Climate Research*, *5*(2), 99–105.

Tacoli, C. (2009). Crisis or adaptation? Migration and climate change in a context of high mobility. *Environment and Urbanization*, *21*(2), 513–525.

Torres, S. (2012). International migration: Patterns and implications for exclusion in old age. In *From exclusion to inclusion in old age: A global challenge* (pp. 33–49). Bristol: Policy Press.

United Nations High Commissioner for Refugees. (2020). *Global trends: Forced displacement in 2019*. Technical report statistics and demographics section of UNHCR global data service. Copenhagen. Retrieved from https://www.unhcr.org/5ee200e37.pdf

United Nations Population Fund. (2000). *UNFPA annual report 2000*. Retrieved 23rd February 2022, from https://www.unfpa.org/sites/default/files/pub-pdf/annual_report00_eng.pdf

Upadhyay, H., & Mohan, D. (2017). Migrating to adapt? Exploring the climate change, migration and adaptation nexus. In S. I. Rajan & R. B. Bhagat (Eds.), *Climate change, vulnerability and migration*. Oxford: Taylor & Francis.

Urry, J. (2012). *Sociology beyond societies: Mobilities for the twenty-first century*. Oxford: Routledge.

Warnes, A. M., & Patterson, G. (1998). British retirees in Malta: Components of the cross-national relationship. *International Journal of Population Geography*, *4*(2), 113–133.

Williams, A. M., & Patterson, G. (1998). 'An empire lost but a province gained': A cohort analysis of British international retirement in the Algarve. *International Journal of Population Geography*, *4*(2), 135–155.

Wodak, R. (2020). The trajectory of far-right populism – A discourse-analytical perspective. In B. Forchtner (Ed.), *The far right and the environment politics, discourse and communication* (pp. 21–37). New York, NY: Routledge.

Wood, D. M., & Graham, S. (2006). Permeable boundaries in the software-sorted society: Surveillance and differentiations of mobility. In M. Sheller & J. Urry (Eds.), *Mobile technologies of the city* (pp. 185–199). London: Routledge.

Younge, G. (2019). The politics of identity: From potential to pitfalls, and symbols to substance. *Identities*, *26*(1), 1–11.

10

NEOLIBERALISM, HEGEMONY AND GOVERNMENT RESPONSES TO SOCIAL INEQUALITY IN THE UK

Steve Iafrati

═══════════ Learning objectives ═══════════

- To recognise the diversity of inequality.
- To explore the role of government in relation to causes and outcomes of inequality.
- To reflect on the way in which neoliberalism and small government limit the willingness and ability of government to tackle inequality.
- To understand a hegemony that privileges agency over structure in the explanation of inequality.

━━━━━━━━━━ **Framing questions** ━━━━━━━━━━

- In what ways is it possible to recognise intersectionality within patterns of inequality?
- Should governments concentrate their efforts of tackling the causes or mitigating the outcomes of inequality?
- In what ways has the role of governments changed in terms of welfare?
- To what extent are there popular beliefs and narratives regarding those experiencing inequality?

Introduction

During the last decade, debate within Social Policy has featured an increased focus on inequality and crises within welfare provision (Taylor-Gooby, 2016, 2017). Recognition of a housing crisis (Iafrati, 2020, 2021; Stephens & Stephenson, 2016), the impact of recession and Welfare Reforms (Farnsworth, 2020; Heins & Bennett, 2018; Dowler & Lambie-Muford, 2015), challenges in health and social care provision (Glasby, Zhang, Bennett, & Hall, 2021; Powell, 2019) and increasing poverty (Bourquin, Joyce, & Norris Keiller, 2020; Francis-Devine, 2021; JRF, 2021) have framed such discussions within the UK. However, social inequalities are broader than our relationship to the economy and services. The Black Lives Matter movement, most prominently, has highlighted racial inequalities within contemporary society and this has significant implications for Social Policy, though there is a need for further research on this topic in the UK (Joseph-Salisbury, Connelly, & Wangari-Jones, 2021).

A starting point of this chapter is to recognise that inequality should not be understood as a random phenomenon that can affect the lives of anyone as if by lottery. Neither should patterns of inequality, poverty and social injustice be understood through narratives of welfare recipients 'sleeping off a life on benefits', as the then Chancellor of the Exchequer, George Osborne, stated at the Conservative party conference in 2012 as he heralded a new era of welfare reform. Instead, evidence shows that certain groups of people are more likely to experience the effects of inequality and also that certain geographical areas and neighbourhoods can be characterised by higher-than-average levels of inequality and poverty. On a thematic level, this includes Black and Minoritised workers, single parents, new arrivals to the UK, as well as vulnerable groups such as those facing mental health challenges, people with disabilities, those leaving institutionalised care, and survivors of domestic abuse. On a geographic level, certain areas of Britain have lower levels of economic growth and more pronounced patterns of persistent poverty (Francis-Devine, 2022a).

The persistent nature of these patterns of inequality suggest that they are caused by structural factors, in other words, the causes of inequality lie beyond the choices and agency of individuals. In this context, structural factors might include discrimination, precarious employment and in-work poverty, as well as the residualisation of welfare. This is not to say that people experiencing inequality have no agency or that poverty and inequality are inescapable, but such escapees are anomalous. Evidence on social mobility demonstrates that poverty and inequality are not only difficult to escape, but that the impact of COVID has exacerbated this situation (Social Mobility Commission, 2021). It is also important to remember that in addition to the personal costs of poverty and inequality, there is also a social cost, in other words, a cost that is borne by all of society.

On a financial level, this might be the increased cost of healthcare and other interventions for those that are homeless (Leng, 2017) or the long-term impacts of child poverty (Hirsch, 2021). For those geographies characterised by concentrations of low-income levels (Harari, 2018 for pre-COVID data), there will be lower levels of economic growth and, possibly, greater impact of economic shocks. Meanwhile, regarding the social cost of discrimination and marginalisation, it is the cost of a divided society where sections increasingly feel disconnected. Importantly, for this chapter, it is both personal and social costs that justifies government intervention to tackle the causes and mitigate the outcomes of inequality. To this end, the history of the modern welfare state that emerged after the Second World War was built on the premise of the five giants, by definition structural inequalities, that were a threat to a fair and prosperous society. The role of government in tackling such inequalities rested on their financial and legal powers to enact change. This chapter will recognise the role of neoliberalism and austerity as key areas where governments have walked away from such commitments in recent years.

When examining the nature of inequality, it is also important to recognise intersectionality in order to move 'an understanding of the axes of power away from the class-capital binary towards the complex interrelations of gender, race and class in the context of a patriarchal and post-colonial capitalism' (Williams, 2016, p. 630). Intersectionality remains a relatively underused concept in Social Policy but is important in understanding the way in which people face multiple barriers and challenges that may shape their experiences of inequality.

Furthermore, when understanding inequality and intersectionality, it is important to recognise inequality as a dynamic process that exists in the context of social, economic and policy determinants. Consequently, as these factors change, so does the extent and composition of inequality. Understanding inequality as a process therefore identifies a context that, at its most basic, includes (i) causes, (ii) experiences and (iii) mitigation. From a Social Policy perspective, the process identifies a key role for government, which is to address causes and mitigate outcomes. This identifies a pre-emptive role for government to put in place measures that prevent inequality occurring, or at least limiting the extent to which inequality does occur. Additionally, mitigation of inequality involves governments operating in a responsive manner to counteract the impacts of inequality once they have come to the fore, such as the disproportionate health impacts from COVID-19.

Social Policy, Ideology and Social Inequality

Within the discipline of Social Policy, inequality has traditionally been defined in terms of the unequal distribution of rewards and resources, though it is also important to recognise the unequal distribution of opportunities and the barriers that people face. Consequently, while inequality might be defined in terms of economic resources, it should also include social factors. Furthermore, it is important for Social Policy to look not only at the indicators of inequality, but also to study the causes and outcomes. In doing so, this recognises opportunities, though not always taken, for government to intervene to address the causes and mitigate the outcomes of inequality in society.

However, since the early-2000s and more explicitly since 2010, the increasing influence of neoliberalism has underpinned a reticence within government to reduce inequality. This has taken place under the banner of committing to a small state, characterised by reduced public spending, less commitment to welfare and an ideological shift in terms of the government's appetite to tackle inequalities (Farnsworth & Irving, 2012; Whitworth, 2016). In many respects, the notion of small government, while used in a somewhat sweeping and nebulous manner by politicians as well as possibly even within Social Policy debates, typifies a government vision of less regulation and individuals taking greater responsibility for their own wellbeing. However, the notion of small state might be questioned on an objective level as the government still retains the same power to influence, has a growing level of taxation, and has broadly similar levels of expenditure (Brien, 2020; Zaranko, 2020). As such, it might be more accurate to understand the concept of small government as being shorthand for a retreat from commitments to reduce inequality. In doing so, this retreat from addressing inequality within a contemporary neoliberal political context positions hegemony as an important concept in understanding government approaches to inequality (Crehan, 2016; Donoghue, 2018; Wiggan, 2012).

Importantly, the concept of neoliberalism should not lead to the development of binary analyses whereby governments are positioned as simply being either neoliberal or not neoliberal. Instead, neoliberalism covers a broad ideology, to which governments may aspire to varying degrees. At its most basic, neoliberalism rests on the twin goals of unfettered market forces and a faith in small government, the latter of which includes welfare provision. In this respect, all governments have a faith in market forces and all governments continue to provide state welfare. The issue is the extent to which this is the case, which can be compared with the extent to which governments are prepared to moderate market forces to limit inequality and the extent to which they are prepared to fund welfare to mitigate inequalities. Since 2010, it can be argued that British governments have become increasingly neoliberal as the commitment to mitigate inequality through welfare has receded.

At the same time, there has been a distinctive political narrative centred upon populist, though inaccurate, perceptions of welfare recipients. Language by politicians, as seen above, has featured a consistent message of welfare recipients being scroungers within a binary of 'workers and shirkers' or 'strivers and skivers' (Hills, 2017). This overlooks the fact that most working age benefits go to households that have at least one member in employment. This demonisation of welfare recipients has been further perpetuated through media sources such as newspaper headlines and television programmes characterised as 'poverty porn' (Jensen, 2014). Importantly, it is this 'common sense' narrative and assumptions that provide populist electoral support for increasing neoliberalism and, as such, constitutes what can be defined as hegemony.

Evidence suggests that the UK is witnessing growing social inequality, perhaps most clearly evident in the growing levels of poverty experienced by many households that find themselves increasingly in need of welfare (Joseph Rowntree Foundation, 2021). Yet, this comes as a time when crises in welfare have become more entrenched and, potentially, reflect an ongoing and established residualisation of welfare (Dwyer & Wright, 2014). However, the impact of Welfare Reform and residualisation should not be seen as indiscriminate or evenly shared throughout the population. It is perhaps obvious to suggest that experiencing the most negative outcomes of Welfare Reform will be those in need of welfare, which are those on lowest incomes. However, with unemployment rates and poverty rates being disproportionately high within the Black and Minoritised population, it can be assumed that a disproportionate number of people of colour will be negatively affected. As an illustration, unemployment for Oct–Dec 2019 before the COVID-19 lockdown and recession for white people was 3.4%, while for those of Pakistani ethnicity it was 7.7% and for Black African/Caribbean/British it was 8.7%. Twelve months later in Oct–Dec 2020 when the impact of recession was palpable, the rates had disproportionately increased to 4.5%, 9.7% and 13.8% respectively (Francis-Devine, 2021) (Figure 10.1).

For some groups such as young Black men and Bangladeshi women, the figures are considerably higher. Similarly, the Social Metrics Commission (2020) found that 50% of Black households were living in poverty compared with 20% of white households while the government's race disparity audit found similar patterns in relation to persistent poverty (Cabinet Office, 2017). Similar patterns exist for those with disabilities, single parents and other vulnerable groups. It might, therefore, be easy to presume that welfare reforms and residualisation will affect all people on low incomes in a sweeping and similar manner. However, what is seen is that a government retreat from mitigating poverty and inequality through welfare provision, as well as being part of a broader drift

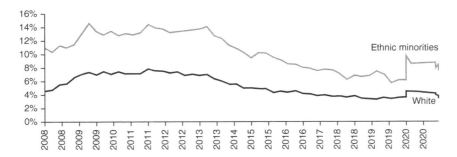

Figure 10.1 Unemployment Rate by Ethnic Background: UK 2008–2021 (Francis-Devine, 2022b)

towards neoliberalism, multiplies inequalities experienced by those groups already economically disadvantaged. It can be expected that this would be a similar picture for other vulnerable groups that are over-represented in those requiring welfare.

Against this background, the COVID-19 pandemic, alongside its economic impacts, exposed the fragility of some people's connections to economic and social inclusion in the context of what has been termed resilience (Bambra, Lynch, & Smith, 2021; Dagdeviren, Donoghue, & Promberger, 2015; Donoghue & Edmiston, 2020). However, it would be wrong to assume that the pandemic created such inequalities. Instead, the pandemic merely exposed and exacerbated the fissures within Britain's economy and society; it had, in effect, a multiplier effect on inequality. While inequalities in contemporary society may be evidenced in economic measures such as growing poverty (Joseph Rowntree Foundation, 2021) and the impact of Welfare Reforms, it is, as mentioned previously, important to recognise that inequality extends beyond economic indicators to include social inequalities. The Black Lives Matters (BLM) movement, for example, highlighted the presence of racial inequalities and discrimination, thereby recognising the importance of social inequalities that may ultimately contribute to economic inequalities. Looking at experiences such as the Grenfell Tower tragedy, policing, the Windrush scandal and the unequal impacts of the COVID-19 pandemic (see case study below), it is clear that inequalities extend beyond economic parameters (Joseph-Salisbury et al., 2021) and that this needs to be a core element of research within Social Policy. In this respect, it is possible to identify inequalities explained in both economic and social dimensions, and while the evidence of the two may be distinct, it is also important to remember how they might overlap and reinforce.

Inequality in UK Society

The aim of this section is not to provide a definitive record of measures of inequality as there exists wide-ranging evidence elsewhere (Byrne, Alexander, Khan, Naroo, & Shankley, 2020; Johnson, Joyce, & Platt, 2021; Shildrick, 2018; Szreter, 2021) as well as through agencies such as the Resolution Foundation, Institute for Fiscal Studies and the Social Mobility Commission. Instead, here the chapter will interrogate the multi-faceted nature of social inequalities. Inequality in terms of Social Policy encompasses a broad range of different peoples and experiences that can be grouped together through shared barriers and challenges. A great deal of Social Policy research has focused on economic inequalities and the outcomes of such inequalities, especially considering austerity and post-recession (Edmiston, 2018; Grover, 2019; Irving, 2021). However, while such research and literature are vital, it is also important to understand inequality in relation to broader non-economic factors such as discrimination in areas including ethnicity and structural racism.

The study of economic inequalities has been a bedrock of Social Policy debate for many years, going all the way back to Rowntree's study of poverty first published in 1901 and the pioneering work of the Webbs that laid the foundations for the discipline of Social Policy in the early 20th century (Knight, 2017). In many respects, this reflects the visibility and relative ease of quantifying economic inequalities. Continuing this trend, one of the key areas of focus in Social Policy during the last decade has been on increasing poverty and the growing welfare residualisation and conditionality based on 'assumptions made by the neoliberal-inspired underclass and workfare discourses' (Carey & Bell, 2020, p. 191). Alongside the impact of Welfare Reforms sits the rise in precarious employment such as zero-hour contracts, gig economy work and underemployment, which also have racialised and gendered dimensions. It has been argued that a growth in precarious work is a key element of neoliberalism in the way it 'equates marketization with the furtherance of human freedom and individual choice' (Kalleberg & Vallas, 2018, p. 8). Alongside the increase in precarious working has been the impact of welfare residualisation (Patrick, 2014) and increased conditionality and sanctions (Reeves & Loopstra, 2017; Watts & Fitzpatrick, 2018; Wright & Patrick, 2019) based on ideology and a hegemony of 'welfare dependency' (Roberts, 2017).

■■■ Case study 1 ■■■

Not all in this together

The COVID-19 pandemic in 2020/21 was a difficult time for many people in Britain in terms of personal bereavement, job losses and the experience of recession. It was portrayed as a time for the nation to come together through doorstep clapping, the celebration of Captain Tom Moore and recognition of the value of community support. At the same time, the Government was praised for its response to the pandemic in terms of the vaccination rollout and the furlough payments. In such times, it is tempting to think that we are all in this together. However, the uncomfortable truth is that the pandemic exposed the intersection of inequalities in race and class. People of colour were over twice as likely to die from COVID-19 compared with the white British population, with those of Black African descent being 3.5 times as likely to die. The first eleven doctors to die of COVID-19 were all people of colour (Otu, Opoku Ahinkorah, Kwabena Ameyaw, Seidu, & Yaya, 2020). However, the disproportionate impact of COVID-19 on the Black and Minoritised population was not due to genetic differences or the impact of other diseases such as diabetes. Instead, it was driven by the increased likelihood of people of colour working in frontline jobs (Otu et al., 2020) and the structural institutionalised racism linked to housing and employment (Patel, Kapoor, & Treloar, 2020). Cuts to local authority public health budgets have been significantly higher in the most ethnically diverse areas (Patel et al., 2020). Without recognising entrenched and institutional racism as a driver of inequalities exposed by the COVID-19 pandemic, it is argued that government responses will 'risk further increasing ethnic inequalities in the UK' (Nazroo & Becares, 2021). However, the government has failed to recognise or address the inequalities exposed by COVID-19 as the government narrative continues to be based on a one-nation vision. In reality, as defined later in this chapter, COVID-19 did not create these inequalities but instead, the inequality of outcomes based on race and class reflects what can be seen as a two-nation Britain.

Neoliberal Responses to Inequality

At the heart of this chapter is an emphasis on understanding government responses to inequality within a context of political economy, which means understanding inequality in relation to both causes and mitigation. As mentioned previously, these are two distinct areas where the government has opportunities to intervene, with the first being to prevent inequalities and the second being to mitigate inequalities once they have emerged. This section proceeds by looking at the political context within which this takes place.

Placing this within a political context, government approaches to inequality have been increasingly framed within a commitment to small government to encourage personal responsibility that can be recognised as increasingly neoliberal (Farnsworth & Irving, 2018), which have contributed to increasing inequality (Ishkanian, 2019). Within this position, neoliberalism is understood to include a governmental retreat from delivering key services such as welfare, leaving voluntary and community organisations to 'enthusiastically, but ineffectually, attempt to mop up the consequences' (Crisp, 2015, p. 3) of austerity, welfare retrenchment and uneven economic development. This was characterised in the early years of the Coalition government 2010–2015 in the language of Big Society as a way of emphasising a positive vision and the 'problematisation of the welfare state' (Deeming, 2016). More recently, the government's explicit rhetoric and vision of neoliberalism through welfare retrenchment and austerity has subsided as a new stability has taken root. Entrenched in a concern regarding what the government has termed 'welfare dependency' at the heart of approaches to addressing causes of inequality, there is a central ideological belief in the agency of individuals and the role of 'bad lifestyle choices' (Patrick, 2014). This agential understanding of the causes of inequality implicitly rests on the assumption that everyone operates on a level playing field of opportunity based on a moral obligation of work and personal responsibility as a way for people to address their own inequalities (McEnhill & Taylor-Gooby, 2018).

However as is frequently the way with unchallenged assumptions, the reality and evidence paint a different picture. Importantly, for debate within Social Policy, it is necessary to go beyond the data and the outcomes by identifying what, initially, allows us to see a political economy of inequality. To this end, narratives of inequality are perpetuated by 'common sense' (Crehan, 2016) articulations and assumptions of deserving and underserving inequality that fails to recognise the needs of the most vulnerable. This shifts responsibility for addressing inequality away from the government and by default on to the individual. Within this agential understanding of inequality, which absolves the government of responsibility, inequality is portrayed as a personal failing based on bad lifestyle decisions rather than failings of the economy and experiences of discrimination. As such, populist assumptions of 'welfare dependency' (Reeve, 2017; Roberts, 2017) among an 'undeserving poor' (Price, Barons, Garthwaite, & Jolly, 2020) underpins a new hegemony of inequality that can be situated in what has been termed 'late-neoliberalism' (McGimpsey, 2017) as a useful demarcation from the approach to inequality taken in the 1980s. Undoubtedly, the process of 'late-neoliberalism' has accelerated since 2010.

The synthesis of political rhetoric regarding inequality and 'welfare dependency' alongside the narratives of moral panic whereby certain groups of people 'become defined as a threat to societal values or interests' (Cohen, 1972, p. 28) is reinforced by 'poverty porn' and media headlines of 'scroungers' (Beresford, 2016; Garthwaite, 2016; Morrison, 2019; Paterson, Coffey-Glover, & Peplow, 2016) that enable the public to abuse welfare recipients and politicians to evidence the shortcomings of Government intervention (Raisborough, Ogden, & Stone de Guzman, 2019). This reflects what might be termed a 'common sense' understanding of the presence of a problem, though common sense is not used here to indicate practical knowledge or an informed understanding of reality. Instead, it indicates part of hegemony (Bocock, 1986; Simon, 1982) with 'popular knowledge [...] and understandings' that are 'crudely neophobe and conservative' (Crehan, 2016). In this respect, it is possible to situate 'common sense' as shared dominant beliefs and populist sentiments in society that, while neither grounded in evidence nor beneficial outcomes, form a prevailing narrative of popularly accepted beliefs. In the respect of this chapter, hegemony includes consensual and popularly accepted explanations of inequality and the role of government. However, the connection of common sense narratives and hegemony with inequality should be understood as extending beyond welfare and economic determinants to also include citizenship and inclusion.

Within this new hegemony of inequality, structural causes of inequality have been disparaged and the new language of blame is based on an agential understanding of the causes of inequality. In Social Policy, this hegemony centres on a binary of those doing the right thing and those making bad lifestyle choices. In doing so, Lavery (2018) identifies the formation of a 'two nation' strategy that uses a 'moralised antagonism' to secure support for welfare retrenchment by casting those in poverty (and presumably other areas of inequality) as a 'subordinate group' that are fundamentally problematic. This has enabled a level of popular consent for government approaches to inequality that lies at the heart of understanding hegemony as a way of using 'common sense' assumptions (Crehan, 2016) in order to secure popular support and maintain policy approaches. The concept of hegemony remains a relatively under-used concept within Social Policy despite its appropriateness for understanding how political ideology and policies are based on popular support and consensus. Hegemony is also an important concept in Social Policy to develop a critical understanding of how inequalities persist and also taking explanations beyond seeing economic determinants as the sole cause of inequality.

Discussion

Returning to the core argument of this chapter, the government has significant opportunity and influence to intervene to address inequality. In this respect, it is possible to see that governments can intervene to prevent inequality arising and also to mitigate the impacts of inequality once they have occurred. However, during the last 15 years, and more so since 2010, governments have chosen not to use the opportunities that are available to them. This is not because government has any less power or potential influence, and neither is it because of economic nor other constraints. Instead, the reduced willingness of governments to intervene to address inequalities is an ideological decision. Understanding the nature of this political standpoint, it is possible to see that governments have become increasingly neoliberal. This neoliberalism, or late-neoliberalism, has been couched in terms of small government. However, it is possible to critique this concept as government is, arguably, no smaller now than it was 20 to 30 years ago. Instead, the concept of small government can be seen as shorthand for a retreat from wanting to address inequality. This represents a changing role for government and a retreat from the fundamental (in theory) role of government to intervene to offset inequalities.

However, inequality should not be seen solely in terms of economic determinants. With potentially disparate groups of people being connected through shared barriers and challenges, it is important for Social Policy to recognise the experiences of those affected by discrimination and inequality. As such, it is essential to recognise intersectionality. In this chapter, intersectionality has been used to recognise how inequality can be understood in terms of multiple barriers and challenges that people may face. It has also been recognised that intersectionality can be about the way in which economic and social aspects of inequality overlap. For example, discrimination against particular groups might also impact on economic experiences of work or areas such as health, which will also impact on economic wellbeing.

Additionally, this chapter has highlighted how inequality can be understood not only as a set of measures that illustrates a snapshot in time but instead as a process. This involves understanding the causes, the experiences, and the outcomes of inequality. Not only does this allow for analysis of how inequality arises and its impacts, but it also creates an opportunity to understand how these factors are dynamic and change over time. From a Social Policy perspective, it also allows for recognition of how governments have opportunities to intervene to address the causes and mitigate the outcomes. The extent to which government chooses to intervene, however, is largely based on political ideology, with increasing neoliberalism in recent governments shaping a growing reticence to intervene. Partly this is because of the way in which inequality is understood by governments as being caused by individual choices, which in turn makes governments believe that intervention is counterproductive if it only enables people to carry on making the same choices and will create further dependency. Problematically, this not only absolves government from taking responsibility to mitigate inequality, but it also overlooks the role of government in the creation of inequality. However, the extent to which government intervenes has also increasingly been shaped by a commitment to small government, which is an overarching understanding of the role of government in our lives.

Ultimately, this chapter has argued that a drift towards neoliberalism leads to greater levels of inequality as the government relinquishes its ability to both prevent and mitigate inequalities. Problematically, this is more alarming for certain groups of people who are most likely to be disadvantaged by the vagaries of the market and in need of welfare to address their vulnerabilities. At the same time, the entrenched and pervasive hegemony of welfare provides the necessary support for this drift towards neoliberalism even though it might not be in the best interests of those providing this support. For the 'red wall' constituencies that voted Conservative and areas such as the North-East of England that voted for Brexit, there is no evidence that their areas will benefit in any way from welfare reforms or leaving the European Union. In fact, evidence suggests quite the opposite. However, the neoliberal shift could not happen without the partnership of hegemony.

████████████████ Chapter summary ████████████████

This chapter has explored the impact of social policy on inequality in the UK, and has included the following topics:

* An understanding of inequality
* Social policy ideology and social inequality
* Inequality in the UK
* Neoliberal responses to inequality

Conclusion

There has been a range of different concepts and elements covered in this chapter such as neoliberalism, or what might be defined as late-neoliberalism, narratives understood in terms of 'common sense', and the increasing primacy of agency in framing government responses to inequality. All of these elements have changed and become increasingly entrenched since the 2010 election. Initially aggregated within a vision of a 'Big Society', the 2010 election heralded a period of rapid change in Social Policy and academic debate, at the heart of which were questions regarding the role of government. Over a decade later, this has moved from a position of rapid change and flux to become a long-run and established approach of government to inequality. With this long-run position in mind, it is possible to reflect on the way in which the ideology of late-neoliberalism, the articulation of agency, and government approaches to inequality coalesce. This can be understood in terms of a new hegemony of inequality that recognises an established and entrenched position and points to the fact that government approaches to addressing inequality are unlikely to change in the near future. Recognising inequality as a process, this means that there is no indication that government will do more to address the causes of inequality or be more proactive in mitigating the outcomes. In fact, understanding the long-run position of this hegemony of inequality, it might be expected that the government retreat will continue and that there will be even less intervention. As such, the experiences of inequality that are evident in Social Policy research are unlikely to improve at any point in the near future.

Questions to Reflect Upon

- Why is it important to understand intersectionality when examining inequality and how might this impact on the effectiveness of Social Policy to address inequality?
- To what extent do people have power and agency to address their own challenges and inequalities?
- The chapter recognises inequalities as being multifaceted and, at its simplest, a two nation approach from government. What might be the long-term implications for those experiencing inequality?
- How do neoliberalism and/or hegemony help analyse inequality?
- Hegemony defines a political system based on consent rather than coercion, even when policies might not be in our interest. To what extent has welfare reform and austerity been in our interest?

Further Reading

Byrne, B., Alexander, C., Khan, O., Nazroo, J., & Shankley, W. (Eds.). (2020). *Ethnicity, race and inequality in the UK: State of the nation*. Bristol: Policy Press. (This book looks at the societal issues facing the UK in terms of rising and persistent inequality set against the backdrop of Brexit, and the rise of right-wing ideology. It brings together some of the UK's foremost scholars of race and ethnicity to look at evidence across a wide range of sectors of society.)

Chattoo, S., Atkin, K., Craig, G., & Flynn, R. (2019). *Understanding 'race' and ethnicity*. Bristol: Policy Press. (This book by Chattoo and colleagues explores how UK policy and welfare provision have been influenced by race and ethnicity, examining the impacts upon minority groups in different settings. Advocating for inclusivity, equality and fairness it demonstrates how minorities can be denied welfare through institutional racism.)

Craig, G. (Ed.). (2017). *Community organising against racism: 'Race', ethnicity and community development*. Bristol: Policy Press (Exploring, through the use of case studies from across the world, this book looks at various community development projects which have been successful in empowering marginalised communities to challenge discrimination and disadvantage.)

References

Bambra, C., Lynch, J., & Smith, K. (2021). *The unequal pandemic. Covid-19 and health inequalities*. Bristol: Policy Press.

Beresford, P. (2016). Presenting welfare reform: Poverty porn, telling sad stories or achieving change? *Disability & Society, 31*(3), 421–425.

Bocock, R. (1986). *Hegemony*. London: Ellis Horwood: Chichester and Tavistock.

Bourquin, P., Joyce, R., & Norris Keiller, A. (2020). *Living standards, poverty and living standards in the UK: 2020*. London: Institute for Fiscal Studies.

Brien, P. (2020). *Public spending: A brief introduction*. House of commons library briefing paper 8046, 16 October 2020.

Byrne, B., Alexander, C., Khan, O., Naroo, J., & Shankley, W. (2020). *Ethnicity, race and inequality in the UK. State of the nation.* Bristol: Policy Press.

Cabinet Office. (2017). *Race disparity audit.* London: The Cabinet Office.

Carey, M., & Bell, S. (2020). Universal credit, lone mothers and poverty: Some context and challenges for social work with children and families. *Critical and Radical Social Work*, 8(2), 189–203.

Cohen, S. (1972). *Folk devils and moral panics: The creation of the mods and the rockers.* Palladin: St. Albans.

Crehan, K. (2016). *Gramsci's common sense. Inequality and its narratives.* Durham and London: Duke University Press.

Crisp, R. (2015). Work clubs and the big society: Reflections on the potential for 'progressive localism' in the 'cracks and fissures' of neoliberalism. *People, Place and Policy*, 9(1), 1–16.

Dagdeviren, H., Donoghue, M., & Promberger, M. (2015). Resilience, hardship and social conditions. *Journal of Social Policy*, 45(1), 1–20.

Deeming, C. (2016). Rethinking social policy and society. *Social Policy and Society*, 15(2), 159–175.

Donoghue, M. (2018). Beyond hegemony: Elaborating on the use of Gramscian concepts in critical discourse analysis for political studies. *Political Studies*, 66(2), 392–408.

Donoghue, M., & Edmiston, D. (2020). Gritty citizens? Exploring the logic and limitations of resilience in UK social policy during times of socio-material insecurity. *Critical Social Policy*, 40(1), 7–29.

Dowler, E., & Lambie-Muford, H. (2015). How can households eat in austerity? Challenges for social policy in the UK. *Social Policy and Society*, 14(3), 417–428.

Dwyer, P., & Wright, S. (2014). Universal credit, ubiquitous conditionality and its implications for social citizenship. *Journal of Poverty and Social Justice*, 22(1), 27–35.

Edmiston, D. (2018). *Welfare inequality and social citizenship. Deprivation and affluence in austerity Britain.* Bristol: Policy Press.

Farnsworth, K. (2020). Retrenched, reconfigured and broken: The British welfare state after a decade of austerity. *Social Policy and Society*, 20(1), 77–96.

Farnsworth, K., & Irving, Z. (2012). Varieties of crisis, varieties of austerity: Social policy in challenging times. *Journal of Poverty and Social Justice*, 20(2), 133–147.

Farnsworth, K., & Irving, Z. (2018). Austerity: Neoliberal dreams come true? *Critical Social Policy*, 38(3), 461–481.

Francis-Devine, B. (2021). *Poverty in the UK: Statistics.* House of commons library, 31 March 2021.

Francis-Devine, B. (2022a). *Poverty in the UK: Statistics.* House of commons library, 13th April 2022.

Francis-Devine, B. (2022b). *Unemployment by ethnic background.* House of commons library research briefing 6385, 25th February 2022.

Garthwaite, K. (2016). Stigma, shame and 'people like us': An ethnographic study of foodbank use in the UK. *Journal of Poverty and Social Justice*, 24(3), 277–289.

Glasby, J., Zhang, Y., Bennett, M., & Hall, P. (2021). A lost decade? A renewed case for adult social care reform in England. *Journal of Social Policy*, 50(2), 406–437.

Grover, C. (2019). Violent proletarianisation: Social murder, the reserve army of labour and social security 'austerity' in Britain. *Critical Social Policy*, 39(3), 335–355.

Harari, D. (2018). *Regional and local economic growth statistics*. House of commons library, briefing paper 05795 5 September 2018.

Heins, E., & Bennett, H. (2018). Retrenchment, conditionality and flexibility: UK labour market policies in the era of austerity. In S. Theodoropoulou (Ed.), *Labour market policies in the era of pervasive austerity: A European perspective* (pp. 225–251). Bristol: Policy Press.

Hills, J. (2017). *Good times bad times: The welfare myth of them and us*. Bristol: Policy Press.

Hirsch, D. (2021). *The cost of child poverty in 2021, centre for research in social policy*. Loughborough: Loughborough University.

Iafrati, S. (2020). *Supporting tenants with multiple and complex needs in houses in multiple occupation: The need to balance planning restrictions and housing enforcement with support*. Cambridge: Social Policy and Society.

Iafrati, S. (2021). Out of area housing by local authorities in England: Displacement of vulnerable households in a neoliberal housing crisis. *Journal of Poverty and Social Justice, 29*(2), 137–153.

Irving, Z. (2021). The legacy of austerity. *Social Policy and Society, 20*(1), 97–110.

Ishkanian, A. (2019). Social movements, Brexit and social policy. *Social Policy and Society, 18*(1), 147–159.

Jensen, T. (2014). Welfare commonsense, poverty porn and doxosophy. *Sociological Research Online, 19*(3), 277–283.

Johnson, P., Joyce, R., & Platt, L. (2021). *The IFS Deaton review of inequalities. A new year's message*. London: Institute for Fiscal Studies.

Joseph Rowntree Foundation. (2021). *UK poverty 2020/21*. York: Joseph Rowntree Foundation.

Joseph-Salisbury, R., Connelly, L., & Wangari-Jones, P. (2021). 'The UK is not innocent': Black Lives Matter, policing and abolition in the UK. *Equality, Diversity and Inclusion, 40*(1), 21–28.

Kalleberg, A., & Vallas, S. (2018). Probing precarious work: Theory, research and politics. *Research in the Sociology of Work, 31*, 1–30.

Knight, B. (2017). *Rethinking poverty. What makes a good society*. Bristol: Policy Press.

Lavery, S. (2018). The legitimation of post-crisis capitalism in the United Kingdom: Real wage decline, finance led growth and the state. *New Political Economy, 23*(1), 1–19.

Leng, G. (2017). *The impact of homelessness on health. A guide for local authorities*. London: Local Government Association.

McEnhill, K., & Taylor-Gooby, P. (2018). Beyond continuity? Understanding change in the UK welfare state since 2010. *Social Policy and Administration, 52*(1), 252–270.

McGimpsey, I. (2017). Late neoliberalism: Delineating a policy regime. *Critical Social Policy, 37*(1), 64–84.

Morrison, J. (2019). *Scroungers: Moral panics and media myths*. London: Zed Books.

Nazroo, J., & Becares, L. (2021). *Ethnic inequalities in COVID-19 mortality: A consequence of persistent racism*. London: Runnymede Trust.

Otu, A., Opoku Ahinkorah, B., Kwabena Ameyaw, E., Seidu, A., & Yaya, S. (2020). One country, two crises: What covid-19 reveals about health inequalities among BAME communities in the United Kingdom and the sustainability of its health system? *International Journal for Equity in Health, 19*, 189.

Patel, P., Kapoor, A., & Treloar, N. (2020). *Ethnic inequalities in Covid-19 are playing out again – How can we stop them?* Institute for Public Policy Research. Retrieved from https://www.ippr.org/blog/ethnic-inequalities-in-covid-19-are-playing-out-again-how-can-we-stop-them

Paterson, L., Coffey-Glover, L., & Peplow, D. (2016). Negotiating stance within discourses of class: Reactions to benefits street. *Discourse and Society, 27*(2), 195–214.

Patrick, R. (2014). Working on welfare: Findings from a qualitative longitudinal study into the lived experiences of welfare reform in the UK. *Journal of Social Policy, 43*(4), 705–725.

Powell, M. (2019). The English national health service in a cold climate: A decade of austerity. *Social Policy Review, 31,* 7–28.

Price, C., Barons, M., Garthwaite, K., & Jolly, A. (2020). 'The do-gooders and scroungers': Examining narratives of foodbank use in online local press coverage in the West Midlands, UK. *Journal of Poverty and Social Justice, 28*(3), 279–298.

Raisborough, J., Ogden, C., & Stone de Guzman, V. (2019). When fat meets disability in poverty porn: Exploring the cultural mechanisms of suspicion in too fat to Work. *Disability & Society, 34*(2), 276–295.

Reeve, K. (2017). Welfare conditionality, benefit sanctions and homelessness in the UK: Ending the 'something for nothing culture' or punishing the poor? *Journal of Poverty and Social Justice, 25*(1), 65–78.

Reeves, A., & Loopstra, R. (2017). 'Set up to fail'? How welfare conditionality undermines citizenship for vulnerable groups. *Social Policy and Society, 16*(2), 327–338.

Roberts, C. (2017). The language of 'Welfare dependency' and 'benefit cheats': Internalising and reproducing the hegemonic and discursive rhetoric of 'benefit scroungers'. In A. Mooney & E. Sifaki (Eds.), *The language of money and debt.* London: Palgrave Macmillan.

Shildrick, T. (2018). Lessons from Grenfell: Poverty propaganda, stigma and class power. *The Sociological Review, 66*(4), 783–798.

Simon, R. (1982). *Gramsci's political thought. An introduction.* London: Lawrence and Wishart.

Social Metrics Commission. (2020). *Measuring poverty 2020.* London: The Legatum Institute Foundation.

Social Mobility Commission. (2021). *State of the nation 2021: Social mobility and the pandemic.* London: Social Mobility Commission.

Stephens, M., & Stephenson, A. (2016). Housing policy in the austerity age and beyond. *Social Policy Review, 28,* 63–85.

Szreter, S. (2021). *The history of inequality: The deep-acting ideological and institutional influences.* London: Institute for Fiscal Studies Deaton Review of Inequalities.

Taylor-Gooby, P. (2016). The divisive welfare state. *Social Policy and Administration, 50*(6), 712–733.

Taylor-Gooby, P. (2017). Redoubling the crisis of the welfare state: The impact of Brexit on UK welfare policies. *Journal of Social Policy, 46*(4), 815–835.

Watts, B., & Fitzpatrick, S. (2018). *Welfare conditionality.* Abingdon: Routledge.

Whitworth, A. (2016). Neoliberal paternalism and paradoxical subjects: Confusion and contradiction in UK activation policy. *Critical Social Policy, 36*(3), 412–431.

Wiggan, J. (2012). Telling stories of 21st century welfare: The UK coalition government and the neo-liberal discourse of worklessness and dependency. *Critical Social Policy*, *32*(3), 383–405.

Williams, F. (2016). Critical thinking in social policy: The challenges of past, present and future. *Social Policy and Administration*, *50*(6), 628–647.

Wright, S., & Patrick, R. (2019). Welfare conditionality in lived experience: Aggregating qualitative longitudinal research. *Social Policy and Society*, *18*(4), 597–613.

Zaranko, B. (2020). *Spending review 2020: Covid-19, Brexit and beyond*. London: Institute for Fiscal Studies, Green Budget.

11

RESEARCHING INEQUALITIES

Ruby C. M. Chau

━━━━━━━━━ Learning objectives ━━━━━━━━━

- To understand the role of culture in research on social inequalities
- To understand the meaning of ethnocentrism and how it generates and reinforces social inequalities
- To explore how different cross-cultural approaches to social research can eliminate ethnocentric views and reduce social inequalities

━━━━━━━━━ Framing questions ━━━━━━━━━

- How is culture relevant to the study of social inequalities?
- How do ethnocentric views lead to and reinforce social inequalities?
- How to use different approaches of cross-cultural research to eliminate ethnocentric views and promote social equalities?

Introduction

Culture is a very broad term. It is made up of elements such as values, beliefs, behaviours and material objects which constitute people's ways of life (Macionis, 1997). To discuss the relevance of culture to research on social equalities, this chapter focuses on the cultural elements that guide people to engage in social relationships. Confucianism, one of the most influential ancient philosophies in contemporary Chinese and East Asian societies, is used as an example for illustration. The discussion will be supported by the case study of the provision of health care for Chinese migrants in the UK (see Box 1).

This chapter is organised into five parts. The first provides an overview of Confucian ideas concerning social relationships. The second part highlights four ethnocentric interpretations of these ideas and their counterarguments. The third part discusses how these interpretations may reinforce inequalities. This is followed by the discussion of four approaches to cross-cultural research that can be used to eliminate ethnocentric views and to reduce social inequalities. The concluding part provides a summary of the main arguments developed in this chapter.

Confucianism

Although Confucianism is named after Confucius (551–479 BC), not all Confucian ideas originated from him. Some ideas were from previous leaders in the Zhou Dynasty and some were developed by Confucian scholars (such as Mencius and *Xunzi*) in later generations. This section highlights three core Confucian ideas which are still frequently referred to by national leaders and scholars at the present time. These are '*Ren*', '*Li*' and '*Da Tong*' (the Commonwealth).

'Ren'

Confucius' view of social relationships is closely associated with his view on how to strengthen people's moral capacity. According to him, people have the potential of taking care of each other. By helping each other, not only those being cared for benefit but so does the moral capacity of society as a whole. This idea of linking self-cultivation to meeting other people's needs is reflected in his understanding of *Ren*.

Ren is translated variously as goodness, benevolence, humanity or human-heartedness (Ching, 1986). Confucius believed that *Ren* is a universal virtue, which can make human beings morally perfect and thus become 'moral gentlemen' (*Junzi*) (Ching, 1986; Fung, 1952). The Chinese word *Ren* is composed of two characters meaning 'man' and 'two' respectively. It is seen to embrace all those moral qualities, which should govern a person in relationships with others (Fung, 1952). In specific, *Ren* can be seen as a manifestation of genuine human nature based on loving others and concern over others' well-being. Confucius assumed that people can find a rule within themselves for the similar treatment of others. As he said: 'do not do to others what we do not like ourselves' (quoted in Fung, 1952, p. 73). When asked about five things in the practice of *Ren*, Confucius replied that those were respect, magnanimity, sincerity, earnestness and kindness (Fung, 1952).

Ren can be achieved by nurturing a harmonious relationship between people. On the one hand, those who care for others can see the practice of *Ren* as a benefit because their moral status can be enhanced. On the other hand, those who receive care can be seen as beneficiaries because their caring needs are fulfilled.

'Li'

One of the essential ways of practising *Ren* is to follow *Li*. Analects recorded these sayings of Confucius (quote from Fung, 1952, p. 70):

> *Ren* is the denial of self and response to *Li*.

> If not *Li*, do not look, if not *Li*, do not listen, if not *Li*, do not speak; if not *Li*: do not move.

The meaning of *Li* in ancient China was very wide, representing not only the present-day definition of 'politeness' or 'courtesy' but also the entire body of usages and customs, political and social institutions (Fung, 1952). It entails the normative principles that guide people in major social relationships to meet their role expectations.

For example, Confucius identified five key relationships in the society and the corresponding ideal character for each role in four of these relationships (Chau & Yu, 1997):

- between the sovereign and ministers of the state – benevolence and royalty;
- between father and son – kindness and filial piety;
- between husband and wife – righteousness and compliance;
- between elder and young brothers – goodness and respect;
- and between friends.

Confucius assumed that different social systems are closely related to each other. As it says in the Analects (1.2): 'Rare are those who are filial to their parents and deferential to elder brother yet are fond of causing trouble to their superiors' (Rozman, 2014, pp. 45–46). This also implies that by learning to obey their father in the family, people are at the same time learning to be loyal to their sovereign. In return, the sovereign is expected to rule the country as he manages the family as a father.

In short, *Li* can be seen as a cement of the entire normative sociopolitical order. When people follow *Li*, they are expected to behave according to the role, status, rank and position within a structured society (Schwartz, 1985).

'Da Tong' (The Commonwealth)

Confucius' ideal society of 'the Commonwealth' (*Da Tong*) was recorded in a conversation between Confucius and his pupils in the article '*Li Yun*' in the Book of Rites (Chung & Haynes, 1993, p. 38):

> The world becomes a commonwealth; men of talent and virtue are selected, and mutual confidence and harmony prevail. Then people not only love their own parents and care for their own children, but also those of others. The aged are able to enjoy their old age; the youth are also to be fully employed; the juniors respect their elders, widows, orphans, and handicapped are well cared for.

In short, the Commonwealth is founded on the normative principles advocated by Confucius:

- Members of this ideal society practice *Ren* by looking after other people's needs.
- They should follow *Li* – for example, by taking care of their parents and children.
- Following *Li* can be seen as members' voluntary attempts to take care of others and in turn, strengthen their moral capacity.

Ethnocentric Interpretations of Confucian Ideas and Counterarguments

Ethnocentrism refers to the application of one's own culture as a frame of reference to judge other cultures, practices, behaviours, beliefs and people, instead of using the standards of the particular culture involved (Walker & Wong, 2004). This section discusses four ethnocentric interpretations of Confucian ideas and the counterarguments. Some of these ideas can be dated back to the 19thcentury when China was invaded by multiple foreign powers. Some are more recently developed when China adopted an open-door policy in 1978 to accept Western knowledge such as social work. Some are generated in the interaction between Chinese migrants and local people in Western countries such as the UK. These ethnocentric interpretations have far-reaching effects not only on conception of people of different ethnic origins but also on the equal access to health and welfare services for these communities.

Ethnocentric Interpretation I: Confucian Ideas are Inferior to Western Thinking

The Ethnocentric Interpretation

Confucian ideas are seen as inferior to Western ideas. For almost a century since the middle of the 19th century, China had been heavily affected by imperialism and colonialism. With technological advancement after the industrial revolution, foreign powers (such as Britain, France, Germany and Portugal) not only invaded China with their military force but also forced China to open its ports for Western goods, technologies and knowledge. Many Chinese traditional values and practices, including Confucianism and Chinese medicine, faced unprecedented challenges both within the country and from these foreign powers. Some national leaders advocated for importing knowledge from the West, especially concerning weapons and technology (Hsu, 1995). Others simply argued that Western ideas are superior to Confucianism and other traditional practices. For example, traditional Chinese medicines were negatively judged in the context of Western science, as shown in the following quotation (Morse, 1933, pp. 3–7):

> Chinese ancient medical beliefs and practices showed not a little real knowledge by Chinese practitioners of the art of healing. They not for a thousand years possessed, and do not now possess, the habit of constantly searching for facts combined with a willingness to discard any previous opinion as soon as a new truth points the way to further improvement.

This quotation shows that some analysts have ignored the value of traditional beliefs and practices and assumed that Western ideas are superior to traditional Chinese thinking.

Counterarguments

Some scholars pointed out that Western ideas may not be superior to those in traditional China. Instead, they believed Western inventions such as medicine and science have been used as an instrument to promote imperialism. Cai (1988, p. 527) made this argument by citing the views of some missionary physicians:

> The best way of introducing Christianity to China is through medicine while the best of selling more merchandise in China is through missionary activity... When Western cannons even lift a bar from China's door, Dr Parker opens the gate of China with his lancet.

It is important to note that Western science is not the only Western idea regarded as an instrument for promoting imperialism in non-Western territories in the past. Others such as Western welfare ideas and international social work practices are suspected of carrying similar functions in modern days. Midgley (1981) argued that when Western ideas (such as individualism, liberalism, and work ethics) are transferred to developing countries, they could serve the interests of developed countries and establish a new colonialism. Healy (2012) pointed out that the exploration of international social work practices unremittingly raises concerns that the concept embodies imperialistic notions for two reasons: social work was introduced to some countries in Asia and Africa by colonial government officials; and to some newly independent nations by Western consultants and educators under the auspices of the United Nations. Gray (2005, p. 235) attributed professional imperialism to the dominance of Western paradigms in the field of social work:

> Unless we have the insight and ability to step outside our Western paradigms and to view international situations through a cultural lens and to approach them with humility, we run the danger of perpetuating professional imperialism.

These counterarguments show that the assumed superiority of Western ideas is contestable. Western ideas can be an instrument to promote imperialism both in the past and at the present time.

Ethnocentric Interpretation II: Confucian Welfare Systems Are Very Different From the Others

The Ethnocentric Interpretation

The differences between welfare systems with and without a Confucian cultural root tend to be over-emphasised in contemporary welfare literature. Esping-Andersen (1990) presented his seminal work of *The Three Worlds of Welfare Capitalism* which has led to many related studies of welfare typologies. Some analysts suggested that the East Asian countries and territories sharing the Confucian heritage are different from the others and should be grouped under the fourth world of welfare capitalism. For example, Jones (1993, p. 214) argued:

> Conservative corporatism without (Western-style) worker participation; subsidiarity without the Church; solidarity without equality; laissez-faire without libertarianism; an alternative expression for all this might be household economy; welfare states – run in the style of a would-be traditional, Confucian, extended family.

However, as East Asian and other non-Western welfare systems have long been excluded from comparative welfare research, there is limited empirical evidence to confirm the above observations.

Counterarguments

Other analysts stated that the fact that these countries and territories only occupy a marginal position in the studies of welfare typologies is an example of ethnocentric bias (Walker & Wong, 2004). Their observation shows that many studies of the classifications of welfare regimes are mainly drawn on the experiences of advanced capitalist parliamentary democracies which are members of the Organisation for Economic Cooperation and Development (OECD). These studies convey a message that welfare states are a capitalist-democratic project and therefore justify the little attention given to those societies without either one or both of the supposed core institutions – a capitalist economy and a Western parliamentary democracy, even though these societies may have similar welfare arrangements. About this point, Walker and Wong (2004, p. 118) argued this:

> ...the Western welfare state paradigm is an ethnocentric construction. Their (Asian countries and territories) exclusion is not based on the policy content or institutions of welfare in those countries, but on other institutional requirements that are not concerned with the welfare state per se but rather its cultural, economic and political context.

These counterarguments suggest that Western and non-Western welfare systems may not be as different as assumed. This is especially true when many countries, Western or not, are facing similar problems such as an ageing population and climate change. It is not uncommon that these governments refer to each other's experiences and/or work together to find solutions to the problems.

Ethnocentric Interpretation III: Confucianism is a Monolithic Cultural Idea

The Ethnocentric Interpretation

Confucianism is seen as a monolithic idea. The emphasis on *Li* in Confucian ideas has made some analysts believe that all Confucian societies are hierarchical. For instance, the principles of Three Obediences and Four Virtues that were applied to women in the past are often cited as proof of the gendered social hierarchy in China [*sic*] (Chau & Yu, 1997):

- the obedience of a girl to her father, a married woman to her husband after marriage, a widow to her son (the Three Obediences);
- performing appropriate behaviours conforming to the moral code, being careful in her speech with no-nonsense comments, keeping the appearance modest, and being diligent in the management of domestic duties (the Four Virtues)

These principles are commonly used to justify the unequal gender division of labour in the family in ancient China and contemporary Chinese societies. As research shows the traditional patriarchy and gender division of labour remain influential in socialist China; the tenet of 'Men in charge of the outside world and women in charge of the internal affairs' still prevails; and working women continue to bear the double burden of paid work in the workplace and unpaid domestic work in the family (Ji, Wu, Sun, & He, 2017, p. 767).

Counterarguments

The patriarchal and hierarchical social order is only one dimension of Confucianism. As shown earlier in this chapter, Confucius emphasised in the Commonwealth that 'people of talents and virtue are selected; and the youth can be fully employed' (Chung & Haynes, 1993, p. 38). This implies that in this ideal society not all adult women are expected to stay at home playing the role of informal care provider; they can take part in the work economy as much as male adults. The Commonwealth also stresses that 'people not only love their own parents and care for their own children but also those of others… widows, orphans and handicapped are well cared for' (Chung & Haynes, 1993, p. 38). This means not all the care responsibilities are supposed to be taken up by women at home. Instead, people's caring needs can be met collectively outside the private domain of the family.

As mentioned earlier in this chapter, Confucianism has evolved over the Chinese history. Many ideas are still subject to debate even among contemporary Confucian scholars. By assuming Confucian ideas as monolithic, one may lose sight of the complexity of the ideology.

Ethnocentric Interpretation IV: Chinese People and Supporters of Confucianism Are Inflexible Followers of Traditional Ideas

The Ethnocentric Interpretation

Some analysts stressed that Chinese people and other supporters of Confucianism have a strong attachment to their traditional beliefs and practices. For example, there is an influential view that Chinese migrants in Britain prefer to remain attached to traditional practices that have become a stumbling block to their participation in mainstream society. Jones (1979) argued that Chinese people in Britain were never concerned to develop social relationships outside their own closed communities. Moreover, they were keen to maintain their Chinese culture and continue to identify with their kinsmen at home rather than the host community. As shown in the quotations below:

> There were over thousand years of feudal history in China. Feudal customs would more or less affect everybody...Many of the residents (of a Chinese hostel) migrated to Britain in their middle or old age. It is not easy for them to accept new concepts and they enjoy keeping their Chinese customs. Some of them have been here over 30 years, they are still not used to English food, even English tea. (Bao, 1996, p. 27)

> The practical obstacles to Chinese integration are very real, but it is also true that historically the Chinese community had a cultural confidence and a sense of self-sufficiency that has made their isolation to some degree voluntarily. This has been reinforced by the benevolent indifference of the host culture. (Victim Support, 1997; quote from Chau & Yu, 2001, p. 111)

According to these analysts, the main reasons for Chinese migrants not being able to integrate into the British ways of living are their strict adherence to traditional customs and refusal to make changes.

Counterarguments

Yu and his colleagues (2000) contested that the responsiveness of Chinese people to other cultures is often underestimated. For example, Chinese migrants in the UK often adopt both traditional diets and Western medicines to promote their health (Yu, Chau, & Law, 2014). Besides, many of them are keen for their children to integrate into the British education system and attain good academic results (Yu, 2000). It is also worth noting that Chinese people have a long history of learning from foreign countries. Cai (1988) proved this point by showing examples of medical literature from India recorded in the Record of Classics in the Book of Sui compiled in 656 AD containing prescriptions of Brahman Immortals, Brahman recipes and Methods for Incensing by the Boddhisattva Nagarjuna. Thus, the assumption that Chinese people are strict followers of traditional ideas is incongruent with the observations of their interest in foreign knowledge and practices both in the past and at the present time.

The discussion in this section shows that ethnocentric interpretations of Confucian ideas are often based on partial understanding. These interpretations could be the result of a sense of cultural superiority, an oversight of the complexity of the ideology and/or other reasons. Nonetheless, they have affected people's perception of this traditional ideology and the social institutions, values and practices associated with it. In the following part, the implications of these interpretations on social equalities are explored. A summary of the discussion can be seen in Table 11.1.

Table 11.1 Presents Examples of Ethnocentric Views and Counterarguments

Ethnocentric Views	Counterarguments
Western ideas are superior to non-Western ideas.	Western ideas can be instruments for promoting imperialism.
Non-Western ideas such as Confucianism are very different.	Overemphasis on differences can contribute to the oversight of potential similarities of Western and non-Western societies.
Non-Western ideas such as Confucianism can be monolithic.	Non-Western ideas may evolve over a long history of transgenerational debates and can be complex and multidimensional.
Supporters of non-Western ideas are inflexible followers.	Some non-Western countries such as China have a long history of learning and integrating foreign knowledge and practice.

Ethnocentric Views and Social Inequalities

The four ethnocentric interpretations of Confucian ideas discussed in the previous part can create or reinforce different forms of inequalities. Firstly, making Confucian ideas and related practices subordinate to Western ideas leads to an unequal recognition of different cultural ideas. Putting into the contexts of health care and social welfare, this to a certain extent justifies an unequal allocation of resources between the development of traditional Chinese practices (such as herbal medicines) and the development of Western practices; and between the development of culturally sensitive practices based on Confucian ideas and the development of practices based on Western ideas.

Secondly, the over-emphasis of the differences between the welfare systems in the countries and territories with a Confucian root and others could lead to the marginalisation of the study of the former in welfare literature. Such academic marginalisation reinforces the bias that countries with a Confucian root do not face the same social problems or need similar kinds of social assistance programs as the rest of the world. Moreover, how welfare is organized in these countries may not be relevant to other countries. Their experiences may be regarded as less worthy to study. Thirdly, seeing Confucianism as a set of monolithic cultural ideas does not give equal recognition to all important elements of Confucianism. Since building an inclusive society based on the ideal of the Commonwealth is often overlooked as a key element of Confucianism, people's preferences for this element does not receive sufficient recognition.

Finally, seeing Chinese and other people in favour of Confucianism as inflexible followers of traditional ideas may result in blaming the victims. The needs of Chinese migrants in the UK for equal access to health and social services as other citizens are often overlooked (Yu, 2000). Their under-use of health and social services has been interpreted as their cultural preferences. This may have given the government an excuse to ignore the need to improve the accessibility of services or to deliver the services in a more culturally sensitive manner.

The discussion of the ethnocentric views of Confucian ideas and how they can lead to unequal treatment in welfare provision and academic studies suggests that it is important to keep an open mind in understanding different cultures. The interpretation of cultural ideas should be based on systematic research instead of ethnocentric assumptions.

Cross-cultural Research Approaches

As mentioned at the beginning, one of the objectives of this chapter is to explore how cross-cultural research can contribute to the reduction of social inequalities. To avoid ethnocentric views that may generate and reinforce social inequalities, it is important for researchers to be aware of a range of potential relationships between different cultures. Four cross-cultural research approaches are discussed in this section – the sameness approach, the difference approach, the diversity approach and the dynamic approach. These approaches are based on different assumptions of the relationship between different cultures and among members of the same cultural group. The sameness approach and the diversity approach are related to the concept of homogeneity. They remind researchers that there could be important commonalities between cultural groups and thus people from different cultural backgrounds may have similar needs and interests. The difference approach and the diversity approach are related to the concept of heterogeneity. They emphasize the potential differences between cultures and also among members of the same cultural group.

The Sameness Approach

The sameness approach focuses on the commonalities of cultural ideas developed by different cultural groups. It is based on the assumption that human beings living in different cultural entities can have important similarities. These may include some of their biological needs (such as physical health) and their needs to respond to the challenges of the global environment (such as global warming). Hence, their views on the meaning of welfare and the ways for achieving welfare can have important commonalities. For example, the concept *Ren* discussed by Confucius has important commonalities with the concept altruism discussed in Western welfare literature. The way that *Ren* influences how people interact with others has some similarities with the inner voice discussed in Etzioni's communitarianism (Etzioni, 1993).

The Differences Approach

The differences approach is based on two assumptions. Firstly, different cultural groups have their ways of defining welfare needs. Secondly, to meet the needs of the service users, the service providers should understand the cultural ideas shared by the service users. In carrying out the difference approach, researchers are expected to explore the uniqueness of cultural ideas of a cultural group, and whether such cultural ideas contribute to different needs and preferences for welfare services.

The Diversity Approach

The diversity approach emphasizes that cultural ideas can be diverse; they may challenge as well as support each other. Besides, members of the same cultural group can have diverse ways of connecting to their cultural ideas. It is also important to note how people organise their lives is affected by multiple factors (such as their gender and socio-economic positions in society or family) in addition to cultural beliefs. By taking this approach, researchers are expected to explore the differences between individual members of the same cultural group in interpreting their cultural ideas, and the existence of sub-groups that have different characteristics.

The Dynamic Approach

This approach regards the opportunity for different cultural groups to interact and learn from each other as important. In this process people may change their attachment to different cultural ideas over time. By adopting this approach, researchers are expected to study how and to what extent different cultural groups reciprocally influence each other, and whether people can change their attachment from one set of cultural ideas to another set or adjust their only views.

Challenging Ethnocentric Interpretations by Cross-cultural Research

The four study approaches to cross-cultural research can be used to challenge the ethnocentric interpretations to Confucian ideas in several different ways. The sameness approach serves to challenge the over-emphasis on the differences between different cultural groups. The knowledge generated from this approach may be able to prevent marginalizing the experiences of some cultural groups in social research. The difference approach serves to contest the emphasis on the universal application of Western ideas to other groups. The knowledge derived from this approach may be able to defend people of non-Western societies against being made to organize their lives based on Western ideas involuntarily. The diversity approach can reduce the over-emphasis of the similarities of the welfare needs of members of the same cultural groups. The knowledge developed from this approach may be able to prevent the oversight of the diverse needs among members of the same cultural group and the over-reliance on a limited variety of services to meet all the needs. The dynamic approach can question the assumption that people are inflexible followers of cultural ideas. The knowledge developed from this research approach may be able to help to recognize the changing needs and preferences of those people who pick up new insights from other cultures.

The implementation of these four approaches can also strengthen different kinds of equalities. The sameness approach stresses the importance of joint international conventions (such as the Sustainable Development Goals under the UN 2030 Agenda) for promoting welfare based on commonalities and equalities between different cultural ideas. The difference approach stresses the importance of ensuring that different cultural groups can have an equal opportunity for meeting their welfare needs in their ways. For example, traditional health-promoting practices can be encouraged alongside Western medical treatments. The diversity approach stresses the importance of giving different members of the same cultural group equal opportunities for meeting their welfare needs in the ways they prefer. These can be achieved by ensuring equal access to both mainstream services and services specialized for specific ethnic groups. The dynamic approach stresses the importance of giving different cultural groups an equal opportunity to learn from each other and share their cultural ideas. These can be encouraged with cultural exchange activities.

Based on the example of Confucianism, this chapter discussed four types of ethnocentric interpretations to cultural ideas, how these interpretations may generate and reinforce social inequalities and suggested four cross-cultural research approaches. The sameness approach enhances the awareness of the potential homogeneity among different cultural groups. The dynamic approach draws attention to the possibility that people from different cultural groups can develop their homogeneity through learning from each other. The difference approach and the diversity approach are based on the idea of heterogeneity. The difference approach emphasizes the differences between different cultural groups. The diversity approach draws attention to the potential differences between members of the same cultural group despite their shared cultural heritage. This implies that in minimizing ethnocentric biases to cultural ideas, it is necessary to pay attention to both the homogeneity and heterogeneity within and across different cultural groups. It is also important to provide people with the opportunities to voice out their views and treat these views with equal respect. By doing so, it may be possible to prevent some people or governments from over-emphasizing cultural homogeneity and/or heterogeneity that in turn create or reinforce political, economic and social inequalities.

■■■■■■■■ Case study ■■■■■■■■

Culturally sensitive health care for Chinese people in the UK

Health care is mainly concerned with promoting people's physical and mental well-being. It also serves to meet other social goals, such as tackling inequities, changing people's patterns of consumption and raising awareness of cultural beliefs (Kumar & Preetha, 2012). However, if health promotion strategies are not culturally sensitive, they may increase inequalities between different cultural groups and reinforce stereotypes.

Evidence suggests that there are six major discrepancies between the healthcare services Chinese people in the UK prefer, and what they actually receive (Yu et al., 2014).

- Chinese people in some local areas are only provided with Western medicine even though they prefer to use traditional Chinese medicine.
- Chinese people use the concepts such as *yin-yang* to assess their health conditions. However, mainstream healthcare professionals may not understand or approve of these concepts. They may not assess the health conditions of Chinese patients in the same way and provide diagnoses and treatments accordingly.
- The needs of some Chinese people for mainstream healthcare services could be neglected because they are assumed by healthcare professionals and other healthcare providers to prefer traditional Chinese medicine to Western medicine.

- Chinese people are commonly assumed to prefer to go to their place of origin to receive medical treatments. However, only those who can afford to pay the costs of travel and medical care can do so.
- Some Chinese people are able and willing to use their knowledge of traditional medicine, such as acupuncture, *Tai Chi* and Chinese herbal medicine to promote the health of the Chinese community and that of other cultural groups. However, their knowledge is undervalued by mainstream society and they have limited opportunities to share their knowledge.
- Some Chinese people use both Western medicine and traditional Chinese medicine. However, few healthcare professionals in Britain can advise on how to make appropriate use of a combination of these kinds of medicine.

To deal with these discrepancies, the four approaches in cross-cultural research mentioned in this chapter may provide the basis for the development of four types of strategies in the provision of culturally sensitive healthcare services:

- The sameness strategy stresses that Chinese people and other cultural groups have similar needs for healthcare services and therefore should be provided with equal access to mainstream healthcare services.
- The difference strategy stresses that Chinese people have their ways of defining their healthcare needs and culturally preferred ways of meeting these needs. This strategy stresses the importance of providing Chinese people with the information and resources for promoting their health in their cultural ways.
- The diversity strategy stresses that members of the Chinese community may favour different ways to meet their healthcare needs. This strategy focuses on ensuring that Chinese people have the equal opportunity of gaining the information and resources for meeting their healthcare needs as they prefer.
- The dynamic strategy recognises some Chinese people's attempts to share their cultural knowledge with other cultural groups. Healthcare professionals should provide the opportunities for them to do so.

Given that the four different strategies address different issues, it is important to ask Chinese people rather than healthcare professionals to decide which approach(es) would be the most culturally appropriate to meet their healthcare needs.

Chapter summary

This chapter explores the role and relevance of culture in research, and covered the following areas:

- Ethnocentric interpretations of Confucian ideas and counterarguments
- Ethnocentric Interpretation I: Confucian ideas are inferior to Western thinking
- Ethnocentric Interpretation II: Confucian welfare systems are very different from the others
- Ethnocentric Interpretation III: Confucianism is a monolithic cultural idea

(Continued)

- Ethnocentric Interpretation IV: Chinese people and supporters of Confucianism are inflexible followers of traditional ideas
- Cross-cultural research approaches
- Challenging ethnocentric interpretations by cross-cultural research

Conclusion

This chapter examined the role of culture in research on social inequalities. By using Confucianism as an example for illustration, it points out four types of ethnocentric responses to cultural ideas, including the following:

- Treating other cultural ideas as inferior
- Over-emphasizing the differences between different cultural ideas
- Assuming certain cultural ideas as monolithic
- Positioning followers of some cultural ideas as inflexible

By referring to the critiques of current comparative welfare studies and the findings of research on the Chinese community in the UK, this chapter argued that ethnocentric biases could underpin social research and government policies that create or reinforce social inequalities.

Four approaches to cross-cultural research on social inequalities were highlighted:

- The sameness approach
- The difference approach
- The diversity approach
- The dynamic approach

Each addresses different issues and has the potential to prevent ethnocentric biases in social research.

Questions to Reflect Upon

- How and to what extent do ethnocentric views affect our understanding of other cultures?
- How and to what extent do ethnocentric views affect our research on social inequalities?
- How can ethnocentric bias be avoided in cross-cultural research?
- Which of the four approaches (sameness, difference, diversity and dynamic) would you prefer in conducting cross-cultural research and why?

Further Reading

Charles, M. (2008). Culture and inequality: Identity, ideology, and difference in 'Postascriptive Society'. *The Annals of the American Academy, 619*, 41–58. (This article highlights three important sociological questions about inequalities and explores the role of culture in the analysis of various forms of inequalities, such as gender, ethnicity and class.)

Li, C. (2012). Equality and inequality in Confucianism. *Dao, 11*(3), 295–313. (This article refers to the ideas of various Confucian thinkers and provides a clear analysis of two forms of equalities in Confucianism – numerical and proportional.)

Yu, W. K., Chau, C. M., & Law, C. (2014). Culturally sensitive health care services for Chinese people in Britain. *Journal of Ethnic and Cultural Diversity in Social Work, 23*(3–4), 256–70. (This article provides details of the four approaches to culturally sensitive health care practice in the UK.)

References

Bao, X. C. (1996). *Special needs of Chinese elderly in Chung Hok house, project for the national certificate course for wardens of sheltered housing.*

Cai, J. (1988). Integration of traditional Chinese medicine with western medicine – Right or wrong. *Social Science and Medicine, 27*(5), 527–529.

Chau, C. M., & Yu, W. K. (1997). The sexual division of care in mainland China and Hong Kong. *International Journal of Urban and Regional Research, 21*(4), 607–619.

Chau, C. M., & Yu, W. K. (2001). Social exclusion of Chinese people in Britain. *Critical Social Policy, 21*(1), 103–125.

Ching, J. (1986). What is confucius spirituality. In I. Eber (Ed.), *Confucianism: The dynamics of tradition* (pp. 63–83). London: Collier Macmillan Publishers.

Chung, D., & Haynes, A. (1993). Confucian welfare philosophy and social change technology: An integrated approach for international social development. *International Social Work, 36*, 37–46.

Esping-Andersen, G. (1990). *The three worlds of welfare capitalism.* Cambridge: Polity Press.

Etzioni, A. (1993). *The spirit of community: Rights, responsibilities, and the communitarian Agenda.* New York, NY: Crown Publishers.

Fung, Y. L. (1952). *A history of Chinese philosophy.* Princeton, NJ: Princeton University Press.

Gray, M. (2005). Dilemmas of international social work: Paradoxical processes in indigenization, universalism and imperialism. *International Journal of Social Welfare, 14*, 231–238.

Healy, L. M. (2012). Defining international social work. In L. M. Healy & R. J. Link (Eds.), *Handbook of international social work: Human rights, development and the global profession* (pp. 9–15). Oxford: Oxford University Press.

Hsu, C. Y. (1995). *The rise of modern China.* Oxford: Oxford University Press.

Ji, Y., Wu, X., Sun, S., & He, G. (2017). Unequal care, unequal work: Towards a more comprehensive understanding of gender inequality in post-reform urban China. *Sex Roles, 77*, 765–778.

Jones, D. (1979). The Chinese in Britain: Origins and development of a community. *New Community, 7*(3), 397–402.

Jones, C. (1993). *New perspectives in the welfare state in Europe.* London: Routledge.

Kumar, S., & Preetha, G. S. (2012). Health promotion: An effective tool for global health. *Indian Journal of Community Medicine, 37*(1), 5–12.

Macionis, J. (1997). *Sociology*. Hoboken, NJ: Prentice Hall.

Midgley, J. (1981). *Professional imperialism: Social work in the third world*. London: Heinemann.

Morse, W. (1933). *Chinese medicine*. New York, NY: Paul B. Hoeber.

Rozman, G. (2014). *The East Asian region: Confucian heritage and its modern adaptation*. Princeton, NJ: Princeton University Press.

Schwartz, B. (1985). *The world of thought in ancient China*. Cambridge: The Belknap Press of Harvard University Press.

Victim Support. (1997). No. 65, summer.

Walker, A., & Wong, C. K. (2004). The ethnocentric construction of the welfare state. In P. Kennett (Ed.), *A handbook of comparative social policy* (pp. 116–150). Cheltenham: Edward Elgar.

Yu, W. K. (2000). *Chinese older people: A need for social inclusion in two communities*. Bristol: Policy Press.

Yu, W. K., Chau, C. M., & Law, C. (2014). Culturally sensitive health care services for Chinese people in Britain. *Journal of Ethnic and Cultural Diversity in Social Work, 23*(3–4), 256–270.

12

CONCLUSION

Anya Ahmed and Lorna Chesterton

Throughout the book, contributors have challenged the epistemological and onto-logical foundations underpinning traditional approaches to understanding and explaining social inequalities. Revisiting historically influential theorists alongside a focus on scholars who have been absent from such discussions provided an oppor-tunity for students of social science to question and evaluate the status of knowledge and problematise historical truth claims. A thread running throughout the book is that Western positions are positions, or standpoints, rather than represent a univer-sality of experience or objective truths. Academia has long privileged Western para-digms and in turn marginalised minority and Indigenous paradigms (Walker, 2003), and of course does not operate in a vacuum. Its part in knowledge production must be acknowledged and held to account, since it has historically been complicit in its use of 'the truth' to benefit a white elite and play a part in the perpetuation of social inequalities through, for example, justifying slavery and oppression across the globe (Bhambra et al., 2018).

Although a focus on decolonising the curriculum has recently been embraced by Higher Education Institutions wishing to increase diversity in teaching and widen participation in academia, there remains evidence that HEI systems and structures remain dominated by white middle class men, reflecting society at large (O'Connor, 2017). White men still occupy the majority of leadership roles in universities and women continue to be 'positioned as outsiders' (Burkinshaw & White, 2020, p. 191). Additionally, many universities continue to operate systems of racial exclusion (Bhopal, 2018) with data from the UK showing that only 0.7% of Professors are Black (160 out of 22,855) with only 35 Black female Professors (Higher Education Statistics Agency, 2021) We should also acknowledge that the drive to decolonise was not proactively implemented by the academy itself, but by students who questioned the whiteness of their education (Ndlovu-Gatsheni, 2018). In challenging the epistemic foundations of hegemonic knowledge, this book has examined the dominance of the West and how it has mar-ginalised and excluded other groups and their voices. While we acknowledge the vast improvements made in academia, it is clear that there is much work still needed in order to create fully inclusive systems and curricula.

A central thread connecting all the chapters presented, is a questioning of how structures, systems and social processes create and embed social inequalities. Unsurprisingly, the contributors conclude in myriad ways that since such mechanisms are controlled by the most powerful in society, they also continue to work in their interests, perpetuating privilege alongside inequality. To address these disparities, there needs to be fundamental changes in social and political policy and rhetoric, and we acknowledge that these changes will not be without resistance. A recent example in the UK demonstrated this, as the Government commissioned report into racism found no evidence of structural racism (Commission on Race and Ethnic Disparities, 2021), and these findings were highly contested by healthcare leaders (Iacobucci, 2021). Indeed, the COVID-19 pandemic highlighted the deep-rooted structural inequalities present in the UK, and how these led to disproportionate mortality in Black and minoritised groups (Haynes, 2020).

It is also clear that the colonial legacy continues to cast a long shadow, with inseparable ties binding the present to the past. We have noted the ongoing connections of discrimination, power and exclusion to historical colonial activity and thinking throughout the preceding chapters. Recently in the UK, leaders have adopted a narrative of imperial nostalgia, evoking the need to return to a time when Britain was an empire (Saunders, 2020). The result of which is that right wing views, previously perceived as marginalised and socially unacceptable, have become mainstream political rhetoric (Worth, 2022, pp. 1–15). Moving forward, as the contributors of this book have argued, there is a need to recognise the damage of colonialism and challenge the myth of nostalgia of empire (Saunders, 2020).

This book has also highlighted the multiple dimensions of social inequality and how this is related to individual's identities and social positioning. By presenting case studies, we have sought to humanise some of the social and psychological impacts of exclusion and discrimination, and the consequential effects on attitudes, and outcomes. Demonstrating how inequality is experienced from a multiplicity of perspectives including class, gender, race, age, disability, sexuality, and mobility and overarchingly how these factors intersect can be useful in improving understanding and shaping future social policy. From these vantage points, such insights highlight previously less heard voices and provide a useful lens through which to make sense of historical and contemporary approaches to understanding social inequalities.

References

Bhambra, G. K., Gebrial, D., & Nişancıoğlu, K. (2018). *Decolonising the university*. London: Pluto Press.

Bhopal, K. (2018). *White privilege: The myth of a post-racial society*. Bristol: Policy Press.

Burkinshaw, P., & White, K. (2020). Generation, gender, and leadership: Metaphors and images. In *Frontiers in education* (Vol. 5, pp. 517497). doi: 10.3389/feduc.2020.517497. Frontiers.

Commission on Race and Ethnic Disparities. (2021). *Independent report foreword, introduction, and full recommendations*. Retrieved from https://www.gov.uk/government/publications/the-report-of-the-commission-on-race-and-ethnic-disparities/foreword-introduction-and-full-recommendations

Haynes, K. (2020). Structural inequalities exposed by COVID-19 in the UK: The need for an accounting for care. *Journal of Accounting & Organizational Change, 16*(4), 637–642.

Higher Education Statistics Agency. (2021). *HE staff data. Who's working in HE?* Retrieved from https://www.hesa.ac.uk/news/01-02-2022/sb261-higher-education-staff-statistics

Iacobucci, G. (2021). Healthcare leaders reject "damaging" denial that institutional racism exists. *BMJ, 373*. doi:10.1136/bmj.n911

Ndlovu-Gatsheni, S. J. (2018). Rhodes must fall. In S. J. Ndlovu-Gatsheni (Ed.), *Epistemic freedom in Africa: Deprovincialization and decolonization*. Oxford: Taylor & Francis.

O'Connor, P. (2017). Towards a new gender agenda and a model for change. In K. White & P. O'Connor (Eds.), *Gendered success in higher education* (pp. 255–282). London: Palgrave Macmillan.

Saunders, R. (2020). Brexit and Empire:'Global Britain'and the myth of imperial nostalgia. *The Journal of Imperial and Commonwealth History, 48*(6), 1140–1174.

Walker, P. (2003). Colonising research: Academia's structural violence towards indigenous peoples. *Social Alternatives, 22*(3), 37–40. https://search.informit.org/doi/10.3316/aeipt.130595

Worth, O. (2022). *The great moving Boris show: Brexit and the mainstreaming of the far right in Britain* (pp. 1–15). Oxford: Globalizations; Taylor and Francis.

Glossary

Afro-feminism: Feminist philosophical and social movement that centres on the realities of African women and women living in Africa. These realities include grappling with the continued impact of Apartheid, colonialism and postcolonialism in Africa. Much like Black Feminism, this strand of feminism engages the intersections of race, class, gender and other markers of identity as they affect women living in Africa.

Allopathic medicine: Approach to medicine linked with Western/Global North 'science'. Linked with clinical medicine.

Anticategorical complexity: Intersectional analysis approach concerned with deconstruction of analytic categories such as gender and race. Interest is in exploring how identity categories are constructed and to what end. This level of analysis is largely deconstructive and focused on the meaning of terms and concepts and not based on empirical research.

Biomedical model of healthcare: Approach to medicine and health care that focuses on treating bodies using clinical or pharmaceutical technologies.

Black feminism: Feminist philosophical and social movement that centres on the experiences of Black women in recognition of their differential experiences of gendered discrimination and marginalisation relative to women as a social group in general.

Bourdieu: French sociologist and anthropologist whose work is fundamental to approaches to class analysis in the 20th and 21st centuries.

Bourgeoisie: Owners of the means of production

Colonial difference: The myth that colonised people were different from/inferior to the 'Western' colonizers was used to buttress colonial rule. As Ali Meghji (2020, p. 21) among others argues, 'colonial difference was the central epistemological, ontological scheme that allowed empires to construct the rest of the world as [...] uncivilised, in need of colonial intervention'.

Colonial matrix of power: Is the set of power relations put in place through colonialism starting in the 16th century, which continue through to the present (Mignolo, 2018). As Ali Meghji (2021, p. 21) points out, this concept bears similarities with terms such as 'neo-colonialism' (Hall, 1996) and neo-imperialism (Mandle, 1967). However, the colonial matrix of power goes beyond understanding of economic relations of exploitation that outlived colonialism. It also captures the epistemological and ontological aspects of such a matrix of power relations.

Colonialism: Refers to a political and economic relation whereby the sovereignty of one nation depends on the power of another nation. The latter may thus be described as 'Empire'.

Coloniality: Refers to entrenched forms of power that are a direct result of colonialism. These forms of power extend to cultural superiority, knowledge production among others. For scholars such as Maldonado-Torres (2007) then, coloniality inevitably survives colonialism.

Coloniality of being: This concept has been theorised by Sylvia Wynter (2003). Central to the idea of colonial difference was the premise that only white Westerners/Europeans had achieved the full status of 'man'. The colonised populations were all varying degrees of sub-human.

Coloniality of time: The colonial world order was maintained around the idea that people in different regions of the world are at different temporal stages of human development. It is this idea of teleological progression in human development that was used to rationalise the 'White Man's Burden' (Kipling, 1899) in the aid of Euro-America's colonial domination of the rest of the world.

Confucianism: One of the major ancient Chinese philosophies which remains influential in many contemporary East Asian societies, such as China, Japan and South Korea.

Cross-cultural research: The research approach that focuses on studying the similarities and differences between cultural groups, and the differences and similarities between individuals in responding to the cultural ideas and alternatives.

Cultural capital: Valuable cultural knowledge and resources legitimated through recognised qualifications etc. It can also be embodied and present through e.g. displays of confidence.

Da Tong (The Commonwealth): The Confucian ideal society that promotes mutual respect, shared responsibilities and inclusion of people with different abilities and needs.

Decolonial feminisms: Characterised by a multiple and diverse thronged approach to addressing gender and sexual inequalities that are understood to be rooted in systems and practices of coloniality and colonisation. Decolonial feminism addresses this via multiple throngs that include political, environmental, cultural, psychological, legal and other sites of domination.

Decolonisation: A process that encompasses political, social, cultural, economic moving away from colonial relationships of power. These relationships are understood to continue even post formal colonial rule and influence the ways that colonised peoples think, relate to themselves and each other through frames of reference and practice that deny their humanity and agency.

Economic capital: Material resources such as property, income and inheritance.

Epistemic racism: A form of racism that disregards the 'epistemic capacity' of people (Maldonado-Torres, 2004, p. 34). It is, thus, a form of 'cognitive injustice' (de Sousa Santos, B. (Ed.), 2007: p. 237). Drawing on the works of Fataar and Subreenduth (2015), and Nyamnjoh (2012), Feldman (2019, p. 149) argues that 'epistemic racism' can be located in the 'refusal to recognise different ways of knowing and the parity among different knowledges' that 'combine to form university cultures characterised by knowledge deficit and dependency'.

Ethnocentrism: The application of one's own culture as a frame of reference to judge other cultures, practices, behaviours, beliefs and people, instead of using the standards of the particular culture involved.

Feminism: A social movement that at its roots aims for equality between the sexes regarding access to resources and the protection of bodily and other integrity of women.

Gender: Referring to a range of characteristics that are attributed to the sexes as 'masculine' and/or 'feminine'. These characteristics are socially constructed and will differ across contexts.

Gender-based violence (GBV): Includes physical, sexual, emotional, economic and verbal forms of abuse. May also include the indirect threat of such abuse. GBV is rooted in unequal access to power and the reproduction of normative expectations of gender and sex that favour men over women.

Global north: Term used to describe 'Western' or 'developed' nations in Europe and North America. Sometimes expanded to include high-income English-speaking countries such as Australia.

Global south: Term used to describe countries south of Europe and the US/Canada. Includes Latin America and the Caribbean, South Asia and Africa.

Health inequities: Observable and preventable unequal health experiences across a population.

Hegemony: The dominance of one state, society or culture over another. In social theory this is used to talk about the way 'Western' or 'Global North' dominate through cultural representations and industries.

Intercategorical complexity: Intersectional analysis approach concerned with the relationship between social groups. This level of analysis is concerned with the structural and other group dynamic aspects of relationships. For example, researchers may be concerned with exploring inequalities between social groups on the basis of set criteria.

Intersectionality: A framework that explores how different aspects of who we are influence our access to resources as well as our vulnerabilities to harmful events and practices. Crenshaw's original conceptualisation of the concept highlighted the inter-sections of race, gender and class in the experience of gender discrimination.

Intracategorical complexity: Intersectional analysis approach concerned with micro-level analysis of identity and how identities are constructed in the everyday. This is empirical focused and concerned with the ways that people live their lives via multiple intersecting identities.

Latin American feminisms: Diverse philosophical and social movement that includes the Caribbeans and which engages effects of colonialism, slavery and marginalisation of African and Native peoples.

'Li': Politeness and the social and political institutions for its practice, one of the main Confucian ideas to maintain human relationships.

Malthusianism: Population theory of Thomas Malthus that argues there is a consistent tension between the power of population growth and the power of food production that threatens sustainability.

Means of production: Refers to all the things that are needed in order to produce – e.g. land, premises, equipment, technology.

Neo-malthusianism: Expansion of Malthus's theory to include tension between population growth and finite nature economic and ecological resources.

Patriarchy: Refers to an ideology of gender superiority that privileges men over women and is inflected with heteronormative belief that includes cultural and social systems of practice, institutions and relationships.

Population health: Political and academic discussion and study of the health of a whole population.

Proletariat: Those who need to sell their labour.

Public health: Political and academic discussion of how the world around us impacts our health.

'Ren': Kindness, another core principle in Confucianism in governing human relationships.

Social capital: Networks and social connections between people and groups.

Social determinants of health: Factors that influence health across the lifecourse which are related to the social world. Includes housing, wealth, education, community relations and race.

Violence: Includes physical, economic, emotional, psychological, sexual forms of harm and/or threat of harm.

INDEX

A

Adey, P., 133
Adur, S., 84
Afro-Feminisms, 57, 58, 64–68
Ageing
  ageing well, 90
  constructions of, 88–89
  cross-cultural, 91
  health inequalities, 95, 95 (table)
  intersectional perspective, 94–95
  migration context, 95–96
  post-colonial thinking, 88
  systemic racism and discrimination, 92
  transnational migrants, 92–93
Ahmed, A., 4, 6–8
Ali, N., 7
Allopathic medicine, 125–127
Andrews, K., 47
Anthias, Floya, 46
Anticategorical complexity, 65–66
Anti-white racism, 43
Appiah, K. A., 18
Arango, J., 132
Asher, K., 19

B

Badenoch, Kemi, 21
Baderon, G., 67
Bakewell, O., 132–133
Balderston, Susie, 6
Beck, U., 83
Beck-Gernsheim, E., 83
Bell, D. A. Jr., 42
Berghs, M., 111
Besemer, K., 77
Bhabha, Homi, 46
Bhambra, G., 17–18
Bhopal, K., 51
Bhopal, R. S., 96
Biomedical model, 119
Bissell, D., 133
Black and Indigenous and People of Colour
    (BIPOC), 121, 122, 125
Black Feminism, 21, 57, 58, 60, 61
Black Lives Matter, 41
Black Lives Matters (BLM) movement, 41, 49,
    51, 141, 148, 152
Boonzaier, F., 67

Bourdieu, P., 26–32, 36
Brown, K., 78, 79
Bruce, D., 63
Buggery Act of 1533, 80

C

Cai, J., 170
Calasanti, T., 93
Campbell, Sarah, 6
Capitalist economies, 15
Capitalist inequality, 16
Capitalist society, 15–16
Carabine, J., 74
Cesaire, Aime, 42
Chakravarty, D., 5
Charity model, disability, 108
Chau, Ruby C. M., 7–8
Chauvin, Derek, 41
Chesterton, Lorna, 4, 6, 7, 8
Cisgender, 77, 79
Civil Partnership Act, 78, 81
Class-based social inequality, 14
Climate migration, 134–136
Coetzee, A., 64
Collective industry, 15
Collins, P. H., 21–22
Coloma, R. S., 93
Coloniality of being, 45, 66
Coloniality of power, 18, 43, 66
Coloniality of time, 45
Comte, Auguste, 2, 4, 9–11, 11 (table), 13, 14
Confucianism, 163, 164
  Da Tong, 165
  ethnocentrism, 166–170, 171 (table)
  Li, 164–165
  Ren, 164
Conversation therapy, 76
Cooper, B., 21
COVID-19, 122–123, 126, 149, 153
Cox, Oliver Cromwell, 42
Crenshaw, K., 10, 21, 31, 37, 60–61, 82, 94–95
Critical Legal Studies (CLS) movement, 20
Critical race theory (CRT), 20–21, 41, 60
Cross-cultural research approach
  differences approach, 172
  diversity approach, 173
  dynamic approach, 173
  sameness approach, 172

Cultural capital, 29–30, 32, 34–36
Cultural scenarios, sexuality, 75

D
Da Tong, 165
Davis, A. Y., 16–17
Decolonial theory
  American parochialism, 42
  civilisational benefits, 40
  civilising mission, 48
  colonial condition, 42
  colonial difference, 40, 43–46, 48
  colonial matrix of power, 46
  epistemic racism, 40, 46–50
  global racial hierarchy, 44
  historical conjunctures, 41
  race and racial inequality, 41–43
  racialising assemblages, 45
  racial naturalisation, 43
  #RhodesMustFall (#RMF) student
    movement, 40
  social upliftment, 42
  Western academy, 41
  white ignorance, 41
Decolonisation, 15, 67
  critical thinking, 3
  cultural and power imbalance, 2
  eurocentric domination, 2, 3
  social and political policy, 3
  sociological theory, 2, 3, 9
  structural factors, 1
  structural inequalities, 4
  Western contexts, 4
Degele, N., 65
De Genova, N., 137
Delanty, G., 18
Delgado, R., 42
de Noronha, L., 137
Development model, disability, 109
Disability, 103, 103 (figure)
  charity model, 108
  colonialism, 104
  colonial models, 107–110
  colonial violence, 112–113
  development model, 109
  economic sustainability, 104
  Global North colonial powers, 105
  intersectional analysis, 112
  legislative and policy responses, 106–107
  medical intervention, 108–109
  Nazi T-4 programme, 105
  Neo-Malthussianism, 109
  Peace and Conflict Studies (PACS), 113
  religious model, 108
  social and collective models of, 110–112
  social death, 109
  stigma and social inequalities, 107
    Ubuntu model, 111
    UN Resolution, 2475, 106
    Whānau Hauā, 111–112
Dossou, J. P., 128
Douglas, A., 60
Drucker, P., 82
Du Bois, W. E. B., 42, 44
Duffy, Deirdre, 4, 7
Durkheim, Emile, 4, 9, 10–11, 12 (table), 13,
    14, 15, 17, 48
Du Toit, L., 64

E
Economic capital, 29–30
Economic inequality, 13–15
Economic migration, 136–138, 137 (figure)
Enlightenment and Industrial Revolution, 19
Epistemic racism, 40, 46–50
Equalising society, 16
Esping-Andersen, G., 167
Essed, P., 43
Ethnicity, 113
  disability, 112
Eurocentrism, 17–18
  Chinese people and supporters, 169–170,
    171 (table), 174–175
  cross-cultural research, 173–174
  monolithic cultural idea, 168–169
  and social inequalities, 171–172
  Welfare systems, 167–168
  Western thinking, 166–167
Everatt, D., 65

F
Faderman, L., 75
Fanon, Frantz, 42
Federici, S., 15–16
Feldman, A., 41, 48
Feminism, 3–5, 10, 15, 16, 19, 22, 110. *See also*
    Gender inequalities
feminist re(imaginations), 58–64
Forced migration
  climate change, 134–136
  involuntary repatriation, 134
  refugee protection, 134
  social process, 133
Foucault, M., 75, 82

G
Gaonkar, D. P., 18
Gautier, L., 128
Gender inequalities, 5, 13–15
  Afro-Feminism, 64–68
  decolonial feminism, 64–68
  disability, 112
  employment opportunities, 57
  epistemic delinking, 65

feminist re(imaginations), 58–64
feminist theories, 56–57
gender-based violence (GBV), 57, 61–62
gender mainstreaming, 68
HIV infection rate, 57
sexual violation, 64
Genealogical approach, 75
Geoffroy, C., 132
Giddens, A., 83
Global North colonial powers, 105
Global South, 41, 64–68, 104–111, 113, 114, 118, 123, 127–128
Go, J., 48
Goldberg, D. T., 43
Gqola, P. D., 64
Gramsci, Antonio, 125
Gregory, L., 5–6, 76
Greiner, A., 94

H
Hall, S., 42
Hannam, K., 133
Health policy, 117
   biomedical dominance, 127
   Ebola strategy, 128
   health inequity, 121–122
   Malthusianism, 123
   medical hegemony, 125–127
   modernity, 127
   Neo-Malthusianism, 123–125
   obesity and unhealthy diet, 120–121
   public health *vs.* population health, 118–120
   and social inequalities, 118
   'task-sharing' initiatives, 127
Healy, L. M., 167
Heleta, S., 48
Hepburn, S., 93
Heteronormativity, 76–79
Homophobia, 79–80
Homosexuality, 73–76, 78
Hugo, G., 132

I
Iafrati, S., 7
Industrialisation, 11–12, 15
Ingram, N., 5, 35
Institutional disciplinary knowledge, 40
Intercategorical complexity, 66
International Monetary Fund, 109
Interpersonal scripting, sexuality, 75
Intracategorical complexity, 66
Intrapsychic scripting, sexuality, 75

J
Jackson, S., 74
Jardine, N., 18–19
Jaspal, R., 84

Jato, M. N., 63
Jewell, L. M., 82
Jones, H., 168, 170
Judge, M., 60, 63

K
Kahn, R. L., 90
Karambé, Y., 128
Katz, J., 76
Kessi, S., 67
Khan, M. M., 94
Kiguwa, P., 5
Kindig, D., 119
King, R., 132, 136
Kobayashi, K. M., 94
Korpela, M., 133
Kouaouci, A., 132
Kurasawa, F., 48
Kuzmin, G., 113

L
Laczko, F., 135
Langan, M., 109
Latin American Feminisms, 57, 58
Lawrence, Charles, 42
Lawrence, M., 80
Lentin, A., 41, 42, 43, 45
Lesbian, gay, bisexual and transgender (LGBTQ+) community, 5–6, 77–80, 83–84
Lewis, D., 67
Li, 164–165
Liberatory queer Black transfeminism, 61
Lorde, A., 61, 67
Lugones, M., 44, 67

M
Maathai, Wangari, 67
Macaulay, Thomas Babington, 48–49
Maldonado-Torres, N., 66
Mallé Samb, O., 128
Malthus, Thomas, 123
Malthusianism, 123
Marshall, B. L., 91
Marx, Karl, 5, 9, 11–12, 13–15, 17, 26–28, 31, 36, 48
Maskovsky, J., 83
Massey, D. S., 132
Mastuda, Mari, 42
Matthews, P., 76, 77, 78
Mbembe, A., 65
McCall, L., 65
McGuire, A., 91
McKittrick, K., 45
McLeman, R., 135
Means of production, 27, 28
Meekosha, H., 111
Meghji, A., 21, 43, 44, 48

Memmi, Albert, 42
Merriman, P., 133
Midgley, J., 167
Mignolo, W. D., 19, 43, 44, 65, 127
Mohan, D., 141
Mohanty, C. T., 19–20, 128
Morrison, M. A., 82
Moyo, D., 109
Mudimbe, V. Y., 47–48
Mulderrig, J., 121

N
Nagy, R., 133
Nandy, A., 18–19
Nash, J. C., 32
Ndlovu-Gatsheni, S. J., 66
Nduna, M., 64
Neoliberalism, 150, 154–155, 157
Neo-Malthusianism, 109, 123–125
Niang, S. M., 21
Norris, M., 89

O
Oliver, M., 103
Omi, M., 43
O'Reilly, K., 132
Osborne, George, 148
Oyewumi, O., 67

P
Patriarchy, 5, 22, 40, 58, 59, 64, 169
Peace and Conflict Studies (PACS), 113
Pedersen, J. E., 13
Pellegrino, A., 132
Pereira, C., 68
Perkins, Gilman, 14–15, 16
Pharmaceutical health inequity, 122–123
Phillipson, C., 94
Piguet, E., 135
Post-colonialism, 17–18
  of modernity, 18–19
Poyner, C., 78
Proletariat, 27
Purkayastha, B., 84
Puwar, N., 36

Q
Quijano, A., 18, 43
Quinn, Gerard, 107

R
Race victims, 32
Rahman, M., 91
Rajan-Rankin, S., 89
Rangiahau, Donny, 111
Ratele, K., 63, 67
Ravenstein, E., 136

Religious model, disability, 108
Ren, 164
Retirement (lifestyle) migration, 138–139
Reverse racism, 43
Richardson, D., 76, 82
Rowe, J. W., 90
Roy, A., 137
Ryan, F., 110

S
Scott, S., 74
Settersten Jr., R. A., 94
Sexuality
  Action Plan, 80–82
  hate crimes, 72, 73 (figure)
  heteronormativity, 76–79
  homosexuality, 73–76, 78
  intersectionality, 82–84
  LGBTQ+, 77–80, 83–84
  Trans Lives Survey, 73
Sexual Offences Act 1967, 80
Shakespeare, T., 103
Sheller, M., 133
Shilling, C., 35
Sibley, R., 132
Skeggs, B., 32, 37
Social capital, 1, 29
Social class
  Bourdieusian mapping, 29–30, 30 (figure)
  class position, 34–35
  confidence and competence, 35
  cultural capital, 29–30, 32, 34–36
  cultural resources, 28
  economic capital, 29–30
  intersectionality, 31–32
  labour power, 27
  social stratification, 28–29
Social constructionist approach, 59
Social determinants of health, 95, 119, 120, 122
Social Policy
  COVID-19, 149, 153
  economic determinants, 156
  employment and in-work poverty, 148
  intersectionality, 156
  late-neoliberalism, 154, 157
  moralised antagonism, 155
  neoliberalism, 150, 154–155, 157
  patriarchal and post-colonial capitalism, 149
  and social inequality, 149–152
  UK society, 152–153
  unemployment rate, 151, 151 (figure)
  welfare dependency, 155
  Welfare Reform, 151–153
Socioeconomic disparity, 21
Song, S., 136
Space-clearing gesture, 18
Spivak, G. C., 19–20

Stoddart, G., 119
Stonewall, 80
Structural racism, 180
Structural violence, 112–113
Sullivan, N., 74, 75

T
Tamale, S., 65, 67, 128
Taylor, Y., 80
Torres, S., 90, 91, 139
Transphobia, 79–80
Trouillot, M. R., 18
Trump, Donald, 20–21

U
Ubuntu model, 111
UK immigration context, 139–140
Unequal mobilities
  economic migration, 136–138, 137 (figure)
  forced migration, 133–136
  migration, 132–133
  retirement (lifestyle) migration, 138–139
  UK immigration context, 139–140
Upadhyay, H., 141

V
Valluvan, S., 46
Vázquez, R., 19, 127

W
Walker, A., 168
Wallerstein, I., 17–18
Webbs, 152–153
Weber, Max, 4, 5, 9, 12, 13, 13 (table), 17,
  26–28, 30, 31, 36, 48
Weeks, J., 75, 76
Welfare Reforms, 148, 151–153
West, C., 58
Western feminism, 19
Williams, Patricia, 42
Willoughby-Herard, T., 61
Winant, H., 43
Winker, G., 65
Winslow, C.E.A., 119–120
Wong, C. K., 168
Wynter, S., 45

Y
Younge, G., 138
Yu, W. K., 170
Yuval-Davis, N., 46

Z
Zimmerman, D., 58
Zola, I. K., 126
Zubair, M., 89